T5-CRP-178

What the Children Taught Me

What the Children Taught Me

The Experience of an Educator in the Public Schools

Jack Greenstein

With a Foreword by Kevin Ryan

The University of Chicago Press
Chicago & London

JACK GREENSTEIN was born in Poland and came to Chicago when he was six years old. After stints in the U.S. Post Office and the army, he worked his way through college and graduate school and started teaching at age thirty-seven. He retired at the age of sixty, and now writes, plays tennis, and composes songs.

The University of Chicago Press, Chicago 60637
The University of Chicago Press, Ltd., London

Printed in the United States of America
90 89 88 87 86 85 84 83 5 4 3 2 1

Library of Congress Cataloging in Publication Data
Greenstein, Jack.
What the children taught me.
1. Teaching. 2. Classroom management. 3. Public schools—United States. I. Title.
LB1025.2.G674 1983 372.11′02′0924 83-3503
ISBN 0-226-30705-0

Contents

Foreword

Each fall many beginning teachers get the surprise of their lives. Teaching turns out to be quite different than they anticipated, from what they had been studying and fantasizing about for months and years. For many the surprise is, at the very least, disorienting. For some, the surprise is pleasant. For some, it is deeply disappointing. At the core of the surprise is the fact that teaching involves much more than they, the newcomers, had considered. It is more complicated and has more dimensions than they had expected. The perspective from the desk up front is quite different from the familiar one at the student's desk. New teachers are struck by the wide span of student abilities and, even more, by the range of reactions to events in the classroom. One group of students lights up when the problem sheets come out; another group moans. Some students take the new teacher on as a long-lost parent. Others shy away and view the teacher distantly and with distrust. And teachers are surprised to find that, behind the familiarity of schooling and the predictability of classroom life, there is much drama in the lives of children, and for some much suffering. About teaching itself, new teachers make a series of startling discoveries. Little things, like transitions from arithmetic to reading, can be like turning a herd of thirsty heifers away from the water trough. Teachers are shocked by how physically tiring, let alone mentally exhausting, teaching turns out to be.

The teacher's surprise is not the surprise of the unfamiliar. New teachers are not casual observers of a strange phenomenon. They have spent much of their lives in classrooms and have observed fifty or sixty different teachers. Further, they have studied education and they have taken courses in educational psychology, focusing on such seemingly relevant topics as human motivation and the characteristics of learners. They have taken courses in methods of instruction which have taught them about empirically verified skills of effective teaching. They have textbooks which have summarized and interpreted research. And still they are surprised.

Courses in education and textbooks on teaching attempt to convey the research, the warranted knowledge, in the field. The low regard among many practicing teachers for education courses and their often open contempt for educational research is usually a troubling discovery for university educators. The issues, though, are quite clear to practicing teachers. For example, in the last two decades great effort and expense have been devoted to identifying the skills of effective teaching. Something of a breakthrough has taken place in the last three or four years in that a variable has been identified and isolated which correlated highly with student achievement. That variable is a characteristic associated with some teachers and not with others. The students of teachers who behave in such a way as to demonstrate this variable on a regular basis get higher achievement grades than others. The variable is called "academic engaged time" or "time-on-task" and refers to the ability of some teachers to keep students engaged in the academic task. Professional journals have devoted much space in recent issues to this research. "Academic engaged time" have been the buzzwords at several important educational research conventions. The average teacher, however, looks upon all of this as a masterful grasp of the obvious. As one experienced teacher recently said, "Any semi-conscious teacher with half a brain knows that kids don't learn unless they're paying attention and on the job. Do we need educational research for this!"

The teacher's frustration can be dismissed as impatience or intolerance for a new and promising area of research. Nevertheless, it does seem that much of the essence of schooling is rarely captured in educational research. Somehow, the reality slips through the nets of our research paradigms. The sadness and frustration of a third grader who hasn't learned to read is not captured. The reason why a seventh grader does wonderfully in mathematics and science but cannot write a complete sentence goes unexplained. The mystery of a sophomore girl who was last year's solid citizen and this year's class ne'er-do-well nonachiever remains. How to teach difficult ideas or concepts is rarely addressed by educational research which becomes devalued when it does not help teachers understand their world or solve their problems.

At the heart of this problem is the educational community's overly narrow definition of research. Instead of searching widely for knowledge that will illuminate and enrich the work of the teacher, current educational researchers have focused on a narrow band of research skills, those drawn primarily from the social sciences. In doing this, teachers and other educational practitioners have been cut off from much of the wisdom of the ages. Teaching and learning and schooling have been with us for quite some time, and we know a good deal about the phenomenon. Much of the wisdom about education has been captured in constructed narrative accounts based on some human experience—or more simply, in stories.

The Story

The story is as old as mankind. Telling a story was mankind's earliest social attempt to try to bring sense out of what William James called "life's buzzing, booming confusion." And we have been telling stories to one another down through the centuries. From the time our distant ancestors huddled around the night fires swapping stories and passing on the messages of racial survival, until the present, the story has been a major part of our lives.

The purpose of the story is usually to amuse, to "spin a yarn," to "while away the time." Often, though, while stories are entertaining, their true purpose is to instruct. It is particularly true of the enduring stories. The members of society perceive the value in a particular story and they want to pass it on, particularly to the young. Take, for instance, the story of young George Washington who, having chopped down the cherry tree, confesses his deed to his father. And the short story of Philip Nolan, the Revolutionary War figure and contemporary of Washington who was guilty of treason, a story that comes to us in "The Man without a Country." These stories are culture carriers. They tell us who we are, the people from whom we have sprung, and, most important, how we should behave.

For a long time in our history the story was our major means of knowing who we were, from where we came, and where we were going. The story was the great teacher, the great explainer. As we developed in our quest to forge meaning out of what seemed the abyss of meaninglessness, we evolved other ways of knowing. And with them other methods of inquiry. We developed philosophy and theology, the natural sciences, and then the social sciences. While these ordered patterns of knowing, these disciplines, have added immensely to our sense of who mankind is and what his relationship is to the environment, they have not lessened our interest in or cultural reliance on the story.

The story has, in fact, found its way into disciplined knowledge, most notably in literature and history. Both the writer of fiction and the historian are trying to tell the truth about the human condition. Both the writer and historian tell a story by putting together statements about human life in an ordered pattern. The writer of fiction draws on imagination and carefully crafts these mental scraps into an integrated whole. The historian draws upon a great range of dispersed facts and constructs them into a coherent whole. Both the writer and the historian use the story to help us arrive at a meaning. And, as we listen to the story, we are getting a larger message about "how things fit together." We are learning what we ought to do. Besides offering answers to these questions, often the story provides us with what James Joyce called "epiphanies" or flashes of insight that reveal new, and sometimes startling, meanings.

From its beginnings of fireside tales, the story evolved into long, versed sagas. Today, the story comes to us in a range of forms from country and western ballads to eight-hundred-page novels. Technology, too, has had its way with the story. For much of our history the story lived only in the telling and in the memory of the hearer. But, then, the story was chipped in stone, was captured on parchment and paper, was transferred to celluloid and airwaves and, more recently, to the electronic dots of our color TV sets. Technology has brought not only new forms but also an explosion of the story. Right now, we are surrounded by the story. And it is possibly because of its very obviousness and availability that we have ignored the true value of the story.

The Story and the Teacher

Like others in our society, teachers know much of reality through stories. These undoubtedly contribute to their "knowing what it is to be a teacher and what to do," even though the exact contribution of the story to the teachers' understanding of their work and development are hidden. But certainly the teacher or prospective teacher must be affected by reading in Helen Keller's autobiography about Annie Sullivan's determined struggle with the young deaf mute, Helen Keller, or of a teacher's clever manipulation of her "Brodie girls" in *The Prime of Miss Jean Brodie*. One can speculate about a number of effects that would vary from teacher to teacher, depending in no small degree on their stage of professional and personal development.

The first effect of the story, and one that may be of particular importance in preservice teacher education, is to provide the student teacher with what Louis Smith has called "concrete perceptual imagery of teaching." While most prospective teachers have a great deal of imagery of classrooms, they have little perceptual imagery from the teacher's angle of vision. Seeing children through the eyes of a teacher cannot be done well through psychological generalizations or the analysis of empirical investigations. However, the story of an insecure teacher's vain attempts to find content of interest to her students and her fears that *she* is really the problem may speak with great power to the teacher-reader.

A second effect of encountering teacher stories has to do with what is sometimes pejoratively referred to as "tricks of the trade." As teachers read, they are picking up the skills, strategies, "teacher moves," and other elements of the teaching craft. Reading that the insecure teacher in the above example tried brainstorming with her students, which both gave her a whole new set of ideas of what to teach and changed the tone of her class, could be very important. These chains of behavior are, in fact, "learned-in-the-telling." They actually may be part of the teacher's past social learning. The story, or the memory of the story, triggers this past learning, and the teacher adapts it to his or her situation.

Third, an empathetic reading or hearing of stories prepares teachers for a wide range of human encounters in the classroom. It helps them perceive the fear and isolation of a student who is failing or is new to the school. Stories of other teachers can help them deal with their own feelings of frustration or powerlessness or, even, having too much power. In a sense, the story functions not unlike what David Ausubel calls an "advanced organizer." The teacher in a concrete situation has the sense of having been there before and knowing what to do.

Preparation for the human experiences encountered in teaching may have particular importance for beginning teachers. When new teachers are in what has been called the "survival stage," their sense of professional competence and self worth is frequently at a very low ebb. For the new teacher to know that others have had these same feelings, these same fears and failures, may make the situation more endurable. "I am not alone" may be the most important message a teacher can receive.

The fourth effect of stories deals with the moral dimension of teaching. Because of its importance, and since little attention has been given to teacher education in the moral domain in recent years, this effect is given particular attention here. From the Greek philosophers to the present, educational thinkers have acknowledged the schools' dual role of developing intelligence and a moral sense of connectedness with others. Schooling is intrinsically a moral activity. Moral matters are embedded in the social nature of classroom life. It is especially evident in the uneven power relationship between teacher and students. Much of the content of schooling, then, both the formal and hidden curriculum, is concerned with, "What is the right thing to do?"

In the last twenty years social science research techniques and perspectives have been influential in teacher education. This has caused a shift away from the value dimension of teaching toward a more objective, value-neutral study of behavior. As a result, many teachers are unaware of the moral dimension of teaching, and many more are ill-equipped to take on the traditional role of transmitter of positive social values. This paradigm of teaching as applied science is increasingly coming under attack for its oversimplification and for its meager yield of usable knowledge. One critic, Alan Tom of Washington University, has suggested that this metaphor ought to be replaced by another, that of teaching as a moral craft.

In this moral realm, in particular, there seems to be an important role for the story. As mentioned earlier, stories have been a major form of teaching moral truths and subtleties. From Plato to Lawrence Kohlberg, from Homer to Walker Percy, men have used stories to incite the moral imagination. Indeed, the moral story may be the most valid and reliable means of moral teaching. The stories of teachers, both fictional and real, are a rich storehouse of the ethical events, confrontations and dilemmas of the profession. And they may be the best means of helping teachers to become, as Tolstoy urges, "good by choice."

One Man's Story

This volume should do much to revive the value of the story in professional education. Jack Greenstein has captured in vivid and compassionate images much of the essence of schooling. In the last fifteen years there has been no shortage of stories about school. In most cases, however, they have a limited value or a flawed vision. In the limited value category are the stories of beginning teachers and their attempts to make sense of their world. The utility is circumscribed to beginning teachers and some teacher educators. In the flawed-vision category are the stories of and by hot-eyed and fast-penned school reformers. These unloving critics of the schools are often better at wagging their fingers and assigning blame than understanding the complex phenomenon of schools.

Jack Greenstein's volume is neither in the mea culpa nor sua culpa category. Greenstein is a seasoned educator, having spent twenty-three years in a range of Chicago public schools. He brings to his writing not only the perspective of a teacher and administrator but also a mature sense of balance. His classrooms and schools are peopled with neither white knights nor villains. He trots out no educational devil theory nor does he sharpen axes for us. His vision of teaching and schooling is that of an extremely difficult human activity that must be carried on with limited resources and by imperfect human beings. Frequently and inevitably, the complex machine breaks down and children get hurt unless compassionate and caring individuals are around to soften the blow and cushion the hurt. In addition, some children carry such burdens of poverty and home neglect that they cannot be saved. In such an imperfect world the author found himself and he has tried mightily, if imperfectly, to help as many as he can.

There is much insight and inside information to be gleaned from Jack Greenstein's stories about his experience as teacher and administrator. He has a great deal to tell both professionals and laymen about what is going on inside schools. At heart, though, Jack Greenstein has a moral vision. He sees through to the human core of schools. Greenstein is a wise educator who with wit and warmth and wisdom has compressed his career and made it available to us in wonderful stories. We are much the richer for his generosity.

KEVIN RYAN

Boston University
October, 1982

Preface

"Why don't you write a book!"

This has been said to me many times after I have recounted a few of the episodes that follow. Really! I have a suspicion that it was sometimes said to shut me up by those who were tired of listening to me. If it was in a book they wouldn't have to read it. No matter. I prefer to believe that they were encouraging me to share my point of view (based, after all, upon a fair amount of experience) with the general public.

I have also been influenced in this endeavor by the reactions of beginning teachers who appeared to listen appreciatively to the advice I gave them, some of which is included here. It has been suggested to me that they had no alternative as I was their "boss" at the time, an uncharitable aspersion which I shall not deign to dispute. In any event, having relinquished my captive audience, I will now try to address myself to a larger one—not only teachers but parents.

I suppose my primary purpose is to present the "real world" of education rather than the one in the textbooks or the movies. This is not the story of the young hero or heroine who becomes a successful teacher in six months, converts an unruly mob into a docile and respectful class, wins the love of all the students, tames the class bully, counsels a girl who is about to commit suicide, and teaches the students to appreciate good music and poetry while at the same time transforming them into better human beings. Some of these accomplishments, perhaps even all of them, are possible, but not as quickly or easily as the fiction writers would have us believe. Many teachers, myself included, have started with an unruly mob and ended with a manageable, even attentive class. However, it was seldom the class they started with. The unruly mob remained unruly. Several years later, when the teacher had become more proficient, the class would miraculously become manageable. A few rare individuals (I was not among them) have effected this metamorphosis in two years, others may take five, and some never achieve it at all. For those teachers who are now in their first, second, or even third year and not doing too well, I can only say, "Don't despair. You may still make it. I hope you do."

I believe I have gained the respect—even affection—of most of my students. I have also incurred the enmity of some—at which times I have consoled myself with the sage observation that "you can't win 'em all." I have tamed the class bully, though not by besting him in hand-to-hand combat; and sometimes I didn't tame him at all. I have even counseled two suicidal girls. It wasn't as dramatic as the movie versions and I could do little to change the conditions that induced them to contemplate such a desperate course. Fortunately they both lived.

This book is not an attempt at self-glorification. While most of the incidents I relate have happy endings and I may come out of them looking pretty good, I have had my share of failures. Indeed, when one has been teaching for a number of years, one begins to feel that there have been more failures than successes. Perhaps that is why I emphasize the latter. I believe they were the most instructive, though I learned from both.

This is a very personal account. It encompasses a career of twenty-three years in the elementary schools, thirteen as a teacher and ten as a principal. I do not claim that this automatically makes me an authority. My tenure was limited to three schools in one large midwestern city. However, I cannot be accused, as I have accused others, of pontificating about the elementary schools without ever having taught in one. I am also unimpressed by the "experts" who, after teaching for one or two years, feel qualified to present their conclusions to the public. If there are professions that can be mastered in such a short time, teaching is not one of them.

1. Accentuate the Negative

When I started teaching, an old principal gave me this advice which I, in turn, have passed along to other new teachers. "Remember that the first year is the hardest. Your second year should be easier. If it isn't, quit."

I suppose I should start at the beginning, but of course there really is no beginning. Something has always happened before—especially in my case. I was thirty-seven years old when I embarked upon my teaching career. My education had been interrupted by several minor incidents—the Depression which forced me to drop out of school for a number of years, and a war to which the president sent me an invitation that I couldn't refuse. However, this is not really an autobiography. It is a collection of some of my experiences as a teacher and principal; so in this case, the beginning is my first year of teaching.

Many first-year teachers probably started in similar fashion, especially if they were placed in an upper-grade class in a lower socioeconomic neighborhood. This is the kind of class that the principal tells you is a "challenge." You usually find other names for it. Everything you learned in school about teaching suddenly seems absolutely worthless. Your big problem is discipline—just getting the kids to keep quiet long enough for you to teach a lesson. And after you've taught it, you wonder if anyone was paying attention. Then you test the class to see how much was assimilated, and you don't have to wonder. You know.

If you are sincere in your desire to teach, which I was, you listen to every suggestion from your peers, hoping to discover the magic formula which enables them to (*a*) keep the kids in their seats, (*b*) persuade said kids to work (or at least pretend to work) dutifully on their lessons, and (*c*) induce them to raise their hands decorously when they wish to speak. The "perfect classroom" where you can hear a pin drop is no longer my criterion of excellence. Who wants to hear a pin drop anyway? But in that first year it was "a consummation devoutly to be wished." All I could think of was trying to keep the class quiet and hoping that the principal wouldn't walk in to see how seldom I succeeded in doing so.

Mr. Duncan, the balding, heavyset, scowling teacher across the hall, favored a simple approach. He combined a loud, rasping voice with the swish of a yardstick on his victim's hand, arm, or backside. When I observed him occasionally through the open door, I had great misgivings about the future of my teaching career. I knew I could never learn to employ his methods. The students feared him and referred to his room as "Duncan's Dungeon." Yet he seemed to be successful, at least insofar as keeping order was concerned, while for me each day was a new and often losing struggle. There were some good days, but these were usually followed by bad ones. Then, I would tell myself that somewhere there was a twenty-one-year-old girl just out of college who was facing problems similar to my own. And if she could manage to persevere, someone my age, with my background, who had been able to survive four-and-a-half years in the army, could do no less. This bunch of rowdy youngsters might leave me bloody, but unconquered. And thus while the native hue of resolution often flickered, it never quite went out. And if that's a pretty mixed-up metaphor, I was pretty mixed up myself at the time. Well, at least this ordeal taught me to have a profound sympathy for first-year teachers. What has always puzzled me is that a number of principals I have known do not seem to share this sentiment. I wonder how they managed during their first year of teaching.

As so often appears to be the case with teachers, my neighboring colleague, the one with the loud, rasping voice, displayed a dual personality. The stern, baleful, sneering countenance he exhibited to his students would disappear completely when he conversed with his fellow teachers. Although his attitude was a bit patronizing, he was genuinely friendly to me.

"I hear you've got Vito in your class," he remarked one day. "You'd better keep your eye on him—in fact, both eyes. I had him last year."

He informed me that Vito, if not the reigning "bad boy" of the school, was at least one of the top contenders for that honor. He was the leader of a group which had been involved in shoplifting and general troublemaking. To wind up the year, the group had vandalized the school. As a reward for his participation, Vito was "non-promoted," and this was his second failure.

As I had not been there the previous year, I was naturally unaware of Vito's reputation. Although he was one of the tallest boys in the class (having failed twice, he was older than the others), he had not attracted my attention. He had been relatively quiet, which was more than I could say for some of the other students. When I mentioned this to my colleague, he replied, "Listen, I know Vito. He's sneaky. You have to watch him every minute. He'll turn on you when you least expect it. Maybe he's just lying low for a while. He'll be back in form soon."

I decided that it might be a good idea to have a talk with Vito and asked him to stay after school. As I returned to the room, after dismissing the class, I was not quite sure what I wanted to say. I looked at him curiously. His skin was sallow, his black hair close-cropped, and he had thick, bushy eyebrows overhanging small, dark, expressionless eyes. In fact, his whole face lacked expression. It occurred to me that he probably was accustomed to staying after school and was more at ease than I was.

"Vito, I want you to know that I'm satisfied with your behavior," I began, "and your work seems to be all right. I understand you got into some trouble last year. Is that right?"

"Yes," said Vito. Apparently he didn't intend to be very communicative.

"That's what I wanted to talk about. I want you to know that what happened is over as far as I'm concerned. I'm a new teacher, and you're starting fresh. If you continue the way you've been doing, I'm sure we'll get along fine."

"I'm not look for trouble," said Vito.

Obviously this was going to be a pretty one-sided conversation. "Well," I continued lamely, "I just wanted you to know how I felt about it—and if you ever have any problems or you don't understand the work, just see me after class."

"I can do the work," said Vito. "I had it before."

"Yes, of course you did. Well, good night, Vito."

"Good night."

The month went by, and it was report card time. My records indicated that Vito had earned all G's. (In our grading system, E was excellent, G was good, F was fair, and U was unsatisfactory.) Hardly the best in the room, but he was in the upper third. I decided to speak to him again after he brought back his report card.

"How's everything going, Vito?"

"O.K."

"You had a pretty good report card—and no check marks. What did your mother think of it?"

"She said it was O.K."

"Do you still hang around with Frankie and that bunch?" Frankie had been his companion in the shoplifting and vandalism episodes.

"Naw, I don't see them much," said Vito. He opened up a little. "I decided to stay out of trouble. I would have been in eighth grade if I hadn't goofed off. I want to graduate and go to high school."

"That's fine. Keep up the good work and I'll see if I can help you. Maybe I can get you put into eighth grade at the end of the semester if your grades are all right. I can't promise anything, but I'll try. How does that sound?"

"O.K.," he said.

I mentioned this conversation to my colleague and he shook his head disbelievingly. "Don't let him con you," he warned. "One of these days he'll explode. You wait and see."

I did wait—with some trepidation. After all, this man knew Vito and was far more experienced than I. The months went by, and there was no explosion. I never got as close to Vito as I did to some of the other students. It never became one of those "Mr. Greenstein, thank you for all you've done for me" situations. Nor can I say that I did anything for Vito. He had decided on his own to turn over a new leaf. This doesn't happen very often, but it happens. As I learned later, this is not the usual pattern. I want to emphasize that. A student who has failed twice is not generally stimulated to greater effort. Usually, it's quite the reverse. However, as we were on the semester plan at the time, the two failures put Vito only one year behind. Now that we have annual promotions, the student who fails twice has fallen behind two years, which is quite a different matter. Beside, Vito was able to do the work, although he probably hadn't made much of an effort the previous semester. His failure had been due to his conduct rather than to a lack of ability.

Eventually, I was able to get him into eighth grade. While my recommendation helped, his age and grades were the deciding factors.

That's all there is to the story. That's the significant point, that nothing happened. No explosion, no confrontation. Looking back in time, after a lot more experience, I believe that what I did was important—or rather, what I didn't do. I *didn't* say, "Vito, I know all about you, and you're not going to pull any of your tricks on me!" I *didn't* pounce on him the first time he spoke out of turn and warn him to watch his step. And I *didn't* use a yardstick on him. If that's so effective, as some teachers claim, I wonder why it didn't work on Vito when he was in my neighbor's class.

I am not a laissez-faire individual. Never have been. I am too cynical to believe that people (children included) will do the right thing when left to their own devices. Some will and some won't. I advocate reasonable discipline in the classroom with the teacher in charge.

As a principal, I have walked into a classroom where the teacher was sitting at the desk like a tranquil Buddha, oblivious to what was happening, while students were throwing paper clips at each other, shooting spitballs, sailing paper airplanes, kicking other students under the desks, or even chasing each other around the room, and maintaining a noise level that was almost deafening. There was an assignment on the board which no one appeared to be doing. When I asked what was going on, the teacher replied, "They refuse to behave. I gave them work to do, but they won't do it." Oh, yes, there are teachers like that. I'm not talking about substitutes or first-year teachers but tenured teachers with many years of service. They are the enemy. We should get rid of them. They cheat the students and demean all good teachers. Unfortunately the union keeps protecting them.

But what about the sincere, hardworking teachers? I have seen many of them who mean well but do not realize the harm they do to some children. They want to carve each child in their own image. They are usually very successful with the nice little girls (or little boys). Yet they fail miserably with the misfits, the "lazy" ones, the "bad" ones, because they are constantly nagging, prodding, warning, cajoling, threatening, punishing, embarrassing and ridiculing them, dragging them to the office, and writing vitriolic notes to their parents. A teacher should try to get the parents' cooperation, but an angry note or phone call every other day is not the way to do it. These teachers manage to create an insurmountable resentment in such children toward them, the school, and perhaps even to society. Remember that such children are probably getting the same thing at home. Just imagine—a constantly nagging mother and a constantly nagging teacher. What an unbeatable combination! It sounds like a double-barreled disaster.

I have compiled a short list of "don'ts" for teachers. Any good teacher can come up with additional items. However, to start with:

1. Don't give too much homework. If the students have more than

one teacher, remember that the other teachers may be assigning homework too.

2. Don't assign endless, boring "busy work" with no educational value. We all do it sometimes, but let's keep it at a minimum.

3. Don't require that the students make notebooks, especially the kind that consist mainly of cutting and pasting, or merely copying things from books word-for-word.

4. Don't make a fetish out of neatness. Neat work should be encouraged. If a paper is illegible it should be done over. However, good penmanship should be rewarded by a grade in penmanship. It does not enhance the quality of an English theme or a history paper.

5. Don't kill the joy of reading by requiring long book reports or testing the students' recollection of insignificant details.

6. Don't give long punishment assignments and then double them if they are not completed. In a short time they can become astronomical. I remember the case of a child who was staying up until midnight for a whole week doing "homework." Her father finally checked to see what was keeping her so busy. He discovered that she was writing "I will not talk in school" hundreds of times, not a very educational activity. She was getting further behind each day because when she failed to complete the punishment assignment it was doubled. Meanwhile, she had no time to do her regular assignments. Her father finally took time off from work to see the teacher and put an end to this absurdity.

7. Don't continually yell and scream at the students. It can be very disturbing to others (including the principal in his office if he is within hearing range), and in the long run it will probably hurt you more than the students.

8. Don't use corporal punishment. This practice is so prevalent, and so strongly defended by many teachers and parents and even some principals, that I will discuss it in greater detail later on.

9. Above all, don't do to your students all the things you used to complain about when your teachers did them unto you.

After all those negatives, perhaps it won't hurt to throw in one affirmative. *Do* listen to the children. That doesn't mean you have to agree with them, but it won't hurt to learn what they want and how they feel. And who knows? If we listen to them, they might even listen to us.

2. Parental Guidance

Note from a parent:

"Dear Mr. Greenstein,

I gave Tommy a laxative this morning, so if he has to, let him."

(He had to, and I let him.)

I had managed to survive my first year of teaching and was hoping that the second year would be easier (as the old principal had prophesied). All things considered, it probably was—or it would have been if Leonidas Johnson hadn't been around. That wasn't his real name. The names I use throughout this book are fictitious, mainly to protect the guilty. Also, as most elementary school teachers are female, I will refer to a teacher as "she" when the sex is indeterminate.

The tallest member of our staff was the gym teacher, an imposing man six feet, three inches tall—imposing to me at any rate as I am five-foot-six. Leonidas was six-foot-four. He was fourteen-and-a-half years old and weighed over one hundred seventy-five pounds. He was practically a nonreader. Although his last test score indicated that he read at fourth-grade level, his performance was below that. When I tested him individually, I found that about all he could decipher were two- and three-letter words (at, if, and, but, the, for, etc.). How had he managed to achieve a fourth-grade reading score? Possibly by cheating (what student would dare to withhold an answer from him?), or perhaps by some lucky guessing. If you answer all questions on a multiple-choice test, you are bound to get some right even if they are written in Chinese. In fact, I recently checked the standarized first-grade reading test used in our school system and, I believe, nationally and was surprised to find that thirty-two of the total of one hundred seventy-two items required a "yes" or "no" response. That's approximately one-fifth of the test. Now it doesn't take an expert to know that even a nonreader has a fifty-fifty chance of getting such an item right. For the whole test, the chances of guessing right are about one out of three. I don't know what the odds are at Las Vegas, but I doubt if they are much better.

This might explain to teachers why some of their students' scores are not in line with their expectations. Yet parents, and even many teachers and administrators, accept a test score as gospel.

If Leonidas was functionally illiterate, why was he in seventh grade? An obvious question, and I'll respond with those dirty words, "social promotion." I have listened with frustration to the heated denunciation of this practice by parents and educators. Why do "spineless principals" promote students who can't read? Well, dear reader, what do you do with a Leonidas Johnson, the terror of the seventh grade? Place him in a second-grade class? He wouldn't stay there if you did. This hulking black youth was obviously out of place even with the twelve-year-olds.

A boy of that size and age in seventh grade is usually a menace to his classmates, a headache to his teachers, and probably an unhappy individual himself. Moreover, I don't believe that keeping him in elementary school till he learns the "necessary skills" for admission to high school is the solution. He may never learn them.

Now for the sixty-four-dollar question. After all those years in school, why hadn't Leonidas learned to read? There I go, falling into the trap set by the headline writers. We see it all the time. "Why Can't Johnny Read?" The fact is that, except for the severely retarded, most children *can* read, though a number of them do not read *well*. Even Leonidas, and he was by far the poorest reader in the class, could decipher some words. But why should he have been expected to perform at the same level as the others? It would make a lot more sense if we realized that all children are not equal in ability, that some learn at a slower rate, and that each should be judged according to his capacity rather than by a standard we set as a norm. I'm not talking about children with hereditary or congenital defects. I'm referring to those who are within the range of what we call normal. Obviously they are influenced by a variety of environmental factors. By the time they enter school at the age of five, there are pronounced differences between them mentally and physically. Ask any kindergarten teacher. We don't expect them to run at the same speed; yet we expect them to learn at the same rate.

Children who speak little or no English are bound to experience difficulties, although this handicap can usually be overcome (and bilingual classes can help). Nevertheless, it is a factor to be considered. There are also differences in attention span, motivation, attendance, and in the quality of teaching. Oh, yes, that's important. I'm not trying to get the schools off the hook. Just to balance the ledger a little. Nor am I willing to blame it all on L.D. (learning disabilities). That's a convenient label employed by psychologists. While I'm sure some children suffer from such an affliction, it's a diagnosis that is applied all too freely to provide educators with an excuse when a child does not respond to their teaching. It sound so scientific.

Back to Leonidas. I don't know why he read so poorly. He had been educated (I use the word loosely) in the South and had been in our school only two years. I have no firsthand knowledge of Southern schools, so I'm in no position to place the blame on them. However, that's another problem we have. We receive a large number of students from other school systems. Many are below grade level when they come to us, and we are held responsible for their poor progress.

A poor student is likely to be a troublemaker. Leonidas was a classic example. He was a bully, he stole from the other children—even extorted money from them, though I found this difficult to prove (anyone who "snitched" on Leonidas was taking his life in his hands)—made lewd advances to the girls, and in his spare time disrupted the class. While I would not say he was uncontrollable, there was a noticeable improvement in the class and my state of mind when he was absent. Unfortunately for me, this rarely happened. Leonidas was in very good health.

One day, when he was giving me even more trouble than usual, I reprimanded him sharply. I don't remember his exact reply, but the tone and the words left much to be desired—at least from a teacher's viewpoint. I was afraid that if I permitted this to go unchallenged, I would lose the respect of the class.

"Come on," I said. "You're going to the office." No doubt I would handle the situation differently today. A second-year teacher, however, usually has not learned all the options.

Leonidas didn't move. I walked over to his desk. "Let's go!" I commanded with more assurance than I felt.

He stared at me for a moment while I tried to look fierce and determined. Then, suddenly, "All right," he said. He untangled his large frame from his seat and walked slowly to the door with me. Once outside the door, he stopped as if to consider the matter further.

"Let's go," I repeated impatiently as I took him by the arm.

"Take your hand off me or I'll kill you," he muttered softly but menacingly.

I was in good physical condition and more than a match for the average fourteen-year-old. Leonidas was not an average fourteen-year-old. I took one look at him towering above me and decided that it would not be prudent to put his threat to the test. I released his arm. Neverthless, I said firmly (at least, I thought I said it firmly), "Come on. We're going to the office."

Let me say, parenthetically, that it was this incident which caused me to resolve never again to use corporal punishment upon a student, a resolution I have kept. After hearing several teachers affirm that "the only thing these kids understand is a good slap," I had begun to believe it. Therefore, although I was always ashamed when I did it, I had occasionally slapped a child—not very hard. Now I realized that if I was afraid to lay a hand on a boy who was six-foot-four, it would be cowardly to strike a boy who was smaller than I was. (I had never slapped a girl.)

We were received by the principal in his office and, without going into specifics, I explained that Leonidas had been rude and disobedient and had bullied other children and that I would like to see his mother. The principal agreed to send for her.

The next morning a portly black woman, about five feet tall, walked into the classroom with Leonidas. "I'm his mother," she asserted.

Rather diffidently, I repeated the story of Leonidas's transgressions.

The little woman turned to Leonidas. "Leonidas, is you been giving this teacher trouble?" she demanded accusingly.

He hung his head sheepishly. "Yes'm," he mumbled.

Whack! Her hand shot out and hit him solidly on the cheek. The class stared in amazement. Leonidas did not move. "Don't you give your teacher no more trouble, you hear!" she cried shrilly.

"Yes'm," said Leonidas.

Again she struck a resounding blow on his cheek. She had to reach pretty high to do it. "Now you behave yourself, you hear me!"

"Yes'm," he repeated, his eyes looking down at the floor.

I knew I should not be permitting this. If his mother wanted to slap him, it should be done in the privacy of their home. It was highly improper to shame him this way in front of the whole class. Then I remembered his threat in the hallway and couldn't bring myself to intercede. I was enjoying this too much. I stood there passively, giving no hint of my feelings. The class too was silent. His mother administered one more blow for good measure, then she turned to me. "He give you any more trouble, you just let me know."

I thanked her for coming, and she left. Leonidas meekly took his seat. I continued the lesson as if nothing had happened. Inwardly, however, a good feeling remained—a sort of glow, you might say. I tried to suppress it. I tried to tell myself that I shouldn't be so pleased at seeing a boy slapped by his mother. Nevertheless, this had been a satisfying, even exhilarating experience.

Leonidas was subdued for several days. Then he gradually reverted to his previous behavior, though not entirely. But he never openly defied me again.

Leonidas was good with his hands, and I managed to get our home mechanics teacher, a very kindly and sympathetic person, interested in him. He offered to take the boy for several periods a day. This made the day more bearable for both of us. Eventually Leonidas graduated. He was sixteen, and it was pointless to keep him in school any longer. He probably wouldn't have stayed anyway.

3. The Butterfly

Students often have their own names for teachers. Mr. Tanenbaum became "Mr. Cannonball," and Mrs. Flynn was "Mrs. Flint," why I don't know. However, when a very dark-skinned black student addressed Mrs. Aldworth, our very fair-skinned clerk, as "Mrs. Allwhite," it made sense somehow.

Writers of books about the gifted child point out that he probably receives much less of the teacher's time than the other children. The lesson is usually geared to the level of the average student, the slow ones are likely to get individual attention and even extra tutoring in an effort to raise them to grade level, and the disruptive children always demand a disproportionate amount of the teacher's time (not that either of them want it that way). The bright child has the teacher's approval but is often left to his own resources as far as the development of his abilities is concerned. As I had made a study of the gifted child when I was in college, I was aware of this fact when I started teaching. Consequently, I made a special effort to devise challenging activities for the brighter students to keep them from getting bored. However, though I didn't realize it at the time, if the gifted child has emotional problems, they are more likely to be overlooked than those of other children. He may appear to be happy and well-adjusted in the classroom. In fact, he probably is, as he is enjoying obvious success and receiving the approbation of the teacher. And if he has problems outside the classroom, the teacher is usually unaware of them. His parents may tend to minimize anything that is troubling him. A well-behaved child who brings home a beautiful report card usually makes his parents happy, and they probably assume he is also. It should be noted that many teachers claim that the emotional problems of children are not their responsibility. This is not due to a lack of concern on their part but rather to the belief that they are unable to offer the necessary guidance. They maintain, quite justifiably, that they are not trained psychologists. Furthermore, that their job is teaching, and they don't have the time to devote to the individual problems of thirty or more children.

Unfortunately, psychologists are not assigned to each school. They generally work out of the district office, each one servicing several schools. Besides, their chief function is to test students who are referred to them by teachers. With rare exceptions, these are students who cause trouble in the classroom or are unable to perform at grade level. (When I became a principal, it became my duty to approve these referrals. I can never remember seeing one for a gifted child.) Upon completion of the tests, the psychologist makes his recommendations. He does not provide treatment. He informs the teacher that the child needs individual attention (the teacher knows that), that he should be given materials to work with at his own level of achievement (the teacher usually doesn't have them, or the time to work with the child), and that he should be provided with activities in which he will experience a feeling of success (good advice, but sometimes the only thing he seems to succeed in is disrupting the class).

The school usually has an adjustment teacher. Can the classroom teacher count on his help? Unfortunately, he also has other duties. Many teachers wonder what they are. Take my word for it, if he is assigned to a large school with a transient population, he has enough to keep him busy. Mostly he is occupied with testing, record keeping, and receiving and sending transfers. Occasionally he may have a little time for tutoring, but seldom for individual counseling. So, like it or not, if counseling is necessary, it is usually done by the classroom teacher or not at all.

As my own background included a degree in psychology, I was prepared to counsel individual students. However, one must first be aware that there is a problem. Annette, one of the brightest students I have ever taught, gave no indication that she had one. She always appeared to be composed and well-adjusted. While she did not talk much to her neighbors, I assumed it was because she was so well-behaved. She paid close attention to the lesson, raised her hand eagerly to answer questions, and worked conscientiously on the written assignments. Her performance was the best in the class in every subject, and she showed no signs of boredom.

As she had been double-promoted twice, Annette, who was eleven years old, was the youngest child in my seventh-grade class. (We were on the semester plan and each promotion was for only one-half grade.) Yet she seemed more mature than her classmates, not only mentally but physically. She was a tall, attractive girl, reserved, though not unfriendly. She played piano beautifully and was often called upon to perform at assemblies. She was a perfectionist and set standards for herself that were unattainable by the others in the class. Even a perfect report card did not satisfy her. She was so accustomed to receiving one that it was no longer an achievement. In spelling, for example, getting an E (excellent) was not enough. She was determined to get a hundred on every test. She almost made it. During the entire semester she missed one word on a fifty-word review test. In my history tests, I purposely included some challenging questions for her benefit. (I think she was aware that I was playing a game with her.) I informed the class that I did not expect anyone to get a hundred—that a mark of eighty or above would be an E. Yet Annette had a hundred on two of the tests, the only student to achieve this.

One day she asked to see me after class. She confided that she was having some difficulty in reading from the blackboard. Also that she was getting occasional headaches and thought they might be due to eyestrain. I promised to change her seat. But the solution, I told her, was to ask her father or mother to take her to an eye doctor. If her headaches were really due to eyestrain, she might need glasses. Assuming that the idea of wearing glasses was troubling her, I assured her that there were many attractive frames and styles and that glasses need not detract from her appearance; that curing her eyestrain and headaches were much more important. I had underestimated her good common sense. She *wanted* glasses. It was her father who was opposed to the idea. He refused to take her to an eye doctor. He had never worn glasses, his father had never worn glasses, and his daughter did not need glasses either, he insisted.

There was no nurse assigned to our school, and I was not quite sure how I could help her. Still I had to do something to justify her confidence in me. "Don't worry," I said. "I'll talk to your father."

I telephoned that evening and asked to speak to him. As I waited for him to come to the phone, I wondered what kind of an ogre could be so insensitive to his daughter's health. Well, I would have to be diplomatic. I told him how well his daughter was doing, what a pleasure it was to have her in my class—all the things I knew a father would like to hear—and gradually broached my concern about her health and the possibility that she needed glasses.

The voice that answered was courteous and pleasant. He thanked me for my interest in Annette and assured me that she was very happy to be in my class. As for the headaches, she was probably studying too hard. She was such a perfectionist. Also she was reading lots of books and practicing piano several hours a day. He would persuade her not to work so hard and to get more rest.

"You're probably right," I responded. "Still it really wouldn't hurt to have her eyes checked. Just a precaution."

"There's nothing wrong with Annette's eyes," he asserted. "I would have noticed it if there were. No one in our family has ever worn glasses. Tell me, Mr. Greenstein, are you a doctor?"

"No, of course not. I'm not saying there is anything wrong with Annette's eyesight. Just that it might be a good idea to check."

"Thank you, but I really don't think that will be necessary. She's tired, that's all. I'll see that she gets more rest. Thanks again for calling."

That ended the conversation. I had accomplished nothing. Perhaps Annette's father was right. Maybe I was too ready to accept a diagnosis made by an eleven-year-old girl. Her headaches could have an entirely different cause.

When I saw Annette the next day, I admitted my failure. She accepted the news calmly. Apparently she had not expected me to be able to persuade her father. "I thought that would happen," she said.

Now my pride was hurt. "Don't worry," I said. "I'll try something else. We'll get your eyes tested yet."

I was not as confident as I sounded. I wondered if I was making a promise I would be unable to fulfill. However, I came up with an idea that I thought was worth trying. I obtained a Snellen eye chart, the kind used by doctors. Then, introducing it to the class as part of a science lesson, I explained its origin and function and proceeded to test every student. It was a novel experience for the class, interesting and educational. It also produced some unexpected results which convinced me to use the test with all my classes in the future. Six students failed the test. I sent notes to their parents suggesting an eye examination and some of them subsequently did get glasses.

As for Annette, the test indicated that her eyesight was about 20/70, which meant that at twenty feet she could see what a person with normal eyesight would be able to decipher from a distance of seventy feet. Assuming that my test was valid, she probably needed glasses. Certainly an eye examination by a physician or optometrist was in order. I was now determined to pursue the matter further, this time in person. I called her father again that evening and asked if I could come over and talk to him. He agreed.

When I saw him, I wasted no time in getting to the point. I informed him about my test and its results.

"So you are telling me that Annette needs glasses," he said.

"No," I replied firmly. "That is for a doctor to decide. I am telling you that her eyes should be examined. If they are all right, there's no harm done. On the other hand, if she needs glasses and doesn't get them, her headaches will continue and her eyes may get worse. I'm sure you wouldn't want to jeopardize the health of your child when a simple examination might solve this problem."

To my surprise, he consented without further protest. Evidently I had found a convincing argument. It was with a sense of satisfaction that I relayed the good news to Annette.

The final vindication of my efforts occurred about a week later when Annette came to class smiling shyly, and proudly wearing her new glasses. Now she could read what was written on the blackboard, and after that she no longer complained of headaches. When she saw me after class, she had another bit of news to confide. The doctor had managed to persuade her father to have his eyes tested as well. He too needed glasses.

Although Annette's immediate problem was solved, there was another one which she had not mentioned. I had noticed that she had no close friends in the class. She was, however, to a great extent, self-sufficient. Her time was occupied with reading, practicing piano, and her studies. She was too mature to participate in the games and conversation of the other students. She was not aloof. She just wasn't part of the group and was content to go her own way. Unfortunately, some of the other girls were not willing to permit this. Strangely enough, it was the good students who resented her most. Whether they believed her to be conceited or were just jealous of her scholastic superiority, I don't know. One day a few of them attacked her. When she entered the classroom, her face was scratched, her clothes disheveled, and she was struggling to suppress the tears in her eyes. It was evident, however, that her hurt was more emotional than physical. I tried to comfort her, then sought out the culprits and sternly reprimanded them.

I was pretty sure the girls would not attack her again, but how could I teach her to cope with their animosity? I sensed her pain, her unhappiness, her bewilderment, and it disturbed me. The following day, when I saw that she had regained her composure, I asked her to stay after school.

I had considered the matter carefully and had come to a decision. I would speak to this eleven-year-old girl on a mature level and hope that she would understand. Though she was a child in years, she was a very grown-up child.

"Annette, I know you've been hurt," I began, "and you probably don't understand why. It may be hard for you to believe this, but the girls who hit you are not really bad. They were wrong. They behaved like—well, like children. That's understandable. After all, they are children. I guess they're jealous because your marks are better than theirs. You want to be the best in what you do. There's nothing wrong with that. When I went to school, I also tried to be the best in my class. I learned that it didn't always make me popular. Sometimes I had to learn the hard way, even as you did. It might be a good idea if you didn't show off your hundreds and your good papers—except to your family, of course."

"I haven't been trying to show off," she protested. "I thought I was being polite. The only reason I show the girls my papers is because they ask to see them."

I smiled. "Yes, I know. I've seen them ask you, but I think it was because they were hoping that they had a higher mark than you did. And that didn't happen very often, did it? You have to try not to do anything that will make the others believe that you think you are better than they are. Being smarter doesn't make one better, you know. I don't want you to get the idea that smart people can't be popular. Just look at Harry Lee [a Chinese boy in the class]. Everyone seems to like him. Yet he is a very good student, almost as good as you are. I guess some people just have the knack of being popular. I'm not sure I can explain why. Maybe you should watch Harry and see how he does it. That doesn't mean I want you to change. I like you the way you are. But here you are a big fish in a small pond. You like music, you like to read, and your interests are not the same as those of the other girls."

She nodded. "They jump rope a lot during recess. I don't like to jump rope."

"Well, maybe you should try. It's good exercise. But that's not the point. Many years ago I learned something that I'm sure you will learn too. This is a small school and you don't have much competition. That's why you stand out. When you get to high school, it won't be so easy to be the best. But you'll find friends there. There will be all kinds of clubs you can join, with students who have the same interests that you do. You'll find kids that like music, poetry, journalism, anything you want. Believe me, it will be a different world."

I had talked quite a bit, and now I waited to see her reaction. I hoped she understood what I was trying to say. Though she appeared to have been listening intently, she remained silent.

"Do you have any friends?" I asked hesitantly. I did not want to embarrass her.

"A few," she replied. "They're my neighbors. None of them are in our class. They're older than I am."

"Well, friends are not something you can make any time you want to, but try to be friendly. And remember what I said. Make the best of things now. It won't be this way forever. You'll see. Once you graduate, things will be different."

There were no further incidents. However, I continued to feel that Annette, though she was trying, didn't fit in. She was too advanced for the class. Her age notwithstanding, it was my firm belief that another double-promotion would be advisable. That would put her into 8-A, and in another six months she would be able to graduate. Considering her grades, she certainly deserved it, and the sooner she got into high school, the better. I was confident that with her size and maturity it would work out well.

I made the recommendation to the principal in writing, and he called me in to discuss it. As the principal and I had always been on friendly terms, I did not anticipate any difficulty in convincing him. I was wrong.

As I entered his office, he turned his ponderous frame toward me. "This girl Annette," he said. "I've been looking at her records. Oh, she's a smart girl, all right. But if I double-promote her, she'll only be twelve years old when she graduates. Do you think that's good?"

"Twelve-and-a-half," I corrected him. "In most cases, I guess it wouldn't be good. I know she's young, but she's tall, she's physically and emotionally mature for her age, and she needs work that will challenge her. There's no question about her ability. I'm sure this is the best thing for her."

"I'm sorry. I don't think I can approve it," he said. "It's against school policy to give her another double-promotion. [Evidently he chose to forget that it was he who had formulated this school policy.] She's already a year ahead."

"I wish you'd reconsider," I insisted. "This girl is not happy here. And she really deserves this promotion."

"It would set a bad precedent for the school," he replied.

"I'm not thinking of the school," I said. "I'm thinking of what's best for this girl. I strongly recommend this double-promotion."

He looked annoyed. "I don't think you are considering all the consequences. She was double-promoted not long ago. She'll miss a lot of work. I'd appreciate it if you withdrew your recommendation."

"I know you can disapprove it if you wish, but I can't withdraw it," I said stubbornly. "I'm sorry."

'Well, I'll think it over," he said shortly.

The principal, though usually dictatorial, did not like arguments. He considered himself an astute diplomat. Perhaps that is why he finally approved the double-promotion, although his attitude toward me changed from then on. I must confess that I felt very noble about the stand I had taken, especially since it had caused me to lose the friendship of the principal. I was sure I had done the right thing, and I was glad I had prevailed.

Annette graduated at the end of the school year, and I did not hear from her for some time. It may have been a year later, possibly more, when I received a phone call from her. She sounded very cheerful. She rattled on about what she was doing in high school, all the activities in which she was involved, and how happy she was. There is one remark in particular that I remember. "You wouldn't know me," she declared jocularly. "I've become a regular social butterfly."

I recalled the prediction I had made. At the time, in my effort to comfort an unhappy girl, I realized that I might have been overly optimistic. It had turned out even better than I had expected.

Annette moved out of the neighborhood, and I only saw her once after that when I received an invitation many years later to attend a piano recital. It was the culminating exercise for her master's degree in music. I was flattered that she still remembered me, and I was happy to attend. She introduced me to her friends in a very complimentary way and talked to me for a while, but she was obviously nervous about her impending recital and had little time for reminiscing.

If this were fiction, I would describe her triumphal performance and her subsequent brilliant career. As this is fact, I can only say that she was very tense and was smoking one cigarette after another. She probably had been under a great strain in preparation for the recital. I can imagine how many hours of practice were involved. Although she looked pale and tired, she performed very well. How she fared after that, I do not know. If she achieved success, it certainly wasn't my doing. Music was the center of her being, and I had never been involved in that phase of her life. But the years of childhood are important. They are difficult years. Sometimes a helping hand from a teacher can make them more bearable. And that much I had offered her.

4. You Win Some

I had written a song for the school. The first two lines were:

More than just a school to me,
Like a second home might be.

The students sang it differently. Their version was:

More than just a school to me,
Like a penitentiary.

I hate to admit it, but I thought their version was better.

At one time in my career I volunteered to be a music teacher. I liked to sing, had a fair voice, and had always had some interest in music. I have never sung in a choir, however, and my experience with part singing or harmony was very limited. Also, I don't play an instrument. On the plus side, I can read music, though hardly well enough to call it sight reading. At any rate, I thought that teaching music would be more compatible with my talents and interests than teaching five science classes, which I was doing at the time. So the music teacher and I, with the approval of the principal, simply traded.

He had become a music teacher in more or less the same way that I had become a science teacher. Our seventh-grade science teacher had transferred and a replacement was needed. The principal informed me that the other seventh-grade teachers, who had more seniority than I did, were either unwilling or unable to take the job, so I had been chosen. Actually, it wasn't done quite that crudely. The principal we had then, a very nice lady, called me into the office and asked me how I would like to be the seventh-grade science teacher. Since science was definitely not my best subject—when I was in college I couldn't even dissect my own frogs—I started to express doubts about my capabilities in this field, but she quickly reassured me. I certainly knew more than the students. And there was a teacher's guide. All I had to do was read the book, and I would do just fine. Nothing to worry about. I saw that I was going to be "persuaded" one way or the other, so I acquiesced.

I must say that with the aid of the textbook and a little outside reading I didn't do too badly. After a few years, some of the students even began referring to me as "Mr. Science." They were convinced that this was my greatest interest in life. I was aware of my own limitations, however, especially when I tried to help students who had a real interest in science which went beyond the limits of our textbook; so teaching music sounded like a sensible and intriguing alternative.

I had my own ideas about how to teach it. My main goals were to introduce some of my favorite songs to the children—classical, semiclassical, popular, folk songs—and to get the students to enjoy singing. I ignored most of the songs in our seventh-grade music books (which led to a few less-than-friendly confrontations with the music supervisor), and brought some of my own records to class.

In the army one learns a cardinal rule of survival. "Don't volunteer for anything." Nevertheless, I was sufficiently encouraged by my success in this new endeavor to volunteer for a music assembly. My classes and I had worked very hard, and finally, after many rehearsals, we were in the auditorium ready to go on stage. My homeroom class and I were the first to be seated. Then the others slowly began to file in. An eighth-grade class had just settled itself in back of us when suddenly, directly behind me, I heard a voice call, "Hey, Greenstein."

The obvious discourtesy of not addressing me as "mister" left me with three choices: reprimanding the offender, condoning his breach of etiquette by responding, or pretending I didn't hear him. I chose the last. After a short pause, however, the voice repeated insistently, "Hey, Greenstein."

A few of my students were now turning around to look, so I decided, rather reluctantly, to answer. I turned and saw that the voice belonged to an eighth grader whom I knew slightly. I had noticed him in the hallway occasionally as he was talking and laughing boisterously with his friends. "Well, what is it?" I asked brusquely, trying to convey by my tone that I was aware of his discourtesy but did not care to make a point of it.

Either the chill in my voice was not apparent to him, or he chose to ignore it. He grinned mischievously and said, "I hear you have a good voice."

His manner warned me that he was not trying to be complimentary. "That's nice," I replied shortly and turned away from him.

Evidently he was not ready to terminate the conversation. "Have you got a good voice?" he insisted.

"That's a matter of opinion," I responded. I hoped that the conversation was now at an end, but he was not to be denied his little game.

"I'll bet your voice isn't that good," he continued. "I'll bet I can sing better than you can."

Under other circumstances, I might very well have reacted like a "teacher," intoning a horrified, "How dare you talk to me like that!" and marching the insolent youngster to the principal's office. However, my class was scheduled to perform shortly and this was no time to create a disturbance. Besides, the boy had cleverly avoided using any words which were clearly disrespectful. If I had to explain the incident to the principal or to his parents, it might not sound like much. I would not be able to reconstruct his offensive attitude. He was probably aware of this and was counting on it to protect him.

I turned to him and, with complete self-control, replied cooly, "I have never claimed that I had a good voice. And since I have never heard you sing, I can't judge whose is better. Actually, I don't care. But I am sure of one thing."

"What's that?" he asked, still grinning.

"That my manners are much better than yours."

This did effectively put an end to the conversation. The assembly program was successful, I received some compliments from several teachers which I later duly communicated to my class, and the incident was almost forgotten. I briefly considered reporting the matter to the boy's teacher but decided against it. It wasn't important enough to "make a federal case."

The next day, as I was grading some papers during my "free" period, I was surprised to see the same boy at the door. "May I see you a minute, Mr. Greenstein?" he asked.

The tone of voice (and the "mister") was noticeably different from the one I had heard the previous day. Nevertheless, I was still a bit wary. "Yes, come in," I replied. "What can I do for you?"

There was no smirk on his face now. His expression was serious and a little downcast. "I came to apologize," he said. "I had no business talking to you like that yesterday. It won't happen again."

I smiled, almost embarrassed at this turn of events. "You know," I responded, "there's an old song that says, 'What can I say after I've said I'm sorry?' I accept your apology. Forget it."

After that I saw the boy in the hallway occasionally and he invariably greeted me respectfully, "Good morning, Mr. Greenstein," or "Hello, Mr. Greenstein."

Well, it's nice to win one now and then.

5. And You Lose Some

It is not unusual for girls to become infatuated with a young and handsome male teacher. However, as I was in my forties during most of my teaching career, I considered this a remote possibility in my case. But apparently it did happen on at least one occasion.

The faculty had been invited to have coffee and cake with the parents after a PTA meeting. I accepted the invitation and was conversing with several of the members when a woman was introduced to me as the mother of one of my students. She looked at me appraisingly from top to bottom, paused a moment, and then said incredulously, "This is the 'dreamboat'?" It was the most crushing compliment I have ever received.

Pamela was awkward and ungainly, the tallest girl in my seventh-grade class. She was bright but very moody, with a talent for making herself unpopular. Although her reading and math scores were well above average, she refused to do any homework or, for that matter, much classwork either. I knew her mother well. She was a teacher at another school and a good one, or so I had heard. The father was also a college gradute. Why, then, were Pamela's schoolwork and behavior so poor? I had intended to send for her mother, but she beat me to it. She came to demand an explanation for the U (unsatisfactory) in reading on Pamela's report card. (Apparently the check marks for conduct did not surprise her.)

"Pamela reads books all the time," her mother told me. "She scored 10.8 on her last reading test. [This was roughly equivalent to almost an eleventh-grade reading level, fourth highest in the class.] How can you give her a U in reading?"

"I am aware of her ability, and I know that she reads," I replied. "In fact, she is often reading a book in class when she should be doing her spelling or arithmetic. I wouldn't mind that if she made up the work at home, but she doesn't. And she hasn't been doing the daily reading lessons, so I had to give her a U. If I marked the students simply on their ability, the bright ones wouldn't have to do anything—and I have a bright class. Pretty soon they would stop progressing."

"If she's reading books, isn't she learning to read?" insisted the mother. "Doesn't that account for her high reading score?"

"There is no question about it," I agreed. "Her reading of books may very well be more important than my reading lessons, but I can't grade her on it. Incidentally, I give extra credit for books read out of class. All she has to do is submit a report on what she has read—not a book report, I don't believe in that—just the name of the book, one sentence about it, and your signature verifying that she has read the book. She hasn't even bothered to do that. Also, she does poorly on her spelling tests; and her arithmetic, when she does it at all, isn't that good either. But I'm really more concerned about her behavior. She seems to be a very unhappy girl, and I'm pretty sure that her poor schoolwork is a by-product."

"I know she's unhappy," the mother agreed quietly, her belligerency suddenly subsiding. "I've just started getting psychiatric treatment for her. I'm afraid it's my fault." She paused. The admission was obviously difficult. Then she continued resolutely, "As you know, for the past four years I've been going to school to get my degree and trying to take care of a family at the same time. It hasn't been easy. I know I haven't paid much attention to Pam. My husband has never been very close to the children. Besides, he often works late and doesn't see too much of them. I guess this is the result. I know she finds it difficult to get along with other children."

"Well," I said, "as long as you recognize the problem, that's half the battle. I'm glad you explained all this to me. You'll have to try to help her at home, and I'll see what I can do with her at school."

We parted on this promising note, and I determined to be more patient with Pamela. Her work did begin to improve, though there was no change in her behavior. At my suggestion, some of the girls tried to be friendly to her. She rebuffed them. At times she even attacked them physically. She continued to be argumentative and arrogant. When I tried to explain to her that I could not permit her to hurt other children, she would become disrespectful. The other girls were upset on my account. They thought that I shouldn't permit Pamela to speak that way to me, and now they began to ignore her completely. Although I was getting a bit annoyed with her myself, I still tried to be patient.

One day she complained about her grade on a reading assignment. Of twenty multiple-choice questions, two had been marked wrong—and she thought they were right.

"Bring your paper up here, Pamela, and I'll check it," I said.

She brought up her paper. After referring to the answer book provided by the publisher, I assured her that the mark was correct.

"I don't see why," she insisted.

"All right," I said. "Let's look at the lesson." I found the sentence to which one question pertained and showed her the correct response. I then located the paragraph which related to the second question she had answered incorrectly and indicated the answer that the author had intended.

She read the paragraphs thoughtfully, then replied, "I see my mistake on the first one, but I still think the second one is right."

I endeavored to explain, but I couldn't convince her. "Well, the author doesn't agree with you," I said mildly.

"Can't the author make a mistake?" she insisted.

"Yes, but he didn't. See me after class and I'll go over it with you."

I dismissed the class a few minutes later. Then I turned to Pamela who was waiting for me. "All right, now read the paragraph again. You see, in a multiple-choice question you are supposed to pick the best answer. Though the one you chose is not exactly wrong, this one [I pointed to the one in the book] is definitely better. The author can make a mistake or there can even be an error in the printing. In this case, however, I happen to agree with them. And I hope you'll admit that I'm still a better reader than you are."

"No, I don't," she said stubbornly.

I looked at her with disbelief. Then, nettled by her effrontery, I asked, "What was your score on our last reading test?"

"Ten-point-eight," she replied with obvious pride.

"Do you know what that means? It means that you read at almost eleventh-grade level—in other words, almost the equivalent of third-year high school. [Technically, this is not quite correct. However, I was in no mood to enter into an interpretation of test scores at this time.] Well, that's very good for a seventh grader, though several students in the class did better. But you know that a teacher has to be a college graduate. Your mother is one. And I am too—which means that I should be a little above third-year high school level in reading. So, since I can't seem to explain it to you, I'm afraid you'll just have to take my word for it that your answer is wrong."

She glared at me obstinately. "Why should I? I still think I'm right and you're wrong."

At this point I lost my temper completely. I upbraided her for her arrogance and insolence. As I continued my tirade, she stood there with her lips trembling. Finally I paused, and she said, "Can I go now?"

"No!" I shouted, and started to scold her again. Then, noticing the tears in her eyes, I paused. I suddenly realized that I had gone too far. "All right. You can go," I said abruptly.

She ran down the stairs, opened the outer door, and turned, her eyes flashing. "Go to hell!" she screamed.

This will hardly shock some teachers who have heard far worse from their students. So have I, for that matter, but it had never been directed at me. I was tempted to run after her, then I stopped, wondering what I had done. More than just the words, what disturbed me was the anger, frustration, and hatred I detected in that anguished scream. That I had evoked such sentiments from a girl whom I had sincerely been trying to help made me realize how badly I had failed in this instance. I began to feel ashamed. While defending my wounded dignity, I had browbeaten a twelve-year-old girl until I had goaded her into open rebellion—not just any girl, but one with deep problems, a very unhappy girl who was receiving psychiatric treatment. And I, knowing all this, had lost my temper and shouted at her. I had really been a great help.

At least I had sense enough not to call her mother and insist that she be punished or to report the matter to the principal and demand that she be suspended, as I'm afraid some teachers would have done. When I saw Pamela again, I made no mention of the incident and neither did she. However, the damage had been done. I was never able to overcome her hostility.

I don't know what effect this episode had on Pamela, but it taught me a lesson. I determined that I would not lose my temper with a student again—a resolution I kept—for almost a year.

6. The Best Teacher in the World

One of my students was doing very poorly in all her subjects and seemed to be making no effort to improve. I called her mother in for a conference. I was hoping, I told her, that with her cooperation a change in the girl's attitude might be achieved.

"I know she ain't doing so good," replied the mother, "but maybe you ain't strict enough with her. When I was a kid, them teachers made us learn. Nowadays teachers don't learn the kids nothin'."

There are many experts, pseudoexperts, and nonexperts who are quite vociferous in their denunciation of our public schools. It has become almost a favorite indoor sport. They don't always agree, however, as to who is to blame for the schools' failure or how to improve their performance. Principals blame teachers and parents, teachers blame parents and principals, parents blame teachers and adminstrators, students blame teachers, and everyone blames the Board of Education. Well, I have never been one of the staunchest supporters of our school system, and I'm sure there is enough guilt to go around. However, in the attempt to fix responsibility, one group, even though it is the most important of all in the educational process, is often ignored. I am referring to the students.

One may argue that, if a company is manufacturing ball bearings and some of them are defective, one does not blame the ball bearings. True enough. But students, the end products of the educational system, are not inanimate objects (though some give that impression). It is reasonable to expect them to take an active rather than a passive role in the pursuit of learning, depending, of course, upon their ability to do so.

The difference in ability is something the critics often ignore. They appear to assume that all children, when they enter school, have equal potential and that their progress from that point on is largely dependent upon the quality of the teaching. Yet, as I previously intimated, factors such as heredity, the immediate environment, the social climate, their parents, peers, economic situation, their health, even their size and appearance, all influence children's attitudes and performance.

To return to the analogy of the ball bearings—if a manufacturer employed a variety of materials, he would hardly expect identical end products. Neverthless, some critics evidently expect the schools to achieve equal success with students whose potential is very different. When they examine reading scores—the only yardstick usually cited to validate the success or failure of the educational process—they seemingly overlook the fact that every school produces students whose scores are above the national average as well as those who score below it. Their only concern appears to be the combined average of the particular school or school system which is, after all, an aggregate of highs, middles, and lows. Teachers, on the other hand, are apt to take credit for the achievement of the good students, while they attribute the failure of the poor students to factors beyond their control—either the inadequacy of the parents or the deficiency of the environment, or both.

I can remember receiving compliments from some parents for the fine job I had done in teaching their children. Although these compliments were gratifying, I was aware that, at best, they were only partially deserved. In most cases these were children whose ability and performance were above average when they had entered my class. I knew that they would have succeeded with almost any teacher.

To keep a good student "on course" is important; to encourage and inspire that student is a worthwhile accomplishment. But at the elementary level, the really good teacher is the one who can change the direction of the unsuccessful student. Often the destructive influence of the outside environment is such that even the best teacher cannot effect this—at least not when there is a class of thirty or more students demanding attention. Still, teachers must try to convince students that they have an important role to play in the learning process.

Many students believe that it is the teacher's duty to teach them and that they are merely the passive recipients of this instruction. The teacher didn't teach; ergo they have no obligation to learn. Too many of them, often abetted by their parents, avail themselves of this convenient excuse. We must make them realize that they themselves are the dominant factor in the educational equation and that their success or failure in school depends primarily upon their own efforts. Perhaps we should remind them that many people who had the desire to learn were able to do so with little or no formal education—Frederick Douglass, for example, that great runaway slave, and his contemporary and friend, Abraham Lincoln.

During the latter part of my teaching career I had an aging and ineffective colleague who taught the grade below mine. I had the feeling that she had once been a fairly good—or at least a mediocre—teacher, but had been beaten down by time, life, and rowdy students. She still went through the motions of teaching, apparently oblivious to what the children were doing. As was to be expected, her students—even the good ones—took full advantage of the situation. They played games, passed notes, talked to each other, seldom bothered with the assignments she gave them, and cheated on the tests.

When the teaching assignments for the following year were distributed, I learned that I was to receive her entire class. On the first day of school I was assigned to playground duty. As I walked around the school yard, one of my new students, whose brother had been in my class the previous year, approached me. He told me that he and some of his classmates were apprehensive about the coming school term. They felt that they had wasted a year due to the inefficiency of their previous teacher and were afraid that I would expect them to know much more than they actually did. Consequently, they would have a very difficult time of it—through no fault of their own.

When my new students had entered the classroom and were seated, I instructed them to remove the books from inside their desks and place them on top. After some commotion, they completed this task (with only two or three dropping books on the floor) and gradually settled down. I waited until everyone was perfectly quiet, made sure that all eyes were directed toward me, and then intoned dramatically, "You are now looking at the best teacher in the world!"

This statement, as I had anticipated, produced an immediate reaction. Several students looked at each other and smiled. They had hardly expected such conceit from me. There were a few excited whispers and some puzzled expressions. I paused until they were quiet again and then continued, "I am afraid some of you don't understand. I didn't mean that I was the best teacher in the world. I was referring to the books on your desk. Each of them was written by an expert who knows much more about his subject than I do. I am just a teacher. The authors of these books are scientists, mathematicians, historians, each an expert in his field. It may have taken the author years to write his book—often with the help of other experts. And now you have these books in front of you containing all this knowledge. You may take them home if you wish. Just remember that books are the greatest teachers in the world.

"If you read these books, you will learn. Naturally, you may need my help sometimes to explain things you don't understand. That's why I'm here. My job is teaching, but learning is your job. If you really want to learn, you can probably do so just by reading those books—even without my help. Of course, I intend to help you all I can. I will try to do my part. But if I don't do it well, you can still learn if you do your part. All you have to do is to read the books that are on your desk."

Over the years I have listened to many complaints from students—and parents—about teachers who don't teach. Unfortunately I have often found these complaints to be valid. Some parents, however, are too ready to blame the teacher for the child's failure. That same child may have done poorly last year and the year before, even with good teachers, but now they claim it is the teacher's fault. I do not object to the criticism of poor teachers. If enough parents complain, maybe we can eliminate some of them. Nevertheless, we must recognize that there is often a convenient transference of guilt to the teacher by parents who know that their own efforts and those of their children have been inadequate. It is natural for a student to blame the teacher for his failure. Parents should not be too ready to accept this excuse.

While books are indeed the best teachers, a good classroom teacher is one who can persuade children to read them. Of course she must have other attributes as well. A sense of humor doesn't hurt. And one would expect her to be friendly and compassionate. Especially important, as I have said before, is her impact upon the poor students and the "bad kids." I don't expect miracles, but I don't think they should come out feeling the way Larry did.

Larry was a fourteen-year-old boy who was referred to me for private tutoring. He had ended up in Montefiore (a school for maladjusted children) for what offenses I don't know and was repeating eighth grade. As he often was truant, it looked like he was going to fail again. However, the school psychologist persuaded the principal to let Larry take an examination to see if he could qualify for graduation. That's where I came in. I was to tutor him during the summer and prepare him for this examination.

At the beginning, although I tried to make the lessons interesting,

Larry's response to them was a sullen indifference. Eventually, however, I managed to convince him that we had a common purpose—to get him into high school—and our relationship gradually improved. At the end of the last lesson, as he was leaving, he turned back to me and said, quite unemotionally, "You know, you're the only teacher I ever had that I didn't hate." I have always considered this my greatest compliment—or is it really a damning indictment of teachers in general? Take your choice.

That I succeeded with Larry (he did pass the test) was not necessarily a great achievement. Tutoring one student is a lot different than teaching an entire class. I've had others like him. Some of them I was able to reach. And with some I failed miserably. If their stories are not included in this account, it is not because I am trying to conceal anything. The failures were usually not very interesting, or maybe I'd rather remember the successes.

Now what about the children, and there have been a fair number, I am happy to say, who have informed me that I was the best teacher they ever had? I won't deny that I enjoyed hearing it. But let's examine that statement carefully. First, I am afraid there's a lot of truth to the remark I've often made in jest: "I'm not really that good; it's just that some of the others are so bad." Second, we have to consider how many teachers are involved in the child's evaluation. Suppose you are a fourth-grade teacher, and the children agree that you are the best teacher they've ever had. You may be terrific, but all they are saying is that you are the best of five. Ordinarily, they have had only four other teachers (kindergarten, first grade, second grade, and third grade). The best of five is fine, but it doesn't place you on the endangered species list. What if you are an eighth-grade teacher? All right. If the accolade of "best teacher" is now bestowed upon you, you have become the best of nine. Even if we stretch a point and include auxiliary teachers (gym, shop, library, departmental, etc.), you are the best of about fifteen. Not bad. In fact, very good; but it doesn't automatically qualify you for teacher of the year.

I am not trying to deflate the good teacher. Enjoy the compliments you receive. Teachers are human and can use some approval too. (Parents and principals, please note.) If even one student thinks you are the best, you must have done something right. But before you get carried away by the praise, ask yourself this: How many students in the class would agree, and what would be the vote of the ones you considered troublemakers?

When I was a beginning teacher, I wanted to know what the

students thought of me and of my teaching. Some teachers, perhaps with good reason, don't. Maybe they don't even care. It's so easy to fall back on the rationalization, "I'm here to teach, not to win a popularity contest." (If they asked the students, many teachers might find there was also reason to doubt their success in achieving the first objective.) In my case, especially during the first few years, I felt that my performance definitely needed improvement, and I reasoned that while the customer may not always be right it wouldn't hurt to ascertain his reactions. Therefore, I devised a questionnaire which I distributed to the students at the end of each school year. I wasn't so crude as to ask "How did you like the teacher?" However, such questions as "How did this school year compare to your previous ones?" and "Did you learn more—less—about the same as in other years?" and my request for comments at the end elicited an opinion of me as well as of my proficiency as an instructor.

I know that such evaluations by students are required at some colleges. It has been suggested that this practice gives the students too much power and creates a situation in which the teacher is afraid to antagonize them. If the completed questionnaires are assessed by a supervisor, this argument may have merit. As the use of this device was voluntary on my part and only I had access to the results, I was not susceptible to student blackmail.

Sometimes the responses surprised me. For example, I found that my spelling lessons, which I had considered dull and uninspiring, received a fairly good rating and I didn't have to keep racking my brains for ways to improve them. I also learned that seventh graders are not as clever as many teachers think they are. Even those students who made derogatory comments seldom bothered to disguise their penmanship. Consequently, although I stressed that no signatures were required, I had little difficulty in identifying the respondents.

Was I doing all this because I craved tangible evidence of the students' approval—perhaps an unconscious desire to be stroked? Well, maybe so. I don't think that's so terrible. The affection of the students is one of the few fringe benefits of teaching. But pleasing them should never take precedence over teaching them. Nevertheless, the responses did cause me to make some changes in my methods and even in the curriculum when I felt that the suggestions had merit or the criticisms were justified. I recommend this procedure to all teachers except perhaps those in the lowest grades whose students may be unable to comprehend the questions or to respond intelligently. The results might prove very edifying.

7. It Pays to Cheat

A questionnaire, designed to stimulate parental involvement in the school, had been distributed to all the parents. One reponse was worthy of a politician. Replying to the question, "Do you think parents should or should not be involved in school?" one woman had written, "Definitely!"

As is the case with many students, Herbert's reputation had preceded him. Talkative, loud, rude, annoying—scholastically an average student—this was the appraisal of his previous teachers. Though he was not one of the worst in the class, none of them seemed to like him. And neither did his classmates, they assured me.

This brings up a controversial issue. Should teachers check the records of their new students and elicit information about them from their former teachers, or should each child start with a clean slate? I have known some good teachers who claim that they never look at a child's previous record because they don't want to begin their relationship with a prejudiced opinion. There is, of course, the theory of the self-fulfilling prophecy, to which many educators subscribe—that children tend to perform according to what is expected of them. But I like to know about my students in advance and, if possible, about their parents as well. This doesn't mean that I have to accept the previous teachers' evaluations. I have often found that the ones they described as "terrors" didn't give me much trouble, while occasionally a student might have gotten along well with his former teacher but not with me. However, forewarned is forearmed. In fact, with my natural sympathy for the underdog, if everyone dislikes a child I will make an extra effort to get along with him.

At first glance Herbert wasn't that bad. He was a chubby, healthy-looking youngster who could express himself fairly well and appeared to have the potential to be a good student. But the charactertistics described by his previous teachers soon emerged. He did talk a lot, he got into arguments with his classmates, and he was annoying. I would like to say that I love all children; that is, I would like to say it if I could say it truthfully. I am sure there are people who do. About the best I can say for myself is that I like most children, I tolerate some, I dislike a few, and I try never to hate any. Herbert was one of those I tolerated.

At this particular time, I had a system for keeping order in the classroom which seemed to work pretty well. It also provided me with an objective criterion for grading a student's conduct. If someone was talking out of turn during an oral lesson, bothering his neighbor, or misbehaving in some other way, I would usually give him a warning. After one or two warnings, I would write his name on the board. I kept a grade sheet on which I put a check mark after the child's name each time it appeared on the board. If there were ten or more checks after his name during the five-week marking period, that student would receive a check mark for conduct on his report card. Some students never got their names on the board, most of them would achieve the distinction a few times, while some had their names on the board daily or even twice a day—as much to my regret as theirs. One virtue of this system was that students who were near the danger point, their names having appeared on the board seven or eight times, were especially well-behaved during the last week of the marking period as they made an effort to avoid reaching the unlucky number of ten.

At first glance, this system might seem to be counterproductive. A student could misbehave nine times without penalty. In actual practice, however, most of the children would stop misbehaving the minute I wrote their names on the board. Somehow, just seeing one's name would act as a deterrent. The system wasn't perfect, but it worked well enough for me and eliminated the necessity of constantly giving punishment assignments. I found, however, that once a child had received more than ten checks he sometimes got the idea that he could continue to misbehave without further penalty. To discourage this tendency, I assigned a spelling lesson for every check above ten. Indirectly this provided another incentive to keep below ten as there were no assignments up to that point.

On one occasion my system did have an unfortunate consequence. The class had been getting noisy. "All right, let's quiet down," I said. One of my best students, whose name had never appeared on the board, continued talking to her neighbor and giggling. I called her name and told her to be quiet. She stopped, but as soon as I looked away she started talking again. This was quite unusual. I looked at her disapprovingly and repeated the admonition. For some reason, she began whispering again almost immediately. She was not really being disruptive, but in the interest of fairness I decided that I could no longer disregard her infraction. I have always abhorred the idea of a "teacher's pet," and I didn't want the class to think that the normally "good" student could ignore my warnings with impunity. As I wrote her name on the board, she looked up in shocked silence, then burst into tears. I tried to comfort her, but she continued crying hysterically. I kept her after school and endeavored to explain to her that putting her name on the board was something I had to do in fairness to the rest of the class and that it would not effect her grades in any way. Although she finally quieted down, I'm not sure that she ever forgave me.

Herbert, of course, was not that sensitive. The appearance of his name on the board, which was a frequent occurence, evoked little reaction from him. While he did not lead the parade, he managed to collect at least twenty checks each marking period, and as a consequence he invariably received a number of check marks on his report card. This pattern continued with monotonous regularity each marking period.

Toward the end of the school year it was my turn to be on recess duty. Duties were rotated among teachers, each receiving a particular assignment for one week and then being free of that task for a long time.

I never minded recess duty as long as the weather was mild. It gave me a chance to talk informally to my present and former students. Generally a few of them would tag along for a while as I patrolled the large playground, then take off to join their friends.

On the first day, Herbert joined me, as did some of the others, but when they left he remained at my side. His behavior in the classroom had never led me to believe that he had any great regard for me, so I was a little surprised. At first I thought he might have some problem which he wanted to discuss, but he just seemed content to walk with me and talk about anything that came to his mind. When he ran out of questions, I asked him about his family, his hobbies—whatever I could think of to keep the conversation going. I learned that his father was a salesman who was on the road for days at a time. It suddenly dawned on me that Herbert was without a father much of the time and that this was probably a factor in his behavior. The bell rang to end the recess period, and I gave the matter no further thought till the following day.

On the second day of my tour of duty Herbert was at my side again. As I walked around and stopped to talk to some of the other students, he stayed with me. We soon ran out of questions to ask each other, so I started to discuss the coming baseball season and the various players. I assumed that most boys were interested in baseball. Apparently Herbert was, and this supplied us with a topic of conversation which carried us through recess.

I was less than enthusiastic when I found Herbert beside me on the third day. There was only so much to discuss about a baseball season that had not yet begun, especially since I was not really an avid fan, and I soon found myself running dry on other topics. It occurred to me that I might be becoming a substitute father figure to a boy who already had a father, and I was not anxious to assume that role. For one thing, I have always believed that a teacher should not compete with a parent for the affections of a child. Teachers have an unfair advantage. Paying attention to the children is what they get paid for, while the parents may be kept very busy with other occupations. Also, teachers can make a conscious effort to be "nice," while parents have the unpleasant task of imposing restrictions and saying "no" on many occasions. Besides, I had four children of my own and felt that I had quite enough fathering to do at home. Nevertheless, I couldn't deliberately discourage Herbert as I didn't want to hurt his feelings. Occasionally I would excuse myself and hurry to the other side of the playground to break up a fight, sometimes real and sometimes one I pretended to see. Invariably Herbert would follow and catch up with me.

On the fourth day, having exhausted all other topics of conversation, I started to discuss his behavior. I had avoided this subject previously since I felt it was not fair to chide him about his conduct during recess, a time of relaxation for him. By this time, however, I was getting desperate.

"Why do you keep getting into trouble?" I asked. "Don't you mind all the check marks on your report card?"

"I don't know. I've always gotten check marks," he replied. "I guess I'm kind of used to it."

"But why do you insult the other kids and get into arguments all the time? Don't you like the kids in our class?"

"Some I do and some I don't. I just say what I think, and they don't like that."

"Well, since what you think is usually uncomplimentary, I can hardly blame them. If someone said something bad about you, how would you like it?"

"Not much, I guess, but that's the way I am."

I have heard adults offer the same excuse for obnoxious behavior, and I was tempted to reply, as I have wanted to say to them, "Then it's about time you tried to change the way you are." However, I decided on a different approach.

"How do your parents feel about your report card?" I asked.

"Oh, they don't like it much, though I guess they're used to it by now. They're always telling me to behave better."

"What do you think your mother would say if you came home with a report card with no check marks?"

He smiled. "She'd probably drop dead."

"We don't want that to happen," I said, "but I'm sure it would make her pretty happy if she saw a good report card for a change. I'll tell you what. Why don't you see if you can go a whole marking period without getting any check marks on your report card?"

He looked surprised. "But I get my name on the board all the time," he said.

"Of course you do, because you keeping arguing with other kids, and talking a lot, and getting out of your seat without permission—and you don't finish your work or do all your homework. There's no reason why you can't change all that."

"I don't know," he said. "I always seem to be getting in trouble. I don't mean to. It just sort of happens."

"Look," I said. "No one expects you to be an angel. At least I don't. Right now you're getting your name on the board about twenty times during the marking period. All you have to do is cut it in half—keep it under ten. And your work isn't that bad. You just forget to finish it sometimes. I'm sure you can improve. What do you say?"

"Well, I don't know. I suppose I could do it."

I chuckled. "Say it like you mean it. Of course you can do it if you really want to. Think what a surprise it will be to your parents."

"O.K.," he agreed. "I'll try. I really will."

For the next week it was obvious that Herbert was trying. If he started talking, I would just have to look at him and he would stop. There was also an improvement in his work. But by the end of the week, I guess the strain of being "good" was too great. He got into a shouting match with his neighbor and I had to put his name on the board. After that, although he still seemed to be making an effort, his name began to appear on the board more frequently. Nevertheless, as I explained to him privately, he was doing much better than he had in the past and still had a good chance of staying under ten checks for the marking period.

By the end of the fourth week my grade sheet showed eight checks after his name. I tried to encourage him by stressing that his record still indicated a marked improvement over previous months. "Just try to behave for one more week," I urged, "and you'll have done it."

Of course Herbert was not the only one whose progress I was watching. Many of the students kept their own tally of how many times their names had appeared on the board, and some of them would come up after class to compare their count with mine. Occasionally they would insist that I had made a mistake, that their records showed one or two checks less than mine (apparently my mistakes were never in their favor), and that they were being cheated. Having dealt with this kind of situation before, I would explain to them quietly but firmly that anyone could make a mistake including myself, but that I was the referee and that my grade sheet was official. In any case, I would point out, if my records showed eight checks while theirs showed seven, they could still stay below ten if they behaved themselves. This would quell any incipient rebellion. All they wanted was a hearing and an explanation.

On the first day of the last week Herbert got into a fight. It was a minor altercation, but enough to give him another check. In fact, I considered fighting such a serious infraction that I often gave two checks for it. In this case I kept it to one for each participant—which meant that Herbert had nine checks with four days to go. Though I had little faith in his chances, I talked to him after class again and assured him that he could still make it. The very next morning he and the boy he had fought with started arguing when they came into the room and appeared ready to resume their combat. I quickly interceded, scolded them both, and ordered them to take their seats. I did not write either of their names on the board. I knew that I was cheating, but I told myself that as the day's lesson had not yet started and as no blows had been struck, no harm had been done.

In that last week there were at least two occasions when Herbert's name should have gone on the board. Each time I gave him an extra warning and hoped no one would notice that he was getting special consideration. I felt very guilty about the whole thing as I had always prided myself on being fair. However, if one must be partial, I reasoned, it was better to err in favor of the perennial transgressors. With all the checks they received, some of them might not be deserved anyway.

So Herbert ended the term with nine checks on my grade sheet, an improvement in his work, and no check marks on his report card. When he saw his report card, he smiled and showed it to me jubilantly, apparently forgetting that it was I who had made it out.

"I did it!" he announced triumphantly.

"You sure did," I agreed. "Congratulations!" I saw no need to mention that he had had considerable help from the referee. After all, he had tried. And even if I had marked him fairly, he would have had about twelve checks, which was a decided improvement over the twenty or more he had usually received.

That summer Herbert's family moved to California. He had obtained my address before he left and wrote me one letter which I answered, and then I heard no more from him. This was as I expected. Relationships with students last for the school year and sometimes even the next one, but they seldom go beyond that. One can't even hold on to one's own children, much less someone else's. They grow up.

About five years later, during summer vacation, as I was clipping the privet hedges on my front lawn, a young man approached me with a smile. "Hello, Mr. Greenstein," he said.

As I lived two blocks from the school, it was not unusual for some of my former students, most of whom still lived in the neighborhood, to greet me. I was sure this was one of them, though I couldn't place him.

"Hi. How are you?" I responded.

He obviously was aware that I didn't recognize him. "Don't you remember me?" he said. "I'm Herbert."

This poised, self-assured young man bore little resemblance to the insecure youngster I remembered. I felt like saying something ridiculous like, "No, you couldn't be." Although I had often seen changes like this before, they still surprised me. "So you're Herbert," I said inanely. "I thought you moved. What are you doing here?"

"I live in California. I'm just visiting my aunt. She lives a few blocks away."

I was touched that he should stop by to see me after all these years and immediately invited him into the house. "Tell me all about yourself," I said. "How have you been getting along? How are you doing in school?"

He told me he was a high school senior, was getting good grades, played a number of musical instruments, was in a band which performed professionally at various affairs, and intended to study music in college. "I see you have a piano," he said.

"Not a very good one," I assured him. "It's out of tune. Do you play the piano?"

"Oh, yes," he responded. "That's not what I play in the band, but it's my favorite instrument."

I persuaded him to play. He knew most of the songs I requested, and when I gave him some music he was able to sight read beautifully. I had not been aware of his musical ability and was quite impressed. He stayed for about an hour, then looked at his watch and said, "I guess I'll have to go now. My aunt is expecting me for supper. You know, there's one thing I've always remembered. You were the only teacher in grammar school who didn't give me a check mark on my report card."

I reflected later how strange it was that this should have left such an impression on him. A teacher makes out hundreds of report cards. I always took this task seriously. In fact, I often felt that some of the students were less concerned about their grades than I was. However, I have known teachers whose grades were pure guesswork. It's so easy to give everyone a G (good) if you have no marks in your grade book to go by, or to sprinkle in a few F's (fair) to those who don't behave. And if they decided to give a student a check mark, they might throw in two or three for good measure. It just took a stroke of the pen.

I don't pretend that my action had a profound influence on Herbert's life. Still, it had made an imprint, and I was glad that I hadn't given him that check mark. Sometimes cheating pays.

8. The Wild One

Students are usually given an opportunity to go to the bathroom twice a day. Nevertheless, some of them request permission to leave the room more frequently. This creates a dilemma which many teachers have found insoluble. Parents do not understand the problem. Let me explain it from a teacher's perspective: A request to go to the bathroom is often just an excuse to get out of class. Yet if you don't allow the child to leave and he has an "accident," you are in trouble. On the other hand, if you accede readily to each request, you may suddenly find that you have an epidemic on your hands.

I once had a girl in my class who would ask to leave the room almost every hour. After inquiring each time, "Are you sure it's necessary?" I would reluctantly allow her to go. Finally I told her, "You shouldn't have to be excused that many times unless there is something physically wrong with you. I want a note from a doctor or from your mother explaining why it is necessary for you to go to the bathroom so often."

On the following day the girl dutifully brought a note from her mother. It read: "Dear Mr. Greenstein, Vivian has to go to the bathroom for the same reason you do."

Perhaps it happened fortuitously. At another time I might have reacted differently. Of course, experience was also a factor. I had already been teaching for twelve years.

I had taken the principal's examination a few months previously and had just learned that I had passed. Now it was only a matter of waiting for my apointment to come through. I knew that would take a while, as the list from the previous examination had not yet been exhausted. Meanwhile, I would still have a class to teach—maybe for six months, maybe longer—but it would definitely be my last one. Consequently, I was determined that this would be my best effort. Discipline was no longer a serious problem for me. I had established a pretty good reputation with students and parents, and I felt that each year I had done better than the year before. This year I would outdo myself. I was going to be kind, sympathetic, understanding, interesting, innovative, and, above all, patient. I would not lose my temper under any circumstances. Then I found out who would be in my next class, and I wondered how long I would be able to adhere to my noble resolutions.

I received the news from one of my former students. (The students always seemed to know these things before the teachers did.) "You're getting Ione," she told me.

"Are you sure?"

She nodded, "I saw Miss Morrissey's list. You're getting most of her kids."

As the girl was working in the office, I had to assume that her information was reliable. "Oh, well," I replied nonchalantly, "someone has to have her."

Miss Morrissey had a "low" group, and there were a number of students in her class who were likely to be disruptive, but Ione was definitely the prize package.

In a school the size of ours it is possible that there was more than one Ione. However, when that name was mentioned, no one asked, "Ione who?" I believe her reputation had started in second grade, perhaps even earlier. Often, when I was eating lunch with some of the teachers, I remembered hearing, "Guess what Ione did today!"

As the teacher in whose class she happened to be at the time proceeded to elaborate, there was always a feeling of sympathy for her (coupled with a feeling of relief that Ione was in her class and not yours). On the other hand, having Ione was also a sort of status symbol. Whatever Ione had done, we knew the teacher couldn't possibly be at fault, and when she began, "Guess what Ione did today," people listened.

I was sure that Ione was not as bad as she was painted. No one could be. Probably a little artistic embellishment, a smattering of hyperbole to improve the recital, had helped to establish her reputation. Then again, we didn't have that many girls who were considered troublemakers. We had our share of "bad boys," several of whom could have competed favorably with any I have encountered before or since even in schools with a much worse reputation, but the girls were generally well-behaved. Consequently, Ione won the honors in the "bad girl" competition chiefly by default. She was not very big, and at first glance did not appear formidable, but she was known to be wild, loud, rude, disruptive, a gum-chewer, a talker—and those were her good qualities. She also had a reputation, rare among our girls, as a fighter in and out of the classroom. If she couldn't win an argument verbally, she was quite prepared to debate the issue physically, even if her antagonist was a boy. Such unladylike behavior had to make an impression, especially upon some of our prim, elderly female teachers. Despite these characteristics (or because of them), she had her own circle of friends. No doubt, some of them admired her "nerve" and independent spirit.

Through the years I had discovered that I was usually able to establish a better relationship with the girls than with the boys. (Many female teachers have told me since that they prefer the boys in their class, which has always surprised me as it is common knowledge that girls generally make a better adjustment to school. As a principal, I often considered this "opposite sex" relationship when assigning certain "difficult" students to classrooms.) Ione's sex, therefore, made me less apprehensive about having her in my class than I might have been otherwise. Besides, it probably wouldn't be for long. My appointment could come at any time. Nevertheless, I expected her to make life interesting for me.

As I have said, I was no novice by this time, and I counted on my years of experience to help. Many beginning teachers seem to forget how important this is. They really believe that four years of college (much of it entirely unrelated to their future occupation) has transformed them into teachers—until they face the realities of a classroom. Then, when they encounter problems, instead of admitting their own mistakes (which they often are not aware of), they blame the students. Usually they begin their careers, even as I did, in a poor neighborhood where the students have a reputation for below-average scholastic ability and above-average antisocial behavior, a frequent and predictable combination. Neighborhoods like these, which need the most experienced teachers, generally get the novices. After one or two difficult years—learning years which every teacher goes through—most of them transfer to better neighborhoods. If there is an improvement, they attribute it to the change in the students and the neighborhood. That neighborhoods and students differ is undeniable. But no school and no class is without its problems. The teacher, however, is no longer a neophyte. She has learned to cope with situations which might have demoralized her in her first or second year. In fact, assuming that she has become a successful teacher, if she were now to return to her first school (which she is not likely to do), she would find the students more manageable than she had thought they were.

There was another factor in my relationship with Ione of which I was not aware at the time. It happened that her brother had been in my class several years earlier. He had been a better-than-average student, a little on the impudent side, though within reasonable limits. On the whole, we had gotten along pretty well, but whenever I admonished him for some infraction, I remember him saying with a grin, "Wait till you get my sister."

For some reason, I had never seriously considered this possibility—and now, here she was. I soon sensed, however, that she was happy to be in my class, that she had been looking forward to it. Undoubtedly, this was her brother's doing. He must have put in a good word for me. It was obvious that she was prepared to like me, and all I had to do was to live up to her expectations.

For the first two days Ione was almost a model student. Naturally this could not last. Ione was still Ione. After her initial angelic behavior, she started chewing gum in class (constantly), talking to her neighbors (repeatedly), and arguing and fighting (frequently). Yet, somehow, I found her controllable and even likable. If, when I entered the room, she was involved in a loud and abusive dispute, I would say firmly, "All right, Ione. That's enough. Get to your seat and settle down." And she would do it. At times, when she was about to engage in a fight, I would have to intervene physically. On these occasions, as soon as I was able to induce her to "cool off," she would comply with my orders—not too willingly perhaps, but she would obey. Though she still got into fights on the playground, they were less frequent than in the past.

It would be nice to report that there was also great improvement in her school work, but I have to adhere to the facts. Still, from what I could ascertain from her records, she was doing better than she had in previous years. (As her "cum" card showed almost all U's, anything was an improvement.) Although she was performing at a level below the minimum standards that I had established for a passing grade, she had occasional bursts of energy (or conscience) when she would work hard on her spelling and arithmetic, and sometimes she even did her homework. If I observed that she was talking to her neighbors, or just day dreaming while her notebook lay undisturbed on her desk, I might say, "Ione, why don't you pretend you're doing your spelling?" Then she would resume her work almost cheerfully, as if she had meant to do it all along but had forgotten.

I do not wish to intimate that Ione's reputation was undeserved, but she never quite achieved the promise of her advance billing.

Perhaps she never gave it her best shot. I could see that she liked me, and how could I be angry with her under those circumstances? In a way, despite her bluster, she was a pathetic figure. Her yellow hair was stringy and unkempt. Her nose was straight, but a little too long. Her clothes invariably looked shabby and in need of washing and ironing. Her dresses never seemed to fit properly. They always hung too low as if they had previously belonged to an older sister. I imagine that the boys considered her an ugly duckling and too abrasive and pugnacious. Yet I felt that by the time she got to high school, if she learned to use soap and water and take better care of her hair and clothing, their attitude (and hers) would probably change. I had seen it happen before.

I never met her parents. I decided that they must have been called to school so often in the past that they would welcome the respite, so I never sent for them, and they didn't show up on Parents' Night. I couldn't help wondering why she looked so neglected. Was the family poor? Or perhaps the mother was working and was too busy to take care of her daughter properly, or just too lazy, or possibly she was an alcoholic. Maybe I should have tried to find out, but I never did. My relationship with Ione was satisfactory, and I didn't feel I needed her parents' help.

I never got to regale the other teachers with any "Guess what Ione did today" anecdotes. While she still caused trouble and I scolded her occasionally—after all, I had to act like a teacher—I was seldom really upset. Sometimes I even found her antics amusing, although I tried not to show it.

One day either I was less tolerant or she was more obstreperous than usual, or perhaps it was a combination of the two. I had told her to get rid of her gum at least three times. I don't know whether she faked throwing it away or had an inexhaustible supply. Also, every time I looked at her, she seemed to be talking to a neighbor. And at the end of the day, when I asked to see her work, I found, as I suspected, that she had accomplished very little. By this time I was really exasperated and told her to stay after school.

When the rest of the class had left, I turned to her. "Ione," I said sternly, "you've been talking all day. In fact, that's about all you've done today—except chew gum. Your spelling isn't finished, you've only done two problems in arithmetic, and you haven't even started your history."

"I was going to do it for homework," she replied serenely.

"That wasn't supposed to be homework. You had plenty of time to do it in class. Anyhow, your record for doing homework isn't that good." As I went on about her behavior, her gum-chewing, her inattention to the lesson, she sat placidly as if realizing that she had earned the lecture and that I was just doing my job. If I expected her to be contrite and apologetic, I saw no sign of it, though she listened politely. I tried to work myself into a mood of righteous indignation. Then I suddenly realized that a lecture was not going to change Ione. Tomorrow she would be talking and chewing gum again. Besides, I really didn't feel angry. For some reason, the whole scene appeared incongruous. Suddenly, I started laughing. I paused, tried to resume my lecture, and started laughing again.

"Oh, what's the use," I said. "Go home and finish your work." I shook my head in mock despair. "I don't know why, but I just can't get mad at you."

She picked up her books and started toward the door. Then she turned and grinned at me mischievously. "That's because you love me," she said.

The point I am trying to make is the value of experience. Had Ione been in my class at an earlier time, my tolerance level might not have permitted the kind of relationship we had. Obviously a new teacher will make mistakes. Yet many young teachers whom I have tried to advise refused to believe that they were in any way responsible for the problems they were having. I remember one first-year teacher, after I endeavored to persuade her that her tactics of screaming at the students and chasing them around the room were unproductive, saying to me in exasperation, "Mr. Greenstein, you just don't understand these children!" By that time I had spent twenty years as a teacher and principal dealing with all kinds of children. I am sure there are still some I don't understand and can't control, but I found it quite ludicrous that a first-year teacher should say this to me. I realized that her outburst was the result of her extreme frustration and I didn't respond. Fortunately, she managed to survive. She remained at our school; by her fifth year, the children hadn't changed but she had. Occasionally she even complained to me about the incompetence of some of the new teachers. How soon we forget. Well, experience is a great teacher—especially for a teacher.

I vividly remember four girls who were in my class early in my teaching career. I used to call them "The Four Musketeers" because they were inseparable, always entering and leaving the room together. Ironically, they were a wonderful example of integration. They had risen above race and color to find a kinship, a common ground in mischief, dedicated to making life miserable for me. One was black, one was Jewish, one was Irish, one was Italian, and all were intolerable—at least, as far as I was concerned. Any one of them would have been difficult for me to cope with. The four of them together, each supporting the other, were unbearable.

There was Denise, the Jewish girl, short, dark-haired, pug-nosed, freckle-faced, and rather attractive, but impudent, with a sneering know-it-all smile curling her lips when I spoke to her. Once, when I raised an admonishing finger at her, she shrank back in mock terror. "Don't you dare hit me!" she yelled. "You know you can't hit me. If you do, I'll get you fired."

I sent for her mother. Mrs. Schwartz, a portly, pasty-faced woman, admitted to me that her Denise might be a bit spoiled. "But she is really a good girl. And smart. I've never laid a hand on her," said Mrs. Schwartz proudly.

"Maybe it's time you started," I replied wearily.

I don't want to give the impression that I am an advocate of spanking. I know there are better ways of teaching and punishing a child. Still, I don't believe an occasional spanking by a parent will injure the child's delicate psyche too much. On the other hand, when children are regularly and severely beaten by their parents, they often become discipline problems in school.

The black girl, Erminia, would stare at me blankly with large sullen eyes when I tried to reprove her. Sometimes I would keep her after school and attempt to reason with her quietly. She would listen in contemptuous silence, then walk out without a word when I had finished.

Angela, the Italian girl, was the follower—mischievous, vivacious, talkative, though not as bold as the others. She had some fear of authority and might have been manageable by herself, but she was an able and willing accomplice when her friends started their antics.

And there was Roseanne, the Irish girl, the oldest and tallest of the group and the apparent leader. She was pretty, in a hard sort of way, with curly red hair, sharp blue eyes, freckled white skin made whiter by powder, and a thin red line of lipstick accentuating her lips. (I did not approve of girls in elementary school wearing makeup. However, she was almost fifteen, and I got tired of telling her to remove it.) Sometimes she would be absent, and the others would be a little more subdued, at least for part of the time. She always brought a note which I suspected was forged. In fact, the handwriting looked very much like that of Denise. Reluctantly, for I didn't really miss her, I reported her absences and my suspicions to the office and to her mother. Her mother admitted that she had been unaware of the absences. She did not appear to be overly concerned but promised to "keep an eye on her." Evidently one eye was not enough. Toward the end of the year Roseanne's truancy increased, which probably was an important factor in preserving my sanity. I reported the matter again and decided to let the truant officer take care of it. I was aware that I contributed very little to her education when she was present. I had a feeling that she would soon drop out of school anyway.

Yes, those four were a handful. With more patience, more understanding, more confidence, and above all more experience, could I have gotten through to them? Well, I'll never know. But I do know that if I had had them in my class five years later I would have dealt with the situation differently.

9. The Principal: Man in the Middle

From a speech I made at a faculty meeting:

"Many years ago, when I was a mail carrier, we had a saying, 'All it takes to be a mailman is a strong back and a weak mind.' I have found that the prerequisites for being a principal are even simpler. He doesn't need the strong back."

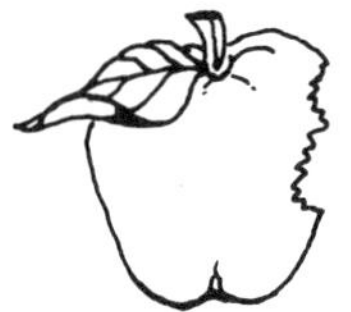

The president of a teacher's union has described the dominant characteristics of a typical principal in this manner: "Lack of educational leadership ability; absence of supervisory ability; low ability to relate interpersonally; job insecurity; 'pass the buck' syndrome; identification of self with the school; 'what's good for the school is good for me and vice versa'; inability to delegate authority; high attitude of 'this is a benign dictatorship'; 'in the middle' or 'between' attitudes because it is safer not to make waves."

There was more, but why go on? Pretty strong stuff! Is he right? Of course, he didn't say *all* principals are like that, just the typical ones. I suppose that means the majority. Well, I've known a lot of principals, and I would agree that there are some like that, but I would not agree that they are typical. Knowing the problems a principal has to face, maybe I'm a little prejudiced. If I wanted to indulge in generalities, I could say that most plumbers, painters, mechanics, TV repairmen, doctors, lawyers, businessmen, teachers—yes, and principals—care more about making money than doing a good job—or should I include the whole human race? I hope that this is too cynical an observation. There are few trades or professions, however, whose members as a whole qualify for sainthood—and that includes the priesthood. From the standpoint of dedication, I would put teachers and principals higher on the list than some of the others. People do not become teachers because they think it is the path to great wealth. And while principals do get paid more, they started as teachers. (In our school system one of the prerequisites for taking the principal's examination is six years of teaching experience.) It occurs to me that most of the principals this union leader is talking about were probably members of his union at one time. Apparently they were the good guys then. Suddenly they have become the enemy.

Perhaps teachers would say, sometimes with good reason, that principals have forgotten they were once teachers. It is unfortunately true that some principals who were severe critics of their superiors when they were in the ranks, so to speak, see things quite differently when they are placed in a position of authority—a not uncommon human trait. Well, things do suddenly become different. While no principal in his right mind would come out publicly with a blanket indictment of teachers, in private they are apt to make some pretty strong statements—though they may not go so far as to say they are describing the typical teacher. Principals are particularly bitter about the fact that they are denied the right to select teachers, and that they find it almost impossible to get rid of bad ones. Yes, it is true that principals and teachers are often placed in an adversary relationship.

And why, after thirteen years of teaching, was I ready to join the opposition? Although several of my friends who had become principals had been urging me for years to take the examination, I still hesitated. For one thing, I really was afraid I would not be able to pass. I had known a number of teachers who had taken it and failed—some of them several times. Besides, I was reluctant to give up my personal contact with students for the impersonal duties of an administrator. I was also aware that teachers, as a group, can be difficult to please, and that a few of my ideas about teaching (which often did not coincide with those of my colleagues) were likely to cause controversy and encounter resistance. (I sometimes even espoused the radical philosophy that children have rights.)

As a teacher I had achieved a certain degree of independence which I knew I would lose if I became a principal. I had done things in my own way with very little interference. Many teachers complain that principals do not permit them the freedom to teach as they would like. While this complaint is often justified, I seldom had that problem. I have generally gotten along well with my principals, although there were some I didn't like. I made a point of not bothering them, and they seldom bothered me. I like to think that they were aware that I was obtaining good results and were not particularly concerned about the methods I used to achieve them. At any rate, I considered myself a successful teacher, and I had no real training or experience for an administrative position although I had taken the required courses. So why, after all these years, should I look for trouble?

Some teachers wish to become principals because of the added prestige. For others the chief motivation is ambition. They may even consider the job a stepping stone to further advancement. For many, I among them, it is a matter of money. I was earning about $8,000 a year and had reached a plateau in the salary schedule. (Teachers' salaries have increased considerably since then, but so, of course, has the cost of living.) It seemed unlikely that I would be able to put four children through college on my salary. Therefore, despite my misgivings, I took the examination and, to my great surprise, I passed.

The school to which I was assigned was old and overcrowded. For many years it had served a stable, middle-class Bohemian community, but now the neighborhood was changing rapidly. The people moving in were much poorer and the families were larger. The school building, which could comfortably accommodate about eight hundred students, now served eleven hundred, and the membership was increasing every year. Over sixty percent of the students were Mexican, though the percentage was considerably larger than that in the lower grades. Our seventh and eighth grades were about fifty percent black. The reason for this lopsided distribution was that the neighboring school, which had an all-black population, only went through the sixth grade. Its students then transferred to our school.

I knew that my position would not be an easy one. Fortunately I had inherited two loyal and experienced clerks. A school clerk is much more than a typist or stenographer. She has many duties, and her value increases proportionately with her years of service and her familiarity with the particular school. A good clerk is important to any principal. To a new and inexperienced one she is invaluable. As for the teachers, they were better than average, though generally conservative and anxious to retain values and standards which were no longer possible in this changing community.

The union president I quoted previously asserted that the typical principal does not make waves. This is not an original observation. It is perhaps the most common criticism made about school administrators. Well, a new principal, if he is wise, will avoid making waves. He may find it is all he can do to remain afloat. My predecessor had been generally popular with the teachers, and I realized that if I deviated too radically from the policies and procedures she had instituted, I would destroy the morale of the staff. The school as a whole, which was going through a difficult transitional period intensified by the constantly growing membership, would be bound to suffer.

Yet I could not avoid taking certain stands which I knew would alienate some of the teachers. For example, it was a rule of the school that the boys wear ties in class. In the staid, middle-income community that the school had formerly served, this had been no problem. Many of the black and Mexican families, however, were large and poor, and this requirement imposed a financial burden upon them which I thought was unjustified. Why should they have to purchase an entirely useless article of clothing? Besides, this was a difficult rule to enforce. I believed there were far more important educational problems which the teachers and I should be addressing instead of wasting time on what I considered a trivial issue. To some of the teachers, however, this was no triviality. It was as if the rise and fall of civilization depended upon the wearing of ties.

As more and more students were sent to me for violating this rule, I decided to place the subject on the agenda for discussion at a faculty meeting. I found that the teachers themselves were equally divided on the issue. The older, more conservative ones insisted that our traditions (and our ties) must be preserved and long-haired boys should be eliminated. The younger teachers were inclined to take a more tolerant attitude. As a new principal, I did not feel secure enough to impose my views upon the staff. For that reason, and because I believed in democratic decisions, I asked for a vote. It ended in a tie (no pun intended). I therefore announced that teachers should decide for themselves whether they wanted ties worn in their own classrooms and that no student was to be sent to the office for disobeying this rule. I realized that even this compromise would alienate the more influential and outspoken teachers, but I could not give a blanket endorsement to a practice which I would never have imposed in my own classroom.

Why did so many teachers have such strong feelings about wearing ties? Partly it was a symbolic thing—the preservation of their mores and values. They were also convinced, as many people are, that a well-dressed student (not only wearing a tie but a white shirt as well) behaved better in the classroom. I know of no evidence to support this theory. It occurred to me at the time that almost all of the teachers who voted in favor of ties were women and had never worn one themselves. I also found it rather odd that at a meeting about a year later, when I asked for a vote on proper attire for teachers, many of these same female teachers threw tradition to the winds and voted in favor of pants suits (as optional attire, of course)—a slight change of attitude where their own comfort was concerned.

The battle concerning long hair for boys was then at its height. Fortunately for me, it was confined chiefly to the high schools. Only a few boys at the elementary level had started emulating this style, so I was seldom asked to make a decision on that question. Or perhaps the teachers suspected that I would not take a firm stand on this issue either and did not care to put it to the test. Personally, I still prefer short hair for boys, but I can't see it as a moral or ethical question. And if it is, what are we to think of our founding fathers? It is hard to imagine Washington, Jefferson, or Franklin with short hair.

The issue of the ties, which I thought had been comfortably disposed of, cropped up several years later. The school membership had grown considerably by then, and as a consequence I had acquired a "freed" assistant principal (one who does not have teaching duties). I had placed him in charge of discipline, and he, with the aid of a committee composed of some of the older teachers, prepared a booklet setting forth the rules of conduct for students. Included was a dress code which, among other things, stipulated that boys should wear ties. He presented the entire booklet at a parents' meeting and received a unanimous endorsement from those present (not a very large number). As he pointedly observed to me, no one had questioned the provision about wearing ties. I reflected that if parents wanted their sons to wear ties they could insist that the boys do so. In practice, however, parents prefer to have the school do the enforcing. They are pretty good at passing the buck too.

A few of the younger teachers, when they heard about it, objected strenuously to the proposed change in policy. I assured them that, while I had authorized the preparation of the booklet, it still required my approval. By this time, I was no longer a new principal and felt more secure in my position. I approved the booklet—after making a few minor amendments and eliminating one item—the one dealing with ties.

After that, the subject of clothing seldom became an issue. Occasionally I would speak to a student (or his mother) when I thought his apparel was inappropriate. (Girls were more likely to require this admonition than boys.) I settled each case individually without threats or punishment and found the parents very cooperative as long as I approached them in a friendly manner.

On the whole, I had a good relationship with the teachers, though I realized that I could never be the kind of "law and order" principal many of them would have liked. One teacher, for example, had a habit of bringing a child to the office and whispering to me, "I want you to scare him." I resented the implication that this was my function as an administrator. To talk to a child, to correct him, sometimes even to threaten him with the consequences if his conduct didn't improve—I could go along with that, but not just to serve as a bogeyman.

One practice, prevalent among the students, which the teachers and I disapproved of, was gum-chewing. As a teacher, I had never permitted it in my classroom. This is not a matter of denying anyone his personal freedom. I have known students to ruin books with gum, place it on a neighbor's seat, stick it on someone's coat, and even put it in someone's hair. It is difficult to get off the floor, and it adheres to people's shoes. Children can (and often do) make loud noises with it when they crack bubbles. All in all, it is a nuisance. Most of the teachers, however, found it almost impossible to control its use. Some resorted to making the offending student place the gum on his nose or forehead, a punishment I have never employed as I considered it distasteful, demeaning, and not particularly effective. (When complying with such a request, a comedian in the class might even display it as if it were a badge of honor.)

One day the unofficial "head teacher" of the eighth grade sent a girl to the office demanding that she be suspended for insubordination. He had told her several times to get rid of her gum. She had done so each time but had started chewing another stick a few minutes later. Finally he ordered her to put the gum in her hair and she refused. The girl was a mature fourteen-year-old with a bouffant hairdo, quite popular at the time, which was obviously the product of a recent and expensive trip to the beauty parlor. Had she acceded to the teacher's command, I could imagine the stormy session I would have had with her mother the following day. I agreed that the girl should be punished for her continual gum-chewing and offered to call her mother, but I balked at suspending her for disobeying an order which I deemed highly improper. The teacher was obviously unhappy with my decision and muttered something about teachers expecting a principal to "back them up." I knew he would communicate his displeasure to the rest of the staff and this would not enhance my reputation, even though I did call the girl's mother to inform her that any further disobedience on the girl's part would not be tolerated. (I did not mention the teacher's action.)

There were a number of other occasions when, in my opinion,

teachers used poor judgment and forced me to make difficult decisions. Sometimes, when I indicated to a teacher that her action was injudicious, she would realize her mistake and thank me for correcting her. For example, a teacher, infuriated by something a child had done, might write a hasty, abrasive note to a parent. After this had happened several times, I requested that notes sent to parents be approved by me. If the note was inflammatory, I would suggest that instead of eliciting the parent's cooperation it would probably provoke anger and resistance. Often, when the teacher had calmed down, she would appreciate the point I was making. There were other times, however, when my role as a moderator was not so well received.

I remember one case clearly, more because of the teacher's reaction than because of the incident itself. A second-grade teacher, exasperated by the unusual noisiness of the class one morning, warned the students that she would put soap in the mouth of the next one who talked without permission. The class was quiet for a while. Then a precocious but mischievous little girl who had been one of the chief culprits started talking again. The teacher felt compelled to carry out her threat. She put a small sliver of soap in the girl's mouth.

A few days later I received a call from my superintendent requesting that I investigate the matter and make a full written report on what action I had taken. He had received a very irate and threatening letter from the girl's mother. After learning the facts from the teacher, I wrote as mild a letter as I could to the superintendent explaining that the child in question had been repeatedly out of order and that the teacher, while using questionable judgment in this instance, was generally conscientious and competent. I stated that I had had a conference with the teacher, during which she had assured me that an episode of this nature would not occur again. I further reported that I had talked to the mother and resolved the matter by promising her that this kind of disciplinary measure would not be repeated. In return, I had received her assurance that she would admonish the little girl for her disruptive behavior.

I permitted the teacher to read my report. She was very upset. She was afraid it would become part of her permanent file in the personnel office and would irreparably damage her professional reputation. I assured her I had the superintendent's word that the report would go no further than his office and would not harm her in any way. I tried to explain to her that I had no choice in the matter as I had to comply with an order from my superior and could not condone her action. She remained hostile and unconvinced.

Some teachers resented my stand against corporal punishment. This was not a personal decision on my part, though I have strong feelings on the subject, but an attempt to enforce a ruling made by the Board of Education. Of course there are quite a few schools where this prohibition is ignored.

To many teachers the most important attribute of a principal is his attitude toward discipline. If he takes a firm, punitive approach toward students who are sent to him for "counseling" (really for punishment), the teachers are likely to overlook or forgive other shortcomings. Most teachers are convinced that the principal's chief duty is to enforce discipline and that his method of doing so is the determining factor in the behavior of the students. I don't agree. I learned very early in my teaching career that (1) a principal cannot be depended upon to enforce discipline and (2) that good discipline depends primarily on the teacher. (Of course, well-behaved students and cooperative parents always help.)

During my first year of teaching I sent no students to the principal although I was often tempted to do so. I was afraid that if I did it would appear to be an admission that I was unable to manage the class. Actually, I wasn't, but I certainly didn't want to advertise this fact to the principal. I was on probation, and after all the years I had worked to become a teacher I was anxious to avoid doing anything that might jeopardize my position. Sometimes, when I was having difficulty with a student, I would warn him that if he did not behave I would send him to the office. This was a bluff on my part as I really had no intention of doing so. Usually it had the desired effect, at least temporarily. However, during my second year, after I had made this threat to a misbehaving student several times, he responded nonchalantly, "Go ahead."

I had not yet learned the maxim, "Don't make threats you can't (or don't intend to) carry out." I now had no choice but to send him to the office. This unusual action on my part had a sobering effect on the rest of the class. I was beginning to think I had made a good decision, until the student returned with a big grin on his face and a note for my perusal. Its contents explained the boy's reaction. The principal, who regarded himself as a very progressive individual, was advising me that his solution to my problem was to appoint the errant student a patrol boy. It was his theory that a disruptive student's behavior can be modified by giving him a position of responsibility.

I have no quarrel with this hypothesis. In later years I have sometimes employed this method successfully myself. But when a teacher has sent a student to the principal for correction, he hardly expects to find that the student was rewarded for his transgressions. Nor is this likely to have a salutory effect upon the class. Yet, in retrospect, I have often felt that the principal did me a favor. I learned the hard way that if I was to succeed as a teacher it would have to be through my own resources. In the years that followed, I may occasionally have requested that the office send for a parent on my behalf, but aside from that I handled all disciplinary matters myself.

I do not want to leave the impression that teachers should never send students to the office. There are times when it may be necessary to request a medical or psychiatric examination of a child, place him in another class, suspend him, or determine that he be sent to a special school, all of which are beyond the authority of the classroom teacher. Even in lesser cases, when a teacher is unable to solve the problem, she should be able to ask for assistance. I am saying, however, that there are teachers who believe their job is only to teach and that discipline is the responsibility of the principal. No principal can help these teachers. He can stay in the classroom for an hour and not a single child will be out of order. I know. I have done it. He can request to see some of the parents. He can punish the recalcitrants. But the minute that teacher is left to her own resources, the pandemonium resumes. When the children know that the teacher cannot or will not control them, they are quite ruthless. Actually, they are doing what comes naturally—trying to have a good time. It might be nice if all students were docile, well-behaved, and interested in their lessons. (I say "might" because I am not sure that children should always be docile.) Occasionally a teacher may even have such a class, though personally I can never remember being that fortunate. Discipline—or perhaps we should call it control—is part of the job, except perhaps at the college level.

During the time of a teacher shortage, two erudite, elderly gentlemen were assigned to our school. They had no teacher training or experience. They were sincere, hardworking, scholarly, anxious to please, and had absolutely no idea of how to handle children. As they were substitutes—without status or tenure—I had no difficulty in terminating their employment, which I did regretfully though not soon enough. They were nice people, and I kept hoping they would improve. I should not have retained them as long as I did. I was cheating the children and I knew it. I must accept the blame for that. However, there are many incompetent teachers with tenure whose rights are protected by the teachers' union. Yes, there is a very complicated procedure set up for removing them. I've tried it. So have many principals. About the best I or any principal I know has accomplished is to have them transferred to another school where someone else has had to put up with them. Just a game of musical chairs. A fine solution!

Some teachers who have good control of their classes send a student to the office so rarely that, when they do so, the principal realizes that the circumstances must have warranted this action. In such cases I would do all I could to resolve the problem. Others, however, cry wolf so often that one cannot distinguish the legitimate complaints from the minor infractions that the teacher should have been able to handle. Teachers like this take up so much of the principal's or his assistant's time that the more important cases do not receive the attention they deserve, and the whole school suffers as a result.

One substitute who had been assigned to our school for the day sent twelve students to me within the first hour. I disposed of them by giving each one an assignment and placing them in other classrooms (with the consent of the teachers). This consumed almost an hour of my time. Then I went to the substitute's classroom to see what was going on. The class, or what was left of it, was now in pretty good order—no great accomplishment under the circumstances. The teacher thanked me profusely for my cooperation. After lecturing the remaining students for a minute (they probably didn't need it, but I didn't want any more sent to me), I left. I was not going to criticize the teacher in front of the students, an action which I consider highly unprofessional (and I know there are principals who do this). Later I notified the area substitute center that I would not accept this teacher at our school again.

As I have intimated, the principal who "takes no nonsense" from the students is more likely to please the teachers than one with a more tolerant attitude. They would like him to make it clear that the teacher is always right (a rather difficult task sometimes). He is expected to reflect this uncompromising attitude in dealing with the students' parents as well when he speaks to them about their children's transgressions.

While being a "teachers' principal" may please the faculty, what is the reaction of the community? Actually, unless the principal becomes unduly abusive and dictatorial, it can be quite favorable. Many of the parents want strict discipline, something they are often unable to achieve at home. Some parents will proudly manifest their commitment to this goal by giving the teacher or principal permission to spank their child. (This "permission" cannot supersede the rules of the Board of Education.) Generally, however, parents are more likely to be in favor of law and order when it is the other person's child who is being punished. There is often a complete reversal of attitude when their own child is the subject of disciplinary action. In fact, one of the common complaints of the parents whose children are most often in trouble is, "How come that so-and-so and so-and-so do such-and-such things and get away with it, but the minute my child does one thing wrong you call me!"

All in all, the principal who "runs a tight ship" is likely to win the approval of most, if not all, of the faculty and even a good number of the parents. He may not be equally popular with the students, but who listens to them?

10. So What Does He Do all Day?

In one episode of a television series, a principal said to his clerk, "I'll never forget January 10th."

"Why?" she asked. "What happened on January 10th?"

"Nothing," he replied wistfully. "Absolutely nothing!"

I knew exactly what he meant.

The job of a principal! I doubt if I can adequately describe it. It varies considerably with the size of the school, the kind of school (Parent-Child Center, primary, Kg–6, Kg–8, junior high, vocational, high school), and the nature of the community. However, certain elements of the job are the same—a lot of responsibility and a limited amount of authority. Although the engineer is in charge of the physical plant (the building itself), the principal orders furniture and equipment, decides where they go, consults with the engineer on rehabilitation and repairs, is the intermediary for teachers' complaints about the cleaning and maintenance of classrooms, and is involved in many other decisions concerning the school building.

A teacher tells the principal her piano needs repairing. He orders it to be done. Simple enough. He instructs the clerk to type the requisition and he signs it. A month later the teacher reminds him that her piano hasn't been fixed yet. He calls downtown and is caustically informed that he isn't the only one who wants a piano repaired, that there are five hundred schools in the city, all of which apparently have pianos that need repairing, that there are only ten (or eight, or five) repairmen to take care of all these pianos, and that he'll just have to wait his turn. Two months later the teacher reminds him again. He calls downtown to find out where he stands on the list. They can't find the requisition. Is he sure he sent it in? Positive? Well, the man who takes care of it is on vacation. Maybe he'd better send the order in again just to make sure. He takes two aspirins, tells the clerk to type up another requisition, signs it, makes sure it's in the school mail, and waits another two months. The teachers wants to know how she is supposed to teach music without a piano. She sounds hostile. He gets the feeling that she thinks he never placed the order.

He calls again. Yes, they have the requisition. They even found the first one. Isn't that funny? He isn't laughing. His school is now only twentieth on the list. How long will it take? It's hard to tell. They can't work on repairs right now because a lot of pianos need tuning. Every school wants a piano tuned for graduation, and they have to start early or they'll never get to them all. The principal suddenly remembers that his order to tune the piano for graduation hasn't gone in. He tells the clerk to get it out right away and hopes he isn't too late. (Graduation is only four months away.) Two more months go by. The teacher informs him that she has gone almost a whole school year with a piano that has no middle C. He is tired of hearing about it. He wishes she played harmonica or guitar. Well, there's only one thing to do. He should have done it long ago and avoided all this aggravation. He hires a repairman and pays him out of school funds. It is finally done, and the teacher is smiling at him again.

Eight months later (this is the next school year) the repairman from the Board of Education shows up, an unexpected but by this time a not particularly welcome surprise. Since the piano he came to repair has already been taken care of, and there are others in the building that need service, the principal suggests that the repairman fix the piano in room 209. Nothing doing. His ticket says to repair three keys on the piano in room 105. But that has already been done, explains the principal patiently. After all, a piano is a piano. Why not repair the one in 209 instead? Or possibly he could tune the piano in the assembly hall. It never did get tuned for graduation. The repairman becomes belligerent. His ticket says room 105 and that's the only piano he'll work on. A call downtown elicits a predictable response. If the principal wants the piano in room 209 repaired, he must send in another requisition. The principal gives up in disgust.

At different times I have arranged for the purchase of paper, ditto fluid, basketballs, record players, and other items. They were paid for with our own school funds—money obtained by selling taffy apples, student photographs (my chief source of school revenue), and various fund-raising projects sponsored by our parents' organization. All of these items are in the supply catalogue and should have been charged to our supply fund, but the teachers couldn't wait forever.

Is it the fault of the bureaucracy? Not always. There have been paper shortages, truck strikes, and other foul-ups. I'm sure the people downtown can give you their side of the story and tell you how tired they are of being pestered by irate, misinformed principals. But the principal's only recourse is to make repeated phone calls or write nasty letters couched in very proper language. Meanwhile, he continues to get complaints from the teachers (and sometimes the parents) face-to-face.

I remember filling out a report in which I was supposed to itemize how I spent my time and what percent of it was spent on each task. I was tempted to respond that I spent a great deal of my time completing stupid reports like that one. Actually I did write that, but not quite so bluntly.

Composing official letters is another chore. There are people downtown who are not convinced that the telephone can function as an instrument of communication. They will listen patiently while you explain your need or complaint, and after you have finished they will say, "Write me a letter." Although I resented the additional work, I found out that it was a good idea to do it anyway and to keep a carbon copy so there was a record of what had transpired if the question ever came up. Time-consuming, but one soon learns that it's necessary.

Does this give you any idea of the work of a principal? I doubt it. A large part of the job is supposed to be the supervision and evaluation of teachers. The principal should visit each class at least twice a year and observe the teacher's performance for about a half hour or more. I always meant to do this, but seldom got around to it. No time. In a school with sixty-five classrooms, it would take over three school months at the rate of one a day to visit them all—and the days can be very short when you're busy. There are many other people you have to evaluate too—teachers who don't have classrooms (adjustment teacher, speech teacher, master teacher, etc.), teacher-nurse, truant officer, teacher aides, clerks, security guards, and even substitutes who have been at your school for a week. You are supposed to know what all of them are doing and how well they are doing it, and meet with them when necessary (and it often is) to discuss their work and their problems. How do you evaluate all these people objectively? You know them all, except perhaps the substitutes, and you have a pretty good idea of how they are functioning, but in many cases you have insufficient data to make a really valid judgment. You can lie a lot and grade high, or you can try to be fair and make enemies. The poorer the teacher, the more likely she is to complain about the grade you gave her, even when you know it was higher than she deserved. Those who received a superior rating won't complain. Unfortunately, they are likely to boast about it to a colleague whom you only graded excellent, and that teacher will demand an explanation.

I will not say I always graded fairly. I often thought I was overly generous, though sometimes a new teacher may have received a lower grade than she deserved because I wanted to see how she would function under different conditions. A teacher may do well with a top group. How will she do with a low one? Conversely, if she is not doing well, it may be that she has a very difficult class. Let's see how she'll do next year with a better one.

"How can he know what I'm doing?" some teachers complain. "He never visits me." Yet many of them prefer not to be visited. It's an awkward situation for the teacher, the students, and the principal. Does the teacher act the same way when the principal is not present? Is this how the children usually behave? Personally, I could tell more about what was going on in a classroom by just looking through the door occasionally when I passed by, which I often did. Sometimes, when I was in doubt about a teacher's grade, I would visit the classroom after school to look at the lesson plan book and at the work of the students displayed on the walls. This would give me a pretty good indication of what the teacher was doing. (In one case the papers on the wall were four months old and were graded incorrectly.) A capsule comment: I believe it would be much better all around if the present grading system for teachers was supplanted with just two grades, satisfactory and unsatisfactory.

There are many other things a principal has to do. He sees book salesmen, makes out (or at least supervises) book orders, attends district meetings, teachers' meetings, parents' meetings, plans the curriculum, prepares duty schedules, places teachers and children in classrooms, assigns substitutes every morning, inspects the lunchroom, even checks the weather to see if the children should have indoor or outdoor recess—and of course there are always reports to complete and letters to write. If he has no freed assistant, he also takes care of discipline problems.

Our school membership kept increasing until I finally was entitled to a freed assistant. I put him in charge of discipline, but gave him few other duties. From my own experience, I knew it was a big job and would keep him busy. I had never handled it as well as I would have wished because I had too many other things to do. Of course a good administrator should know how to delegate authority. I must confess that this was not one of my strong points. I once knew a principal who was really good at it. I often found him asleep in his office while his assistant practically ran the school. I can't say there is a connection, but she has been dead a long time now; he outlived her by many years.

Some principals distribute a number of tasks among the teachers. They use better judgment than I did. Having been a teacher for so many years, I remembered how I had resented being assigned extra duties. I felt that teaching, making lesson plans, and grading papers every night was a full-time job. I realize that I spent more time on these chores than most teachers do. A few may not find it necessary (gym teachers, librarians, shop teachers). Others are too lazy. And many have to shop, cook, and take care of their own children and don't have the time.

Of necessity I did allot jobs to teachers. Some accepted these assignments without protest and performed them well. Others agreed that I should delegate more of my responsibilities—but not to them.

I have often noticed, as I'm sure most people have, that the father in a television series apparently has all day to devote to his family's problems. We know vaguely that he does something for a living, but if he is a banker we hardly ever see him banking, or if he is an architect we never see him architecting. Similarly, a school principal on television appears to be constantly involved with teachers and students and their problems—which he should be—but we seldom see him doing anything else. I realize that a half-hour show on the preparation of a room utilization report would not be very exciting, but much of the principal's time is actually spent on routine duties of that nature. That is why I have attempted to delineate some of the tasks which occupy the working hours of a busy principal. It should be understood that the episodes which follow were highlights against the background of my ordinary, mundane, everyday activities.

11. Who Knows What Danger Lurks?

One of our students was making life extremely difficult for his fifth-grade teacher. Although she tried to cope with his antics, she would send him to me when her patience was exhausted. This began to be a regular occurrence.

One day the boy's mother called. She had to leave on an errand and wanted me to give him a message.

"Please tell him to take his little sister home when he gets out of school and to watch her till I get back."

I assured her I would take care of the matter and sent a note to his teacher. "May I see Rodney?" I asked.

Back came Rodney with her reply: "Yes—every morning, noon, and night if you like!"

The principal of a large school—or any school for that matter—soon becomes accustomed to dealing with a variety of situations. For example, one or two children would be injured on the playground almost daily. Usually the wound was minor and the clerks would take care of it. Occasionally, if they were busy and I happened to be in the outer office, I would take care of it myself. More severe cases were sent to our gym teacher who was an expert in first aid, unless I decided that the student should not be moved, in which case I would send a message to have the gym teacher come to the office. Then I would have to find somebody to take his class. Sometimes there was no one available, and I would proceed quickly to the gym and take care of the class myself till he had completed his diagnosis or treatment. If he thought there was a possible fracture or that the wound required stitches, I would instruct one of the clerks to notify a parent while I called for a police car to take the injured child to the hospital. On rare occasions, when I believed there was a real emergency, I might even call for a fire department ambulance.

A fight on the playground was not uncommon, but the teacher on duty was usually able to take care of it. There were times, however, when she needed help and would send for me. Then I would hurry outside, separate the antagonists, and take them to the office. Often a number of witnesses would follow, all anxious to testify, especially if one of the combatants was their classmate. I meted out punishment for one or both, depending on my analysis of what had occurred. While I considered fighting a very serious offense, I believed that the circumstances should be taken into consideration. If it was a first offense and no particular damage had been done, I contented myself with a lecture on the dangers and folly of fighting, followed by an admonition that a second offense would call for a more severe penalty—probably a suspension. I then recorded the incident on a file card, making sure that each of the students involved was aware of this. As there were few second offenses, I considered this method reasonably effective. Many teachers disagreed. They maintained that both participants in a fight should be suspended immediately, even when the evidence clearly indicated that one had attacked the other. They did not believe in wasting time with an investigation. Nor were they particularly concerned with due process, or that someone is presumed innocent until proven guilty. Apparently, democratic principles are not supposed to apply to children.

Occasionally there was a false fire alarm. This was very disturbing as the school would have to be evacuated pending an investigation to make sure there was no fire. Once the alarm had rung, the fire department would respond quickly. The end result was a waste of time and effort for everybody. After order was restored, I would try to find the culprit, an endeavor in which I was often successful. With all the investigations I had to conduct, I became a pretty good detective—as well as a prosecuting attorney and judge. If the offender was a small child, I would scold him severely and notify his parents. When an older student was involved, one I considered more responsible for his actions, I might have him taken to the police station. His parents would then be called to pick him up. Following such an incident, I would discuss the problem at an assembly or visit some of the upper-grade classrooms, as many as I had time for, to explain the seriousness of such an act—that it cost the city about seventy-five dollars, and that a real fire might get out of control while firemen were busy responding to a false alarm. I would also recount an actual case in which a fire truck, which had been dispatched in answer to a false alarm, had accidentally killed a woman. The incident had precipitated a riot in the community.

At times a class would become very noisy and unmanageable, especially if the regular teacher was absent. The teacher would then send a messenger to me, and I would run up the stairs two at a time (not so much because of the urgency of the situation as because I thought I needed the excercise) to take care of the emergency. As the students were usually aware that I was on the way, they often would have settled down by the time I appeared on the scene. The mysterious grapevine which disseminated the information that I was approaching was not really so mysterious. The source was the messenger sent by the teacher, or sometimes the teacher would warn them I was on the way. As a lookout stationed at the door spotted me, I could hear, with concealed amusement, the loud whispers announcing my arrival. "The principal is coming!"

Whether it was due to my many years of experience, the prestige of my position, or both, I cannot say, but I never had any difficulty in breaking up a fight or quelling a disturbance. (Of course I had often done it as a teacher too.) I thought that this would enhance my reputation with the teachers, but most of them were probably not even aware of it. How many teachers are likely to disclose that their class was out of order and that they had to call for assistance from the principal? On the other hand, some teachers believed that my permissiveness encouraged these disturbances, or that my punishments were not sufficiently severe. Here was a contradiction that often puzzled me. There was never a doubt that I had at least the outward respect of the students. Rare indeed was the occasion when a student would be insolent in my presence. Yet many teachers insisted that the students misbehaved because they had no fear of the principal. And how could I explain to these teachers that as a teacher or a principal (after all, I was still the same person) I wanted children to like and respect me—not to fear me?

Of course the teachers who had control of their classes did not need my help, and for those who could not maintain order my assistance was only transitory. The latter always found it easier to blame the principal or the "permissive atmosphere" than to admit their own inability to cope with the situation. I sometimes felt that in order to satisfy these teachers I would have to boil every offending student in oil (an expensive proposition these days), then dismember him for an encore. At the very least, they wanted every student they sent to me suspended immediately no matter what the offense. As some parents were likely to object to the first solution, and as my superintendent had issued a directive deploring the excessive number of suspensions in our district, my options were somewhat limited.

There were other problems with students. One of them might complain that someone had stolen money from him, or that he had been threatened or beaten up. Or I might hear of an incipient racial conflict. This I would try to avert immediately. Nevertheless, some racial clashes did occur, and neighborhood gangs often became involved.

Like a doctor who becomes accustomed to seeing people who are injured or in pain, I developed, if not a callousness, at least an ability to take these situations in stride. However, there was one incident which occurred during my first year that differed from any I have ever encountered before or since. Although it never was reported in the newspapers, I am sure it would have been if the outcome had been different.

One cool autumn day, shortly before the end of the lunch hour, three eighth-grade girls rushed into the outer office which was the domain of my clerks. I could hear them shouting hysterically and assumed they were reporting a fight. Hastily I went out and tried to calm them sufficiently so I could obtain a comprehensible statement. They were all talking or screaming at once. One had tears in her eyes and the others were gasping for breath, either from running or from excitement, I wasn't sure which.

"Quiet down!" I commanded. I pointed to the one who seemed most composed. "You. Tell me what happened."

"There are two big boys on the girls' playground. They got knives! They're chasing some of the girls! They're trying to kill them!"

I was accustomed to exaggerations. The situation was seldom as bad as the students would intimate. However, big boys with knives on the girls' playground—this could hardly be taken lightly, especially as the two other girls were nodding their heads in agreement.

"Our boys?" I asked.

"No, bigger. High school boys!" one of them responded.

This sounded extremely serious and required some immediate decisions. How to get the girls out of danger—what to do about the boys who were attacking them—what assistance was needed? I knew it would be advisable to get help from some of the male teachers—the gym teacher and a few of the other more athletic ones, but that would take time. Meanwhile, someone could be seriously hurt—perhaps already had been. There were a lot of little girls out there who were particularly vulnerable. The danger to them was not only from the boys but from other students in case of panic. I had to get out on the playground to do what I could and try to obtain help at the same time. I glanced at the clock. The lunch hour was almost over anyway.

"Ring the bell," I instructed one clerk. "Let's get the kids into the building."

I turned to the other clerk. "Call the police. Tell them it's an emergency."

Then—back to the first clerk. "See if you can get some of the men teachers." I was already on the way out as I called back, "I'll be on the playground."

I don't know how many things can enter one's mind at one time. However, as I ran down the short flight of steps from the office, and then the fifty feet or so to the side door, a number of thoughts did come to me—not in any particular order, but almost simultaneously. What I was doing didn't make sense. Was I trying to be a hero, or was I just being stupid? The boys were probably bigger than I was and had knives. I was unarmed. Maybe I should have found a stick or something. Too late now. What chance could I have against them? I didn't mind being a hero, but I had no taste whatever for being a dead one. The logical thing to do was to wait for reinforcements. But there was no time for logic. If I procrastinated, someone might be badly injured—even killed. This was "my" school. These were "my" girls. I couldn't escape the responsibility. (Yes, a principal does identify with his school as the union president I quoted stated in his criticism. Is that always so bad?)

Another thought—this was my first year as a principal. Would it be my last? After all I had gone through to get the job, that would really be ironic. And what about my four children? They still needed a father. I had an obligation to them to be careful. I realized I was getting melodramatic and letting my imagination run away with me. I was probably exaggerating the danger just as the students often did. It wouldn't be the first time I had seen girls become hysterical with very little cause. Well, I would just have to play it by ear.

By this time I was out on the playground. In accordance with my instructions, the clerk had rung the bell, and most of the students were already in the building. Some were still crowded at the entrances and frantically trying to push their way in. The playground was almost deserted. Not quite. As I looked around, I saw two big boys. Facing them at a distance of about twenty feet were some of the eighth-grade girls. They looked frightened. The boys looked menacing, and they were advancing slowly, though I couldn't see any weapons. Quickly I ran between them and the girls. The boys stopped.

"Get in the building," I ordered the girls. Then I turned to the boys and said resolutely, "Let's go. You don't belong here. Let's go!"

I didn't want to sound too threatening. I knew that that could have a contrary effect. "Just play it cool," I said to myself. "Let them know you aren't afraid and are very sure of yourself" (which, of course, wasn't the way I felt at all).

Suddenly one of the boys turned and ran. I felt a little better. At least I had bluffed one of them. The other stood motionless. He wasn't very tall—maybe five-ten, appeared to be about eighteen years old, rather thin, of medium-brown complexion, and was wearing a heavy, dark-blue pea coat. We had eighth-grade boys who were bigger than he was. If it came to a struggle, I figured I could hold my own until help arrived. However, he had one hand under his coat, and it was what might be in that hand that was bothering me.

As if in answer to my thoughts he said roughly, "Don't you come near me, or I'll cut you. Just don't you come any nearer."

Well, at least he wasn't attacking. I had no intention of coming closer. I didn't want to excite him, but I held my ground and stood facing him. "You'd better go," I said evenly. "The police are on the way."

He started backing away slowly, still facing me.

"Don't come any nearer or I'll cut you," he repeated.

My apprehension was beginning to subside. The girls were gone by this time, and I could see that if I didn't attack him he wasn't likely to attack me. Maybe he didn't even have a knife. However, his hand was still under his coat, and I didn't intend to find out. He kept backing away and I stood watching him. Finally, as he got to the open gate, he turned and ran.

As I realized that the crisis was over, I felt myself shaking a little. I didn't feel too heroic. I hadn't captured the attackers single-handed. I hadn't even tried to. They were gone and the girls were safe. That was the main thing.

I walked quickly back to the office. Some of the girls were still there. "Was anyone hurt?" I inquired.

"I don't think so," one of them replied. "They didn't catch us. Mostly they were after Eloise, but she got away."

"He grabbed me," said another. "He tore my coat, but he didn't get me. I ran."

Just then two policemen came up the stairs. I met them at the landing, explained the situation briefly, and told them in which direction the boys had headed.

"Come on!" one of the officers said to the other. "Maybe we can still catch them." Out they went to the squad car and I heard them drive away.

Now, with the situation more relaxed, I ushered the girls into my office, instructed them to sit down, and tried to get a clearer picture of the whole incident. The girls were still pretty excited. To avoid frequent interruptions, I ordered them to speak one at a time and asked each girl to give her story.

There was general consensus on the facts. Apparently the whole affair had started at the beginning of the lunch hour in a department store about a block away. The girls had been seated at the food counter and had just ordered something to eat when two youths walked in. Eloise recognized one of them. He lived on the same block that she did. She called to him.

"Hi, Limpy," she said.

According to Eloise, and the other girls corroborated this, everyone called the boy "Limpy." It was not his real name but the only one by which they knew him. He limped a little on one leg, hence the nickname. Eloise had meant no harm. He had never previously objected to being addressed in this way, but this time it seemed to infuriate him. An argument ensued between the boys and girls and it soon got out of hand. The manager of the store was summoned and tried to quiet them down. The boys reacted belligerently, called him names, and may have done some minor damage—I never got this cleared up. The manager now ordered all of them out of the store. The girls, who were frightened by this time, ran out, and the boys followed. The manager then called the police. When my clerk called, the police were already on the way, which explained their swift arrival at our school. Meanwhile, the girls ran to the playground. The boys ran after them, and it was here that Limpy pulled out a knife and gave the impression that he was quite prepared to use it. His friend, as far as I could determine, was not too deeply involved either in the argument or the subsequent attack. He was just going along with Limpy. One girl's coat had been either cut or torn, I wasn't sure which, but that was the extent of the damage. However, there was no mistaking the fear and emotional trauma these girls had experienced. They were convinced that Limpy would have injured or killed them if he had caught them.

By the time I had gotten this much of the story straightened out, one of my clerks called to me. "The squad car is back. They've got someone in the back seat."

I asked Eloise to come with me in case an identification should be necessary and went outside. They had Limpy. He looked somewhat the worse for wear, with blood trickling from his lip and a red bruise on his head. However, he did not seem to be seriously injured. He was handcuffed, and he sat silently with his head bowed, looking very dejected. After our identification, one of the officers stayed with him, and the other accompanied me to my office.

The officer looked young, not more than twenty-five, with blue eyes and curly blond hair. He entered my office and, as I closed the door, exclaimed exultantly, "Well, we got him! He really gave us a hell of a chase. He ran into an alley and we had to go after him on foot for a couple of blocks. You know," he confided, "I shot at him three times. I don't know how I missed the son-of-a-bitch. Anyway, we found the knife."

I was appalled, though I didn't respond to his remark. So far, all I knew about the young man was that he had threatened the girls and me. Although I was glad he had been apprehended, I didn't feel that he deserved the death penalty without a trial, especially as there was no evidence that he had injured anyone. I was relieved that he had not been shot. Judging by the marks on him and the trickle of blood, I assumed the officers had handled him pretty roughly anyway. Well, it was no use asking questions about that.

"I suppose you'll want a statement," I said rather formally. My initial impulse to congratulate him had faded. His obvious pleasure at another human being's misfortune had turned me off completely. He didn't seem to think of the boy in custody as a human being at all. I wondered if it was because of the boy's color, or just that they were on opposite sides of the law.

The officer evidently didn't notice my coolness. "Yeah, I'll need your statement and the girls' too. You wouldn't happen to know if he's over seventeen?"

I understood the significance of the question. Unless the boy was over seventeen, he would be considered a juvenile. He would be taken to the police station and very possibly get off with a station adjustment—which meant he would receive a lecture and would then be released in the custody of his parents. If the girls' parents or I pressed charges, we might be able to get him before a judge, but the result would probably be the same. However, if he were over seventeen he could be charged and tried as an adult.

"I have no idea," I answered. "The girls might know. I'll get them."

I recalled the girls from the outer office and they repeated, for the policeman's benefit, substantially the same story they had given me, but added one significant fact. Eloise remembered that Limpy had once attended our school.

"In that case we should have his records," I said. "I could check his age if I knew his real name."

"Oh, I've got that," responded the officer. "We got him to cooperate," he added with a grin.

He gave me the boy's name, and I went to the outer office to check our files while he jotted down the girls' statements. I soon returned with the information. "Yes, we have his record. He's over seventeen."

"That's good," the officer said jubilantly. "He's not going to get away with any station adjustment. We'll nail him good!"

I had to agree that chasing the girls with a knife and threatening the principal of a school were crimes that deserved a more severe punishment than a lecture by the police sergeant. As long as he received a fair trial, I would be satisfied. I completed my statement, carefully specifying that, although the girls claimed they had been threatened with a knife and although a knife had apparently been recovered, I had personally not seen a weapon. The threat to me, while I considered it very real, was verbal. I also indicated that the boy was backing away, rather than coming toward me, at the time. According to the officer, this still constituted aggravated assault. I didn't feel like the victim of an aggravated assault, but I took his word for it.

After the officer had gone, the older of my clerks, who had been at the school for many years, said to me, "You know, that policeman looks familiar. Did you get his name?"

"Yes, I did. I wrote it down. Why?"

"Just a hunch. What was his name?"

I obtained it for her and returned to my office. She knocked on the door a minute later and silently handed me a registration card. The policeman was also a former student of ours. His grades had been poor, and he had consistently received a U in conduct.

"I thought he looked familiar," said the clerk.

At the risk of being redundant, I had better interject that this is not fiction. I have not embellished the story for dramatic purposes. Both Limpy and the officer were former students of our school and both had had poor records. Scholastically, the officer's grades were the better of the two. His marks in conduct were worse. I'm not sure if there is a moral here, so I'll just stick to the facts.

Another fact was the nature of my reception the next day. I was greeted with smiles by a number of teachers who had heard that I had been attacked and wounded, and were surprised at my quick recovery. The students who saw me were even more astonished—and some seemed a little disappointed. Nothing personal—but my appearance spoiled an exciting rumor. The word had spread that I had been killed. I assured them that the news of my death was greatly exaggerated. This line had evoked a big laugh when Mark Twain used it, but I didn't even get a chuckle. I don't think they wished me any harm, but school is pretty boring most of the time, and now they thought they were in the middle of some real excitement. I guess they pictured news headlines, and even television interviews—especially for the "eyewitnesses" who had been on the playground at the time of the incident. Then I show up without a scratch and spoil it all! I was really sorry I had let them down. Well, anyway, I was still a celebrity—for one day.

Next came the matter of the trial. This was my first experience with our judicial system, and it turned out to be a learning experience (that's good educational jargon for anything unpleasant). On the designated day, I took time off from work and made a trip to court with the three girls I had selected as the most competent witnesses. The manager of the department store was there too. We had both signed complaints against Limpy. The attorney for the Board of Education was also in attendance and briefly checked the facts with me. Then the arresting officer entered the courtroom and sauntered over. He greeted me effusively, took me aside, and in a conspiratorial tone said that it would be a good idea to review my testimony.

"Now remember that this boy came at you with a knife and tried to stab you," he said.

"Well, he threatened me, but I didn't actually see the knife," I reminded him.

"But he probably had it under his coat," the officer insisted. "In fact, I'm sure he did. It will sound better if you say that he came at you with a knife in his hand."

Better for whom, I wondered. "Don't worry, I'll know what to say," I responded noncommittally. I was offended by his suggestion that I perjure myself. At the same time, I found the situation somewhat amusing. Here was a very young policeman with a very limited education coaching me on how to comport myself on the witness stand. Obviously he was extremely anxious to get a conviction. For the moment, however, what we got was a continuance.

It was simple. We sat and waited for several hours. Finally, the case was called. The defense attorney formally requested that it be continued at a later date. The judge granted the request, set a date for several weeks later, and that was the end of it.

The board attorney told me what to expect at the second court date. He said I probably would not be called to testify, but I would have to be there anyway as he couldn't be certain. When I protested that I couldn't afford so much time away from my job, he offered to phone about a half hour before the case was called, which would still allow me plenty of time to get to court and would save me hours of waiting. This arrangement made me feel a little better. The case had been scheduled for the morning, but the attorney did not call till early in the afternoon. I got into my car and rushed to the courthouse. I needn't have hurried. We still had more than a half hour to wait. The store manager had been there for hours. He agreed with me that the wheels of justice grind slowly, and grumbled that he was getting pretty tired of the whole affair, especially after I told him what the board attorney had predicted for this day's proceedings. The prediction turned out to be correct. The case was called, and the disposition was short if not sweet. Another continuance.

The next court date was set during spring vacation. My clerks were sorry that I would have to go "on my own time." Apparently no one realized that when I went on "school time" I had to make up the work I missed. Even without such interruptions, I usually stayed after school to finish my work and often did some work at home during the weekend. I realized that I was not indispensable and that my assistant could take charge while I was gone. However, I would have to brief him on appointments I had made, placement of substitutes for the day, and other matters that might come up. In addition, some conferences I had scheduled with students, parents, and consultants would have to be postponed. Whenever I was gone from my office for one reason or another, I invariably had to work longer and harder for the next few days. All in all, I was glad that I would be going on my own rather than on school time.

The attorney had advised me to come about an hour later than the scheduled time for our case. This day, he assured me, it would be the real thing. No more continuances. In accordance with his instructions, I picked up the girls who were to appear as witnesses (after getting their parents' consent), and arrived at the time he had indicated. Naturally we were early. As I waited,the officer approached me to review my testimony.

"Don't forget," he reminded me. "He came at you with a knife."

I didn't care to discuss the matter. I knew what I intended to say. I just nodded without comment.

Finally the case was called and, to my relief, it proceeded briskly. Limpy's supervisor at work provided a character reference—it turned out that he had a job as a laborer with the Park District. I thought this was a nice gesture. Maybe he wasn't as bad as I had supposed. In fact, one of the girls had told me that he usually wasn't aggressive and that she believed he was drunk at the time of the assault. As this was not mentioned at the trial, I don't know if it was true. Nevertheless, I reasoned, if someone is killed or injured by a drunkard, he's just as hurt or just as dead. And even though we were not physically hurt, I felt that the girls and I had been injured.

There were short statements from the arresting officer and the store manager. Then the girls were called upon to relate their story. They identified the knife and described the attempted assault. My testimony followed. I recited the facts as I remembered them—that Limpy had definitely threatened me but had made no move to attack me. While I had reason to believe that he had a knife, I had not actually seen one. That concluded the evidence.

Limpy was sentenced to three months in jail. I was satisfied with the verdict. The officer was clearly disappointed. I expected him to reproach me for not having given more damaging testimony, but his anger was directed at the judge.

"These judges are too easy," he said bitterly. "That mother ------ should have gotten at least a year."

I am not writing an exposé of the police department. I have described the attitude and conduct of one officer. In the course of my duties I later had many contacts with the police. Most of them were favorable. The police department tries to cooperate with the schools. However, the attitude and performance of some officers leave much to be desired. As is true in any other profession, there are good ones and bad ones.

As I have indicated, I approved of the verdict in this case. I believe that an assault upon students and a school principal should not go unpunished, especially if it occurs on school grounds. The parents need some reassurance that their children will be protected. The teachers also need assurance that such attacks will not be tolerated. In this case, the reputation of the school was involved and my own reputation as well. But I did not want vengeance, only the satisfaction that justice had been done.

12. Reading Is Not Enough

A parent came to see me one day. "This is my son's report card," she said.

I examined it appreciatively. "Very nice," I observed. "I see he has all E's."

She looked embarrassed. "That's why I'm here. There have been some changes made on it." She paused, then continued quickly, "But Jerry didn't do it. Please tell his teacher not to blame him. You see, he showed me his report card and it had all F's. 'Young man,' I said, 'I want those F's changed to E's.' His five-year-old sister heard me. She likes Jerry and wanted to help him, so she—well, she got hold of a pen and changed all the F's to E's."

While I was in college, I came across something in one of my textbooks which I resolved never to forget when I became a teacher. I never have. I used to read it periodically as a reminder to myself, almost a ritual, especially at the beginning of a new school year. When I became a principal, I made copies for all of the teachers. I often read it to the staff at our first meeting for the benefit of the new teachers and to refresh the memory of the others. Many of them probably got tired of hearing it. I don't know if they were particularly moved or impressed the first time they heard it, but for me it conveys a message which has never lost its significance. The author is anonymous. Here it is:

I Taught Them All

I have taught in high school for ten years. During that time I have given assignments, among others, to a murderer, an evangelist, a pugilist, a thief, and an imbecile.

The murderer was a quiet little boy who sat on the front seat and regarded me with pale blue eyes; the evangelist, easily the most popular boy in the school, had the lead in the junior play; the pugilist lounged by the window and let loose at intervals a raucous laugh that startled even the geraniums; the thief was a

> gay-hearted Lothario with a song on his lips; and the imbecile, a soft-eyed little animal seeking the shadows.
>
> The murderer awaits death in the state penitentiary; the evangelist has lain a year now in the village churchyard; the pugilist lost an eye in a brawl in Hong Kong; the thief, by standing on tiptoe, can see the windows of my room from the county jail; and the once gentle-eyed little moron beats his head against a padded wall in the state asylum.
>
> All of these pupils once sat in my room, sat and looked at me gravely across worn brown desks. I must have been a great help to those pupils—I taught them the rhyming scheme of the Elizabethan sonnet and how to diagram a complex sentence.

A pretty cynical appraisal of our educational goals, but it taught me a few things. First, that there was a lot more to life than the inside of my little classroom—that if Eddie failed his spelling test or Sam didn't finish his homework they were not doomed for all eternity. And second, that there is a lot more to teaching than just teaching, if that makes any sense. The feelings, emotions, and attitudes of the children must be considered, and how we teach may be more important than what we teach.

That teacher's soliloquy has a more personal meaning to me now. I have lived long enough to see my students grow up and to find out how some of them turned out. I can honestly say I have always tried to do more than teach them how to diagram a complex sentence. (I was never big on diagraming sentences anyway.) However, I realize that my efforts were only a small part of their total school experience. If they succeeded, I tried to remember that my contribution to their success was probably very minor. By the same token, I did not reproach myself for their failures. Yet the total school experience has to make its mark upon every child, and I am afraid that the impact upon some children, made by well-meaning teachers who are fully convinced of the importance of what they are teaching, is a negative one. (If I wanted to get psychoanalytical, I would say that these teachers have to believe it's important. It would be too injurious to their egos if they didn't. At the moment, however, I am not concerned with protecting the fragile egos of teachers—especially the bad ones.) Undoubtedly there are children who should be pushed, prodded, and persuaded to do better. But there are others—and anyone who has taught for a few years has seen them—whose capacity is limited. All too often, when such children are unable to perform at the prescribed pace they are labeled as failures and are soon made to feel that way. Perhaps that is why I become vexed, perturbed, and exasperated when I hear the continuous cacophony about reading scores.

I am not trying to minimize the importance of reading. It is fundamental to the process of formal education. I worked hard to improve the reading of my students (mostly by persuading them to read books); and the improvement in their scores was very gratifying. Nevertheless, I realized—contrary to what parents, educators, and the media appear to assume—that success or failure in life (either with a small "l," by which I mean financial success, or with a big "L," having a good life, which I shall not attempt to define) is not necessarily dependent upon reading. I have known poor readers who made a pretty good adjustment to life and good readers who didn't. Yet education, at least at the elementary level, is almost always equated with reading—or, to put it more accurately, with a test score purporting to measure it. I'm not sure whether educators have convinced the general public that this is what it's all about, or whether the parents and the editorial writers have seized upon this most tangible (though hardly most reliable) yardstick to hold up to educators as a measure of accountability. But if reading is what it's all about, why aren't the schools given credit for the good readers, those who go on to college and become doctors, engineers, architects, and, of course, teachers? They must be learning something.

It happens that there are a few subjects besides reading which I believe we should be teaching—and some of us even try to teach them. In fact, if reading scores have indeed deteriorated, one of the reasons may be that our society has become more complex, and there is much more to learn than there was years ago. Oh, I know the answer to that one. Quit teaching all those other things and let's get back to basics. I agree that we should teach the basics. My definition of the term, however, is probably a lot different than that of the people who advocate this position. Their use of the word "basic" implies that we should teach those subjects that were applicable to the society of fifty or a hundred years ago and in the same way they were taught then. But society has changed. We can't go back. Children have to learn how to function in the world of today. I don't think this is being given adequate consideration at any level—elementary, high school, or college.

As far as I can remember, we learned very little science when I went to elementary school. However, right after Sputnik, the country seemed to become paranoid about falling behind the Russians in the space race. Science suddenly became very important and very basic. Later the "new math" hit us. Its premise was that students should understand the reason or theory behind computations before performing them. While this had some merit in the instruction of bright students, it was ineffective when teaching the average or below-average students. Personally, I found it was all I could do to teach them how to perform the computations correctly without going into the "why's" or "wherefore's." I refused to get on the bandwagon. When I became a principal, I managed, with great difficulty, to obtain some "old math" textbooks for our teachers—which they greatly preferred. Now that the science kick has faded a bit and the new math has become suspect, it is time to embark on another crusade which, like the others, is being overdone.

I don't believe anyone will object to having reading, science, spelling, and arithmetic included on the list of "basics." Then which subjects are the frills? Some people say we should eliminate art and music from the curriculum. I have even known principals who agree. Yet these subjects were taught when I went to school, and my teachers considered them important. Of course, during my school days we learned nothing about the Depression, World War II, the Korean conflict, and our involvement in Vietnam since none of these events had as yet occurred. I don't know how much students learn about them today. Probably not too much, though I'm sure those episodes are mentioned in their history books. A lot of people who experienced them not as history but as a crucial part of their lives, including myself, might consider them pretty basic. If children had a better understanding of the times their parents lived through, it might even help to bridge the generation gap. And what about consumer education and learning about different vocations? After all, the kids who are now in school will live in that outside world someday—a world which contains plumbing, and automobiles, and television sets, and repairmen.

Well, just in case no one is arguing with me so far, I'll go on to something more controversial—sex education. (In school we use the more genteel term, "Family Life Education," but I won't mince words.) Also, drug education. I have seen pregnant thirteen- and fourteen-year-old girls, and I've seen youngsters on drugs (including alcohol). Teenage pregnancy is reaching epidemic proportions, and drug use does not seem to be decreasing. I don't see how we can ignore these statistics. Some people who oppose the teaching of these subjects claim that our courses aren't doing any good. They may even be right! If that's true, we must try to do a better job. Sex and drugs won't go away if we pretend they don't exist. Our children are aware of them at an earlier age than we care to admit. As to those parents who claim they can teach these subjects at home, how many know enough biology to present the facts about reproduction properly (even if they aren't too embarrassed to do it)? How many are as familiar with the names and uses (or abuses) of various "uppers" and "downers" as their children are? What do they know about the pleasures and perils of acid or the joys and jeopardies of mainlining? And if parents can indeed teach sex and drug education effectively, why is there no evidence that they are succeeding? (Incidentally, there could be a beneficial side effect to the teaching of these subjects. When our classes started studying family life education, the teachers reported to me that the interest level was high and that the students were reading the textbooks. This might improve their reading.)

Maybe the schools do attempt too much. We are overextended. But there are so many problems that children have to face in this complicated existence that I don't think we—both parents and teachers—do enough. Raising reading scores a few points, while certainly desirable, is not going to solve everything. When the police brought a child to me who had been caught shoplifting, or had run away from home, or was involved in a burglary, or had been truant for weeks—even months—my first concern was not with his reading score. A few examples, actual cases, may illustrate my point.

Christina had been a student at our school for quite a while. She was now in eighth grade, but I had not been aware of her existence until her mother came to see me. Christina's mother was a short, middle-aged Bohemian woman. Although she had been in this country for about fifteen years, her English was halting and she spoke with a heavy accent. She informed me that her daughter, who had always been a good student and a good girl, had changed recently. She didn't like school anymore. In fact, she had been absent (truant) all week. Could I help? I had heard such petitions before, and the "good student" usually turned out to be about average or below. This was not the case with Christina. Her records revealed that she had always been a straight E student. Her IQ and reading scores were well above average. What had gone wrong?

"Tell Christina I want to see her," I said. "Tell her it's very important. I'll see what I can do."

Christina came to my office the next morning. I don't know what I expected her to be like, but I know she was different than I had expected; tall, pretty, physically mature, composed, looking and acting very grown up—it was hard to believe she was only fourteen years old.

"Tell me," I began, "why don't you want to go to school?"

"It's boring," she replied. "I'm not learning anything."

I had witnessed her teacher's performance recently and had not been too impressed. I was afraid that her statement had some merit and decided not to challenge it. "I know school can be boring," I said. "We don't have writers like they do for every television show. I'll bet if you ask your father he'll tell you his work is often boring, but I'm sure he doesn't stay home anytime he feels like it. He has a job to do—supporting his family. And you have a job to do—preparing for your future. You only have a few months till graduation. Then you'll be in high school, and things will be a lot different. You've been an excellent student all these years. Why spoil it now?"

"I don't know. Sometimes I just don't feel like going to school."

I glanced at her attendance record. "It looks like it's more than just 'sometimes.' Your attendance has been getting steadily worse, and now you've been absent a whole week. Your mother came to see me. She's very upset."

Christina did not reply. Her reaction, or lack of it, prompted my next question. "How do you get along with your parents?" I asked.

"All right, I guess."

That didn't sound too convincing. I suspected that I had hit upon the real problem, or at least an important part of it, but I hesitated to probe further. I didn't know Christina and didn't want to invade her privacy unless she volunteered the information herself.

"Anything you want to talk to me about?" I ventured.

"No, I guess not."

"What do you do when you're not in school?"

"Not much. I watch television most of the time."

"Doesn't that get boring too after a while?"

"Sometimes. I don't always watch it. I just have it on."

"Well, I certainly don't want to get the truant officer after a good student like you. And it would be a shame if you didn't graduate. Why don't you do us both a favor and come back to school? How about it?"

She seemed to be thinking it over. Then she replied, without much enthusiasm, "I'll try."

"That's good." I said, ignoring the fact that she had not actually committed herself. "I'll expect you in school tomorrow. Remember, I'm going to check to see if you're here, so don't disappoint me."

There was a pause as she waited to be dismissed. I waited too, hoping she might open up a little, but she was silent. I wasn't sure if I had accomplished anything. I didn't feel that I had established any kind of personal relationship. Maybe I ought to make one more effort.

"I've raised two daughters. One is in high school and the other in college, so I think I know something about fourteen-year-old girls. If you have any problems you want to discuss, just come to see me. Will you remember that?"

She nodded her head. "Yes, sir."

"O.K. And remember—I'll expect you in school tomorrow."

When one is running a school of over sixteen hundred students, one has little time to spend on a single individual. In fact, with all the administrative functions I had to perform, I sometimes thought—and I am sure many of the teachers agreed—that I was spending too much time with students at the expense of some of my other duties. Yet, as far as I was concerned, I had no choice. We had no counselor. Aside from the assistant principal, there was no one to whom I could delegate such matters, and he was busy with day-to-day discipline cases. Of course, the teachers were closer to the students than I was and could be expected to be aware of their problems, but they were busy too. Besides, sometimes they were part of the problem. I made a note to myself to check Christina's attendance for the next few days. I did so and was gratified to learn that she was coming to school. However, I wasn't sure that the matter had been resolved. As she had made no attempt to see me, I decided to take the initiative. A little follow-up never hurt. I sent for her and asked her how she was getting along.

"A little better," she said.

"Do you still find school boring? You can tell me. I won't get mad."

She smiled. "Yes, it's still boring," she affirmed.

"I guess it's that time of the year. When I went to school I always got spring fever about this time. Actually, I think I started getting it in the middle of winter. I couldn't wait for vacation to begin. The month of June was always the hardest." I changed the subject. "How are your parents?" I asked innocently.

The smile disappeared. "They're all right," she said.

"Your parents weren't born in this country, were they?"

"No, they're Bohemian."

"But you were born here, weren't you? That makes it pretty difficult—for you and for them. You see, their background, their early life was a lot different than yours. Sometimes it must be hard for them to understand you or for you to understand them. I'm afraid you can't appreciate what they went through—coming to a strange country, learning a new language, trying to make a living, raising children. I've raised four children, and I can tell you it isn't easy." (I often brought my children into the discussion when I spoke to students. I thought it made me appear to be more of a human being—if a principal can ever be a human being to a student.)

"My parents act like they're still living in the old country," she protested. "They've been here fifteen years and can't even speak English."

"I've talked to your mother. She speaks English. Not as well as you do, but I'll bet you can't speak Bohemian as well as she does. Do you speak Bohemian?"

"More or less. Why do I have to speak Bohemian? None of my friends do."

"How about your parents' friends? Do they speak Bohemian?"

"Most of them."

"And your relatives—your aunts and uncles—do they speak Bohemian?"

"I guess so."

"Well, maybe your parents feel more comfortable speaking their native language. And apparently they were able to communicate well enough with their friends and neighbors. This used to be a Bohemian neighborhood, you know. It's changed now. Most of the Bohemian people have moved away. Your parents have remained, but they can't change their language and their customs overnight."

"They always want to know where I'm going and what I'm doing."

"Yes, I'm sure they do. That's how parents are. Not just Bohemian parents. You have to be patient with them. Raising parents is not an easy job."

She looked at me uncomprehendingly for a moment, then realized I was joking and smiled. Obviously, here was the classic generation gap—not only of age but of cultures. Well, communication is a two-way street. Maybe I would have a talk with her parents when I had a little more time. Now I had a busy schedule ahead of me. Time to end the interview.

"Don't forget. If you need any help, let me know," I said as I dismissed her.

I sent a note to Christina's teacher instructing him to inform me whenever she was absent. Two weeks went by, and as other students and other matters claimed my attention I almost forgot about her. Then one Monday morning I found her mother waiting for me in the office. Christina had run away from home. When she had come home from school on Friday they had had an argument. Christina had walked out and had not returned.

"Have you spoken to her friends? Have you called the police?"

"I speak to her friends, but they say they don't see her. I don't call police. I don't know if I should do this."

"Yes, that has to be done right away. You wait here. I'll call them for you. They'll send an officer, and you can give him the information. And I'll see if I can find out anything from her friends in school."

I made the phone call, then turned to her and asked, "Are you sure she didn't say where she was going?"

"No, she don't say nothing. She get mad and she go out."

"What did you argue about?"

Slowly, haltingly, she told me the story. Christina had an older sister. They had been very close until the sister got married and moved away. Then a neighbor, a young, attractive divorcée, had taken a fancy to Christina. Christina preferred the company of older people. Girls her own age did not interest her, and the divorcée apparently took the place of the older sister whom she missed. Though the parents were not too happy about this relationship, they tolerated it because they did not want to antagonize Christina. She was a good girl, but she had grown up so fast, she was so smart, they did not know how to deal with the situation.

The divorcée took Christina to various places; the zoo, the movies, restaurants, even the beauty shop; and Christina obviously relished being treated as a grownup and enjoyed going to these places. It must have been very flattering and exciting for a young girl. Then the divorcée acquired a boyfriend, and he soon moved into her apartment. This was too much for Christina's parents to tolerate. They forbade her to visit the divorcée (how could they let their daughter enter this atmosphere of sin?) or go anywhere with her. Judging from the information I received later from one of Christina's classmates, they needn't have bothered. The divorcée, now that she had a boyfriend to occupy her time, was no longer interested in Christina. Naturally, she no longer offered to take her anywhere. Christina was deeply hurt. First she had lost a sister and now her best friend. In characteristic fashion, she blamed her parents. She mistakenly believed that her parents had talked to the divorcée and were responsible for her friend's sudden coolness.

It was a difficult situation all around. I was sorry for Christina. I could imagine how hurt and lonely she must be. And I was sorry for her mother. She could not understand what had gone wrong. She looked bewildered. I helped her give the report to the police and promised that I would try to locate Christina. If I found out anything, I would let her know.

Later that day, I talked to Christina's teacher, explained the situation, and instructed him to notify me if he heard any news about her. I also obtained a list of her friends in the class and spoke to them individually. None of them knew where she had gone, but they promised to let me know if they came across any helpful information.

About three weeks went by without a word or a trace of Christina. Her parents were frantic. Her father could hardly concentrate on his work. Her mother came to see me several times, and each time, when I had to inform her that neither the police nor I had made any progress, she left in tears. Then, finally, a lead. One of her classmates came to see me. She had been walking with her parents late one evening about a mile from the school, and she thought she saw Christina leaving a certain restaurant. It didn't sound like much of a clue, but I obtained the address of the restaurant and notified the police. The result was immediate. Christina had been working at the restaurant as a waitress for several weeks. She had passed herself off as a nineteen-year-old and gotten away with it. Her physical and mental development were such that no one doubted her statement.

Christina's parents were overjoyed at having her back. They hugged her tearfully. Christina's emotions were restrained. I warned her mother that she should try to be tolerant and not ask too many questions. If she pushed the girl too far, Christina would simply run away again. That was the pattern. This was not the first case of a runaway girl I'd had. The number seemed to be growing each year. The mother thanked me for my concern and my help and promised that she would try to patch things up with her daughter. She wanted to know if Christina could return to school. I assured her that we would be glad to have her back. "Tell her I want to see her in the morning," I said.

Christina reported to me the next day. I was curious about a lot of things—where she had lived, how she had managed to get the job, what she had been doing—but I decided the advice I had given her mother about asking too many questions applied to me as well. I would force no more information from her than she was ready to volunteer, which wasn't much. Trying to be convincing, but feeling uneasily that I was just being redundant, I again reminded her that I was willing to help her in any way I could, that I was available for advice or for a discussion of any problems she might have. She thanked me politely—she was always polite, but reserved. I explained to her my policy about graduation—that while her truancy was a very serious infraction, she could still graduate with her class providing she came to school regularly for the rest of the school year. (Her reading and math scores were well above average. It certainly wouldn't do any good to fail her. I wanted her in high school as soon as possible. Maybe she would have a chance there.) Again she thanked me—unemotionally. I tried to make her understand how worried her parents had been, how much she had hurt them. She listened but did not respond. What I had hoped would be a dialogue was becoming a lecture; and I knew that children get tired of hearing lectures. Hoping, despite her outward reserve, that something I had said had gotten through to her, I gave her a note to return to class and dismissed her. She did indeed remain in school and graduate, with her parents beaming proudly in the audience.

A few years later I received a phone call from a hospital. Christina was a patient and the caller wanted information—her grades, her test scores, her adjustment to school, and whatever else I consider pertinent. I countered by asking what was wrong with Christina, who was making the inquiry, and why she wanted the information. She couldn't or wouldn't tell me much. She refused to give me a diagnosis or a prognosis—that was restricted information, she said, but the staff psychiatrist had requested a report about Christina's school background. I responded that our school records were also restricted and I had no intention of disclosing them over the phone. I would have to receive a proper written request, including a signed authorization from the parents, before I would release any specific data. However, I saw no harm in revealing that Christina had been a good student, that her achievement scores had been above average, and that her conduct had always been excellent (at least, in the classroom). I asked if I could see Christina but was informed that she could have no visitors at this time.

We eventually received a form letter from the hospital, signed by the parents, requesting certain information from our school records. I attended to it personally. What had happened to Christina? I never found out. Obviously it was no ordinary physical ailment. Hospitals do not require school records for the treatment of a diseased lung or malfunctioning kidney. It had to be drugs or a mental breakdown of some sort, I concluded.

What could have caused the problem? My own guess was that she had matured too fast and was too pretty for her own good. She had the mind and body of an adult coupled with the inexperience of a child. And the lack of communication with her parents had to be a factor. Well, if we use reading as a criterion, the school hadn't failed. She was an excellent reader.

Xavier was nearly sixteen when I first became acquainted with him. He had recently transferred to our EMH (educable mentally handicapped) class from another school and soon made his presence known. He was in a class of fifteen students, some of whom were only ten years old. Consequently, although he was not tall for his age, he was the biggest and toughest in the class. His reading level was about fourth grade—maybe lower—and he showed little interest in improving it. I guess being in a room with a bunch of "little kids" didn't help his attitude.

I read an article recently in which the author observed that, according to his research, students who failed tended to become discipline problems. As astute observation which I could have confirmed years ago. That was one of the reasons (though not the main one) for my insistence on reducing the number of failures in our school despite vigorous objections from many of the teachers. Naturally that lays me open to the charge that I permitted unqualified students to go on to the next grade. According to many people, this policy results in poor discipline, lack of effort, and inability to read. Well, I have checked the records of many students who have failed, and I found little evidence that this improved their reading, their attitude, or their behavior. If a child fails once, assuming that the failure was due to laziness and not lack of ability, he may try harder (though he often doesn't). However, after a student has failed twice, he usually doesn't care anymore and stops trying altogether. I never instructed the teachers to promote everyone, nor did I, as a teacher, promote all of my students. I liked to keep the option open. I was not above using the threat of failure as a prod to the lazy ones. However, when one of our most experienced teachers wanted to fail one-third of the class, I decided it was time to intervene. Her object was not to punish the children. She honestly believed it was for their own good. (Somehow, those who fail never seem to appreciate that it is for their own good.) She also believed, very sincerely, that we had to maintain our standards—standards that were set years ago when the community was far different from the one we were dealing with now. She realized that many of her present students could not achieve those standards and admitted to me that most of them were working up to their limited capacity. But standards had to be maintained! I couldn't see how failing them would improve their performance any more than shaming or punishing a lame child will teach him to run. Does it make sense to fail a child who is doing the best he can? (Whether Xavier had made an effort to learn in previous years I don't know, but he certainly wasn't doing so now. Failure had definitely not improved Xavier's performance.)

Some superintendents have taken a "courageous" stand (applauded enthusiastically by the news media and most of the public) by ruling that no student will be permitted to graduate elementary school unless he can achieve a reading test score of at least 6.5. Not to be outdone, one superintendent raised the ante to 7.5. I don't know how much courage this took. It's the eighth-grade teachers and not the superintendents who will be stuck with the overage students who can't meet these criteria. I wonder if anyone has bothered to ask these teachers how they feel about it.

Had Xavier remained in elementary school until he achieved the required reading score, he might have stayed there a very long time. Of course it can be argued that Xavier, since he was mentally handicapped, was an exception. A few years ago, the administration, in its infinite wisdom, suddenly recognizing that such students required special consideration, changed the rules for EMH students. It was mandated that these students should graduate at age fifteen (and enter a high school EMH class) regardless of their reading scores. This created a peculiar situation. A student who scored a point or two above the EMH level on an IQ test (which doesn't necessarily make him any smarter than someone who scored a point or two below that level) could not graduate unless he met the minimum reading standard set by the district superintendent (as determined by another test). Yet if he had scored a few points lower on the IQ test, he would have been able to graduate as an EMH student. Somehow, that didn't make sense to me.

By the way, I wonder if the people who are now applauding this new "get tough" attitude are aware that we had similar rules in our district (and probably other districts) about ten years ago. As the neighborhood changed and we received more black students from the South and more Mexican students with language problems, the number of failures increased. Pretty soon, in addition to the thirteen-year-olds in eighth grade we had many fourteen- and fifteen-year-olds. That meant trouble. Most of the fifteen-year-olds no longer cared if they graduated or not. They didn't want to start high school at age sixteen or older. By this time they were sick of school anyhow and were just waiting until they were sixteen so they could drop out. (Some didn't wait that long.) Then along came a superintendent who thought it would be better to get these overage, oversized youngsters into high school, even if only for one year. It was better than having them out on the street. And there was always a chance that some of them, when they were with their own age group, would feel less out of place and stay in school. So we relaxed our standards and graduated many of the older students who were not doing themselves or us any good. This caused a persistent outcry from the high schools. They were getting too many students who couldn't read. If we would keep these students in elementary school until they dropped out, the high schools wouldn't have to worry about them. (It would also make the high school drop-out rate look better.) This attitude is understandable. They don't want students who are not "ready" for high school. So we will now try to get them ready by using a new (actually, a very old) technique. We will teach children to read by threatening them with failure.

And so the pendulum swings again. I am sure some students will work harder and try to pass the reading test. Fine. Some will have to attend remedial reading classes (which have not been too successful in the past), after which they will take the test again. And some will pass. Fine. But before I jump on the bandwagon, I still want to know what will happen to those who can't pass the test. Will the eighth grades once more be filled with fourteen- and fifteen-year-olds? And when they drop out, what will happen to the rate of juvenile delinquency? A follow-up study showing how these students turn out might prove interesting.

Perhaps it would be apropos to quote from a news article about the alarming increase in gangs and juvenile crime in Japan. The Japanese police estimate that there are now 1,730 gangs across the country, and in the first eight months of the year they "collared" 113,000 delinquents. This constituted forty-four percent of all felony arrests. (One example: A fifteen-year-old student stole five sticks of dynamite from a construction site and blew off the front end of a teacher's car because the teacher had scolded him.) What are the causes of this upsurge in delinquent behavior? One of them, according to the article, is "the fiercely competitive school system where failure builds up fury and anger in the young. Japan's compulsory education ends at junior high school; students must pass entrance examinations to go on to high school, then to college. 'The pupils who . . . can't keep up in class get left behind and resort to delinquency or violence to assert themselves,' says Chieko Najima, a writer on delinquency."

Certainly our schools have problems, but they will not be solved by saying "let's get tough" and by failing more students. Are there any solutions? Aside from the obvious ones—better teachers, better schools, better parents, better neighborhoods, and a better society—I have one recommendation which I have been making for years. Let's have more and better vocational schools. Place students in them as early as age twelve if they exhibit no academic interests. I don't mean that we should force them to go. It would have to be with the consent of the parents and the child. We constantly hear about the large number of unemployed teenagers who have no marketable skills. Why don't we give them some? Learning to read is fine—and reading can and should be taught in vocational schools too, but of and by itself it doesn't get one a job. Incidentally, I have known youngsters with very limited reading ability who exhibited a remarkable affinity for automobile motors. And I happen to possess a knickknack shelf which was given to me by one of our poorest students. He made it in our industrial arts class. It won't win any prizes, but it shows a lot more effort and accomplishment than he demonstrated in his other subjects.

Getting back to Xavier—effort and accomplishment were not qualities exhibited by him. The rule about graduating students at age fifteen, however, was not in effect at that time, so we had to keep him. It was not long before his teacher, a good, hardworking lady, was bringing complaints to me. Xavier used profanity in class, terrorized the other children, refused to obey her, and disrupted the class to such an extent that she was unable to teach. There was one ameliorating factor. He was often absent. His teacher, understandably, was not too upset about that. It provided her with welcome relief. On those days, she said, she could at least do some teaching. Nevertheless, she conscientiously reported his frequent absences to the truant officer. The truant officer informed me that there was no father in the home and that the mother's influence upon Xavier and his activities was limited. I could initiate a case report and get him into court on a truancy petition, but that wouldn't make much sense. It would take four or five months before he could be brought to trial. By that time he would be sixteen years old and could no longer be prosecuted for truancy. (We still had a Parental School for truants then. It has since been abolished.)

Maybe his mother's nagging had some effect. Whatever the reason, he did keep coming to school sporadically. His teacher soon lost control of him entirely (she didn't have much to begin with) and began sending him to the office with monotonous regularity. I talked to him, listened to him, cajoled, entreated, threatened—all to no avail, or if there was any avail I couldn't notice it. It was evident that this would not be one of my more successful efforts. Finally, more for the teacher's sake and sanity than anything else, I was forced to do something which I knew made very little sense. I suspended him for three days.

Though most teachers have great faith in suspension as a disciplinary measure, it is only a temporary expedient. When the student returns, so does the problem. For the normally well-behaved student, it can act as a deterrent. However, if overused, it loses its effectiveness. The chronic offender, after the second or third experience, is likely to accept a suspension with equanimity unless there is a determined follow-up by the parents. He may even get to enjoy it, or at least find it preferable to going to school. But suspending a known truant is the height of absurdity. First you try to get him to come to school; then you give him a legitimate excuse to stay home. There have been instances when I suspected that a truant misbehaved deliberately as if he wanted to be suspended. With no parent to supervise him (and there are fewer and fewer parents at home these days), he was free to do as he pleased. Knowing all this, I still suspended Xavier. I had to show support for his teacher, and I couldn't come up with a viable alternative. Besides, she needed the rest.

Xavier did not appear to be particularly disturbed when I informed him of my decision. And after three days he returned, not to learn anything, but probably to see his friends, some of the older boys in the eighth grade. His attendance pattern continued as before—in school a few days, then out a few days. When he was in school, according to his teacher, he spent almost as much time in the hallways and in the bathroom as he did in class. This was a mixed blessing as far as she was concerned. While the class was certainly better off without him, he was still her responsibility, and she often had to leave the room to locate him.

Things went along in this way for a while; then Xavier, a self-appointed champion of Mexican honor, became involved in something worse. To put things in proper focus, an explanation is necessary. Our enrollment reports at this time indicated that the school was about 75 percent Hispanic, mostly Mexican, 12½ percent black, and 12½ percent white. (I referred to them as European white because, while some Mexicans thought of themselves as brown, others considered themselves white, as indeed many of them were as far as their complexion was concerned—and people get very touchy where race or ethnicity is concerned.) But these numbers did not reveal the real picture. Our lower grades were about 90 percent Hispanic. The rest were European whites except for a few blacks averaging about one per class. In our seventh and eighth grades, however, as I mentioned earlier, it was a different story. The school closest to us went no higher than sixth grade. All of its students were black, and most of them would enter our seventh grade and remain with us till they graduated. Consequently, our seventh and eighth grades were 50 percent black, 40 percent Hispanic, and 10 percent "other" white. This led to certain complications. For one thing, hardly any of the black students had been in an integrated situation before seventh grade, and it was sometimes a difficult adjustment for them to make. For another, though they were numerically a minority in the school as a whole, their size (they were, on the average, much taller than the Mexicans) and their number in the upper grades made them a force to be reckoned with, perhaps even the dominant force in the school. Under these circumstances, some racial problems were inevitable.

Most of the students got along quite well, and interracial friendships were common. This is not simply conjecture on my part, but was confirmed by a study I made (see Chapter 18). Nevertheless, and these are the things that draw attention, one or two racial incidents did occur each year. I doubt if we had more fights than other schools, and when they were between two boys (or girls) of the same race, I would punish the offenders, notify the parents, and that would be the end of it. But if the fight was between students of different races, the repercussions could be far-reaching. Often their friends would get involved. The next step would be the entrance of the gangs, usually the Latin Kings and the Deuces. Over the years, I had become accustomed to dealing with such outbreaks. They were never pleasant and sometimes required police intervention. Fortunately (almost miraculously, considering that rocks, bottles, baseball bats, knives, and even guns were sometimes involved) they never got completely out of hand. During my ten years as principal, not one student, as far as I know, was seriously injured in these clashes. Maybe that's why they were never reported in the newspapers. Still, when I received word that a racial battle was imminent, I always had a premonition that this would be the time when my luck would run out.

For a few days now I had heard rumors, sometimes from a student, sometimes from one of the teachers, that "the natives were getting restless again." As usual, it had started with a minor incident, a scuffle between two boys, a black and a Mexican, in which neither suffered any physical damage. A teacher had separated them almost immediately. Each, however, vowed to get revenge for the other's "unprovoked" attack. The teacher didn't know who started it. He interrogated several witnesses, and predictably the account varied with the ethnicity of the witness. He then prudently referred the matter to me, and I sent for the combatants. After listening to their charges and countercharges, I interrupted them.

"O.K.," I said. "Each one says the other started it, and your friends tell the same story. I don't know who is lying and who is telling the truth, so I have two choices. I can suspend both of you, or I can send you both back to class if you promise there will be no more fighting. Nobody has been hurt, and I want it to stay that way. What do you say? Do I suspend you or send you back to class?"

The choice was an obvious one. "Back to class," they muttered, still eyeing each other belligerently.

"All right. I'm letting you off easy, but only on the condition that you behave yourselves. If either one of you starts something, the one who does will be suspended. If I can't find out who started it, you'll both be suspended. Is that clear? And I don't want your friends getting into the act either. Well, do you promise?"

Each waited for the other to respond, then turned to me and mumbled, almost in unison, "I won't start nothin' if he don't." It didn't seem to be the appropriate time for an English lesson, so I summoned a hall guard and instructed him to escort them back to class and to make sure they arrived there without resuming hostilities.

Things were quiet for a few days. Then I heard rumors that there would be an encounter after school and that Xavier was the instigator. A few minutes before the dismissal bell I went outside. As the students poured out of the exits, I observed a small group of black students, the known troublemakers, gathering at one corner. At the opposite corner the Mexican contingent was forming, headed by Xavier. It included a few of our worst "Anglo" students. There weren't enough of them to form their own gang, so they had cast their lot with the Kings.

I walked over to the black group. "Let's go, fellows," I said calmly. "I didn't realized you liked school that much. I know you hate to leave, but it's time to go home." I prided myself on using the light touch.

"What about those dudes across the street?" demanded one tall, pugnacious individual.

"I'll take care of them. You get going. Then I'll get rid of them."

There was a whispered conversation, several of the boys nodded their heads, and they started to leave—very deliberately, to show they had not been intimidated.

I crossed the street and went through my act with the other group. "Let's go. No use hanging around. The party's over. You too, Xavier."

A short conference ensued, and they turned to cross the street. "Hold it," I said. "You're going the wrong way. I don't want you meeting the black kids a block away."

After a few meaningful glances, they changed direction and started to walk away. My usual suspicious nature manifested itself. I hurried rapidly to the next block in the direction taken by the black students. They had to walk two blocks through the Mexican neighborhood before they reached their own "turf." That would be as far as the Mexican boys would dare follow them.

As I had suspected, Xavier and his friends had run around the block and were now converging at this point. They saw me and hesitated.

"O.K., fellows. Go home," I called. "The police could be on the way, and you don't want to get picked up."

I was bluffing, though technically I hadn't lied. I didn't like to lie—and especially to be caught in one. Partly it was a matter of personal ethics, and partly because I wanted to preseve my reputation with the students as one whose word could be trusted. I hadn't called the police—but I hadn't said they were on the way—just that they could be.

There were only about five or six of them, and perhaps they were disconcerted at being outmaneuvered by me. Reluctantly they turned around and left. I waited about five minutes, assured myself that all was quiet on the northern front, and returned to the school.

I went through the same routine the following day and so did the two groups. Aside from some menacing looks and a few shouted insults, the situation remained stable. Another day or two and the tension would probably subside—unless something happened to cause it to escalate. Something did happen. Xavier got into a pushing and shouting match with one of the leaders of the Deuces. I heard from my informants that there would be real trouble after school this time. The word was out that there might be knives and that one boy had a gun, so I called the police.

I had notified a few of the male teachers that I could use some help. They and my assistant principal were on hand at dismissal time as were two or three squad cars. It was a mild, bright, autumn day, unfortunately. Cold weather tended to discourage gang activities and prompted the uninvolved students to go home more quickly. On this day, while the two gangs assumed their respective positions on opposite corners, some students were hurrying home as rapidly as possible to avoid getting hurt, but others strolled along at a leisurely pace, and many more were just standing around so they wouldn't miss any of the action.

My faculty helpers and I went after the two gangs and tried to get them to disperse. We were partially successful. They started walking away on opposite sides of the street, each watching the other suspiciously and regrouping at regular intervals. Meanwhile, the squad cars moved slowly alongside as the officers shouted through the open windows and exhorted the students to keep moving. Occasionally a car would stop and an officer would emerge to break up a group that had formed. It's hard to identify the players without a scorecard, and most of the time they were shouting at students who were innocent, or at least semi-innocent, observers. On the whole, the gang members managed to stay a respectful distance from the police cars. I saw Xavier about a half block away and called to one of the officers in the car nearest me.

"There's the boy I want—the one with the black jacket and the stick in his hand. Do you see him?" I had a feeling that if we neutralized Xavier, we would have a much better chance of ending the conflict.

The officer nodded and began to speed up, but Xavier, seeing the car approaching, ducked into a passageway which led to the alley. Not much use chasing him there.

As I walked back toward the school I saw a lanky youth spread-eagled over the hood of a squad car. An officer was standing behind him and checking him for weapons.

"What's wrong?" I asked. I recognized the boy. He was known to me as a smart aleck, but I was pretty sure he was no gang member.

The boy turned his head. His hands remained on the hood of the car. "I didn't do anything," he shouted to me. "I was just waiting for my little sister."

"Officer, I know this boy. He's not a bad kid," I affirmed. (He was no model of virtue either, but in this instance I was working for the defense, not the prosecution.)

The young policeman turned to me, his face flushed, his eyes hostile. "I told him to move along, and he gave me a lot of lip. I'm taking him in."

"He really does have a little sister," I confirmed. That he was waiting for his brother, his sister, or his cousin was the usual excuse a gang member would give when told to move along, but in this case it was probably legitimate.

"He's going to the station," the officer insisted. "I don't care what they do with him there. He's got a big mouth."

He opened the door of the car and shoved the boy in. Just then I observed the sergeant who was in charge of the operation. I had had contact with him on several previous occasions. He was middle-aged, his hair liberally sprinkled with gray, his pudgy face lined and coarse. His manner was easygoing, as if he had learned to accept life the way it came. He had just emerged from his squad car, and he waved to me. I walked toward him.

"You can relax now," he said, his broad face breaking into a smile. "I think we're in pretty good shape."

"Well, there's a little problem," I said. I told him about the boy in the squad car. "I'll have to call his mother to explain what happened. She's going to be pretty upset. He's not really bad. Just a smart aleck."

"I'll check it out," he assured me, still smiling. "These young officers get a little excited. I'll talk to him."

He approached the car with the boy in it, while I maintained a discreet distance. I thought it would be better if I did not get involved in the proceedings. There was a short conference; then the boy got out, and the officer started the car and slowly drove away.

I called the boy and, as he approached, I said, "You go straight home before you get into more trouble. You're lucky I was here to help you." I was not above taking the credit. If the story got around, it might help my image in the community.

"What about my sister?" he asked. "My mother told me to wait for her."

"Go home," I ordered. "She's probably there by now. If she isn't, tell your mother to call me. Get going—and watch that big mouth."

"There she is!" he shouted as he saw a little girl standing all alone about a half block away, and off he ran.

The street was now deserted. I returned to my office to clean up the work on my desk and call it a day.

I sent for Xavier the next morning, but he was not in school. I knew the feud wasn't over, especially when I heard there had been a "rumble" between the two gangs the previous night in a nearby park. The rumble had been prearranged, and the gangs had met at the specified time and place. Fortunately, someone had called the police just as the action was beginning, and it was broken up before anyone got hurt. The police had picked up a few of the participants but, as they were juveniles, had released them in the custody of their parents. Though Xavier had been there, he was not one of those who had been apprehended.

With the rumble aborted, there was one extra day for tempers to cool. Time always helped in these cases. On the other hand, as nothing had been settled, it was very likely that another rumble would be set up. From a selfish viewpoint, that was not my concern. Fights which occurred during or immediately after school and were on or near the school grounds were my responsibility. The others were not. Just thinking this way, however, made me feel guilty. Someone could be badly injured. The least I could do was to make an effort to prevent that. I called a few of the known ringleaders to the office and made my "pitch"—that they could be hurt, that innocent people (maybe their own little brothers or sisters) could be hurt, that their mothers would be very upset, that the police had been alerted and might not be too gentle, that whichever side lost would want to get revenge, and that this could go on and on if they didn't stop now.

I had done this many times before and was pretty good at it, I thought. Unfortunately, I couldn't reach all the leaders, especially since some of them were high school students or dropouts.

"Well, what do you say?" I concluded. "Why don't all of you just 'cool' it?"

Immediately each group heatedly started to blame the other, but I interrupted them sharply. "Yes, I know. It's always the other guy's fault. Listen, I know everyone of you, and none of you are little angels. I'm trying to talk some sense into you before someone gets killed. If you get in the way of a knife or a gun, it doesn't care who you are. I'm going to have the police out there again, and I'm going to tell them to pick up anyone that gets out of line. I want you to pass the word to the others. Who's going to see Xavier?"

There was a pause as no one volunteered. Then one of the boys spoke up. "Why don't you talk to his girl friend? She sees him?"

"His girl friend? Where do I find her?"

They told me she was an eighth-grade girl named Theresa. Well, it was worth a try. First I asked her teacher about her. He told me that Theresa was fourteen-and-a-half (she had failed once) and was in the lower half of the class scholastically, but she was a quiet, well-behaved girl who seemed to be trying.

I instructed her teacher to send Theresa to my office. As I awaited her arrival, I tried to imagine what Xavier's girl friend would look like. I could hardly think of him as the catch of the season. His swarthy face was pimpled, his nose was large and bulbous, he had poor posture, he was not too bright, he swore, he was a bully, and he was bad-tempered. I could only conclude that a girl whose own attributes were such that no other boy would be interested in her would settle for someone like Xavier.

A girl walked in and inquired, "Did you want to see me, Mr. Greenstein?"

"Are you Theresa?" I asked.

As she affirmed that she was, I inspected her endowments with some surprise. Judging by her looks alone (and what else do boys judge by?) she could hardly be suffering from a lack of prospective boyfriends. She was taller than the average Mexican girl, probably taller than Xavier, slender, well-shaped, with large dark-brown eyes, a small straight nose, smooth light-brown skin—in short, while not a beauty, certainly an attractive girl. Why she would be interested in Xavier, if indeed she was, I couldn't imagine.

"Theresa, maybe you can help me. You know we've had some trouble lately between the black kids and the Mexicans. I happen to know that Xavier is involved. Is he a friend of yours?"

"I know him," she replied unemotionally. "He lives near me."

So that was it. I should have known she was not Xavier's girl friend. They were just neighbors. Or maybe it was a one-way relationship with Xavier referring to her as his girl and without any reciprocity on her part. Should I warn her that Xavier was not the kind of boy for her to get involved with? It probably wasn't necessary. Besides, it was none of my business.

"I'd like you to give him a message. Tell him I've talked to the other boys and they've decided to call a truce. You can also tell him that the police will be out here, and I'll have him picked up if he makes any trouble. Do you think you can get that message to him?"

"If I see him," she replied.

"If you get a chance, maybe you can talk to his mother too. I want to let her know what's going on, but I can't get hold of her. She has no phone."

"I'll try," she said.

I sent her back to class. Well, I'd done all I could. I didn't expect her to have much influence with Xavier. I knew I didn't, but then I wasn't built the same way she was. I called the police and asked to speak to Sergeant Jovanovich, the officer who had been in charge the previous day.

He was called to the phone and, after I had identified myself, he asked, "What can I do for you?"

"I wonder if you can get a couple of squad cars out here after school for two or three days? I think if we can keep the lid on for the next few days we'll be all right. And listen, do me a favor. See if you can get some officers who aren't too 'gung ho.' We're dealing with kids here, not criminals. If they get pushed around, it will only aggravate the situation, and then I'll have to answer to their parents. I've got enough problems as it is."

"Don't worry," he said. "I'll pick the men myself. I won't get any hotshots."

At dismissal time, the gangs again gathered at their respective corners, but they seemed a little less volatile. With the help of a few teachers, my assistant and I dispersed them without too much difficulty. I saw Xavier and called to him.

"You weren't in school today. How come you show up now?"

"I was sick," he replied with a smirk.

"Sure you were. I'm glad you recovered so fast. Now go home and get some rest. I don't want you getting sick again." I walked away, but kept an eye on him to make sure he didn't start anything.

The police were very good. I had never seen them do a better job. The sergeant must have talked to them. As the teachers and I broke up the bottlenecks at the corners, the squad cars just followed along. Their occupants ignored the scattered jeers and insults which greeted them along the way. When the students' progress slowed to a snail's pace, a squad car would pull alongside, a window would open, and one of the officers would call out, "All right, let's keep moving." The whole operation was very low-key. The officers stayed in their cars as they drove slowly around the block and watched for any potential trouble spots. Gradually the crowd thinned out and disappeared, and I gave a sigh of relief. It looked like the worst was over.

As a precautionary measure, I requested that the police come back for a few days, but things were practically back to normal. Although Xavier showed up, he remained in the background. After that, I didn't see him again for quite a while. He never returned to the classroom.

It was quiet for about a year, and then hostilities broke out again. And on the very first day, as I watched the opposing forces line up in their accustomed places, I saw Xavier at the head of the Mexican contingent like a general directing his troops. (I guess generals don't lead troops. Maybe he was more like a captain.)

I walked over and confronted him. "You have no business here," I told him. "You'd better leave, or I'll have the police pick you up."

He gave me the "It's a free country" routine, and I assured him that it wouldn't be for him if I could help it unless he stayed away from the vicinity of the school. He held his ground, so I sent a boy to the office to tell my clerk to call the police. My instructions were purposely given loud enough to be overheard, and naturally by the time the police arrived Xavier was gone.

I checked his records the following morning and discovered, as I had suspected, that he was now over seventeen and no longer a juvenile as far as the law was concerned.

I saw him again after school and approached him. "You're seventeen years old. Do you know what that means?" He didn't respond, and I continued, "It means that according to the law you're an adult now. If the police pick you up, there's no more station adjustment. I'm giving you a last warning. I'm going to instruct the police to pick you up if you're anywhere near the school, and I'll personally swear out a warrant for your arrest if necessary. You don't belong with these kids. You're a troublemaker, and I don't want you around here."

Again I sent someone to the office with instructions for my clerk to call the police, while I stayed to make sure the situation didn't get out of hand. A squad car drove up in about five minutes and Xavier disappeared.

For the next few days I arranged to have the police on hand before dismissal time. I pointed Xavier out to them and they tried to apprehend him, but he knew the neighborhood better than they did. He ducked into passageways and alleys and easily eluded them. This game continued for several days, until Xavier finally became discouraged and stayed away. Meanwhile, a few of the teachers who had a good relationship with the gang leaders had been meeting with them. The tension gradually subsided, and I was sure that Xavier's absence was a factor.

I had been working on a plan to prevent these periodic racial confrontations, and I now put it into effect. I asked the members of each gang to pick their own leaders who would meet at regular intervals with me or with two teachers of their choosing. I called this my "Peace Council." They were also to come to me or to the faculty representatives in case of emergency for arbitration of any disputes. Some of the teachers did not approve of the implied "status" I was giving to the gang leaders by meeting with them. They thought I should meet with the Student Council representatives instead. However, I knew that the Student Council representatives, though they were helpful in talking to the student body as a whole, had little influence with the gangs.

As the gang leaders were usually eighth graders, new ones would have to be selected to serve on the council each year when the incumbents graduated. Nevertheless, the system worked pretty well. Complaints of the truce being violated, brought by one side or the other, were successfully adjudicated, and there was relative quiet, at least on the racial front, for a year or two. During all that time I did not see Xavier and had almost forgotten him. Then, for some reason, his name came to my mind during one of our Peace Council meetings, and I asked if anyone knew what had happened to him.

"He isn't with the Kings anymore," I was told. "He's married now."

This surprised me, especially when I learned that he had married

Theresa. I had given her credit for better judgment. I was further informed that he had a job and lived in a small apartment in the neighborhood. It was hard to imagine Xavier as a solid citizen.

The truce, which had barely survived on several occasions, was broken about a year later by the senior Mexican delegate to our Peace Council, a big, tough, hot-tempered fifteen-year-old named Carlos. A black youngster had had a fight with his cousin and won. As the black youth was almost a head taller than his opponent, Carlos contended it was not a fair fight. He promptly avenged his cousin with a few well-placed punches which inflicted a bloody nose and cut lip upon the recipient, not to mention hurt feelings. The black boy had an older brother, a former student of ours, who was sixteen years old and quite a bit taller than Carlos. The older brother, in turn, decided that the altercation between Carlos and his little brother was not equitable, and he very much wanted to discuss the matter—with his fists. The scenario was a familiar one, and I resigned myself to the same routine I'd gone through a number of times before. I tried to contact the potential adversaries, but they were absent. I learned that they had already alerted their respective gangs and had arranged an after-school rendezvous. Once again I invoked the aid of the police and spent a half hour after dismissal time patrolling the vicinity of the school.

I did this for a few days, returning to my office each day after the streets were quiet and remaining till my desk was cleared of unfinished work. On one of these days, as I left the office quite late and proceeded to my car, I saw a figure coming toward me. The street lights had been on for a while and the shadows were lengthening. As the man approached, his features, hazy in the dim light, became more clearly defined. I thought he looked familiar.

"Hi, Mr. Greenstein," he greeted me as he passed. His head was bent slightly forward, and the brim of his black hat obscured his eyes. He swung a lunchbox in his hand. It looked like Xavier, but I wasn't quite sure. He was already about twenty feet away when, obeying an impulse, I turned and called to him.

"Hey, is that you, Xavier?"

He turned around and nodded. "Yes, it's me."

"Come here a minute. Maybe you can help me." As he retraced his steps, I remarked, "I hear you're married."

"That's right," and with a hint of pride, "I've got a son—two months old."

"Well, isn't that something! Congratulations! How are you getting along?"

"Pretty good."

"Are you working?"

"Oh, sure. I've had this job a couple of years now. I'm working in a factory." He named the place, which I recognized. It was within walking distance, less than a mile from the school.

"That's fine," I said. "Listen, there's this boy Carlos Montego. He's with the Latin Kings and they've been making some trouble. You know, fighting with the Deuces. Maybe you could talk to him."

"Carlos Montego? I never heard of him. I ain't been with the Kings for a long time. Don't have time for that kind of stuff no more." He smiled, as though we were old friends instead of former adversaries. "Sorry I can't help you. Well, I'll be seein' you," he said, and he left.

And that's the way it was—Xavier working, married, and a father. It was hard to believe. Not exactly a success story, but I guess that's a matter of opinion. After all, what is success? A few years ago, I would have given odds that Xavier would be either dead or in jail by this time, depending upon which came first. By contrast, I thought he had done pretty well.

What had made the difference? Certainly not the school. Was it the gentling influence of a woman (actually, just a girl)? Pretty corny, but I'd seen it happen before. I am not about to downgrade the power of love.

Harvey was in sixth grade when I became principal, and that is when I first came in contact with him. As I recall, he was a gangling, skinny boy with lustreless brown hair, sickly white skin, and washed-out blue eyes. His features, his walk, and his speech were on the effeminate side. It was almost inevitable that his classmates would call him a sissy. The boys picked on him mercilessly—seldom hurting him physically, just teasing him to the point where he'd fly into a helpless rage. It was a game they played, and this was the part they enjoyed most. Kids can be almost as cruel as adults.

His teacher had attempted to punish some of the students involved, but catching them was not easy. Usually she had no inkling that anything untoward was taking place until Harvey's screams shattered the decorum of the classroom. Then she would look up from behind her desk only to observe faces that were pictures of innocence. As Harvey accused one or the other of his tormentors, they would deny, in tones of injured virtue, any and all of his charges. At first the teacher was sorry for him, but soon it became a problem for her as well. For one thing, Harvey was constantly bringing his complaints to her; for another, these episodes, and his loud reactions to them, were disrupting the class. Finally, she asked for my assistance, and I instructed her to send Harvey to my office.

"Your teacher tells me that some of the kids are bothering you," I began. "Who is picking on you?"

"All of them," he replied bitterly.

"Well, who are the main ones?"

"They're all doing it—all the boys anyway," he insisted. "They don't like me because they're a bunch of bums, and I won't act like they do. They swear and do a lot of other things, and I won't."

I complimented him, rather half-heartedly, upon his righteous attitude, then asserted, "Someone must be doing it more than the others. I can't accuse the whole class. You'll have to give me some names so I can talk to them."

Obligingly he gave me one name, then another and another, until I had compiled a list of more than ten and he was still going. I managed to get him to reduce the list to five of the "worst" ones and promised that I'd talk to them.

After dismissing him, I sent for these five. I told them I was too busy to listen to their protestations of innocence. All I wanted to hear was the reason for their actions and how we could solve the problem.

They stood there without replying, none of them apparently inclined to admit his guilt. Finally, one spoke up. "He starts it. He calls us names."

"What kind of names?"

"He says we're bums and dummies and things like that."

Another boy chimed in with the old standby. "Yeah, and he says things about my mudder."

"I don't want to hear about your 'mudder,'" I said wearily. "According to him, you swear at him and push him around. Maybe that's why he calls you names."

"Well, you should hear him swear. And right out loud in the room. Ask the teacher."

"Look boys, I can't believe he's making all this up. In fact, I know he isn't, because your teacher told me what's going on. I think you're all involved in this. It's got to stop, or I'm going to call your parents. You'd better remember that, and pass the word to your friends. Now go back to your room."

I sent for Harvey again. He indignantly denied their charges. "They're always lying about me!" he shouted. "They want to get me in trouble."

"Calm down," I said. "Are you sure you never swear at them?"

"Well, maybe sometimes, but only when they get me real mad. How would you like it if they shot rubber bands and paper clips at you and kicked you under the desk?"

I admitted that I wouldn't like it but explained to him that his reactions were only aggravating the situation and that he would have to exercise greater self-control. "How can I blame them for swearing if you're swearing too? And I want you to stop this screaming in class."

"All right, I'll try," he agreed grudgingly. "But they better leave me alone."

There wasn't a great deal of improvement in the situation. The students I had warned reduced their activities. According to Harvey's own admission, they were no longer the "worst" ones. However, when he had told me, "They're all doing it," he had not been far off the mark. Unfortunately he was a very easy target. As he became increasingly sensitive, it took less and less to provoke him. Someone making a face, or even an imaginary insult, could drive him into a hysterical fury, which only caused the class to laugh at him. This frustrated him to such an extent that he would run out of the room to escape his tormentors. His teacher would then report to me that he was missing and that he had left the room without permission, a breach of discipline which she could not tolerate. I agreed that it was time to talk to his parents.

I found out that there were no parents, at least not at home. Harvey, the oldest of three children, lived with his grandparents. How this came about was subsequently related to me by his grandmother, though I never got the story quite straight. My recollection is that his mother (her daughter) was an alcoholic who finally was unable to accept the responsibility of raising the children and simply deserted them, leaving them with their father. Another man may have been involved. The father could not go to work and take care of the children at the same time, so he parked them with the grandparents. I believe he later obtained a divorce, remarried, left the city, and abrogated his responsibilities toward his children entirely. They saw no more of him. There may be some discrepancies in this account, but the end result was that the grandparents were left with the task of raising the children. Actually, as far as I could determine, their grandmother was doing the job alone, which made it even more difficult. I don't remember ever seeing the grandfather.

Harvey's grandmother was a diminutive, wrinkled, nervous, querulous woman whose attitude indicated that she felt the world had conspired against her—which indeed it had. Raising one family is difficult enough. Raising a second one when you're old and tired is an unfair burden, but in this case there was no one else to do it. There were also financial worries. Her husband's small pension was insufficient to cover their needs, so she had to work part-time. And if she complained a lot, who could blame her?

I was aware of her problems as well as Harvey's and tried to be sympathetic. Nevertheless, when she came to see me in response to my call, I explained to her that Harvey's habit of leaving the class without permission placed me in a difficult position. Technically, his transgressions were greater than those of the students he complained about.

"How do you expect him to stay in that room with all those kids picking on him?" she demanded.

I admitted it was difficult but suggested that she talk to him. "He has to learn not to get so upset about little things. Some of the things he complains about aren't really that serious—like the kids making faces at him. If he'd learn to ignore them, the kids might stop teasing him so much. Believe me, I've tried to put a stop to it, but I can't punish the whole class."

"Maybe you can put him in a different room," she suggested.

"That's a possibility," I conceded, "but it seldom helps the situation. If Harvey can't get along with the children in this class, there's no reason to believe that he'll get along any better somewhere else. He's complaining about the whole class, not just one or two kids. And what happens if he can't get along in the next class? He'll want to be moved again. It will just teach him that he can run away from a problem instead of facing it. I've talked to the teacher he had last year. She told me he was having trouble then too, though it wasn't quite as bad. And they weren't the same kids, either. I'm not trying to tell you it's all his fault, because it isn't. I know the kids pick on him. Still, he has to learn that he can't scream out loud in class and rush out of the room every time a kid does something that bothers him. You have to understand that if I transferred every student who didn't like his teacher or his classmates, I would be transferring kids every day. You can see me in a couple of weeks if the situation hasn't improved, and

I'll think about it—though I won't promise I'll do it. Meanwhile, it's his teacher's complaint I have to consider. No teacher can permit a student to disrupt the class and run out of the room without permission the way he does. It undermines her authority. If there's a problem, he should bring it to her."

"He does tell her, but she never does anything about it," she insisted.

"She has tried to help him and so have I. We'll do what we can, but I want you to talk to him. We can't help him if he doesn't help himself. Incidentally, the kids tell me he swears at them."

"My Harvey doesn't swear. Those kids are a bunch of liars. You don't know what they're like. The neighborhood has changed. I wish I could move, but I can't afford it. These kids are mean. Sometimes they knock him down when they get him outside. He comes home with his clothes dirty and torn and I haven't got the money to buy him new clothes."

"I hadn't heard about that. I can't stop the teasing, but I won't tolerate any physical abuse. If that happens, tell him to report it to me. But remember, I can't help him if he's the one who starts the trouble."

"He never starts it. He's a good boy. They know he can't fight with them." Nevertheless, she agreed to talk to him about his behavior in class, and that ended our conference.

Harvey was, at best, an average student. He could read well enough, and his teacher's assessment was that he had the ability to do better. However, his emotional problems prevented him from concentrating on his schoolwork.

He started coming to my office after school occasionally to talk to me, explaining that he wanted to wait till the other kids went home so they wouldn't bother him. As I always remained after school to complete my work, I usually permitted him to stay for a few minutes.

"They know I won't fight them," he often told me. "I could if I wanted to, but I promised my grandmother I wouldn't fight, and they know it."

I would suppress a smile and agree that fighting was not the answer. It certainly wouldn't have been for him. I had once separated him in a scuffle with a girl (he claimed she stuck him with a pin, she said he pulled her hair), and he wasn't doing too well at the time. Fortunately for him she wasn't a very big girl. I knew that the real reason he wouldn't fight any of the boys was that he had no chance of winning, but I didn't want to puncture his alibi. If this pitiful attempt to rationalization helped him, why not? His ego needed all the help it could get.

Some parents try to teach their children to stand up to a bully and show him they aren't afraid of him. Occasionally, this tactic will work. If the child can give a good account of himself, even if he loses, the bully may then decide to leave him alone. Of course it works even better in the movies, where the weakling, after being humiliated by the class bully, secretly takes boxing lessons and eventually turns the table on his tormentor while the heroine is watching. Real life is seldom like that.

I tried to teach Harvey what I myself had learned as a kid growing up in a tough neighborhood, that if someone says something that hurts you, you pretend it doesn't. If the kids laugh at you, you laugh with them. Pretty soon you're not fun anymore, and they pick on someone else. (There is a time to fight back too, but for Harvey I didn't believe this was the time or that he had the capability.) It was not an easy lesson for him to learn. He appeared to understand what I was saying and promised many times to heed my advice, but his resolution was usually of short duration. Days and even weeks would go by with only minor altercations. Then there would be another eruption.

On one such occasion, he burst into my office screaming, "I won't stay in that room anymore! I'm leaving. I'm not coming back to your school! You don't care what those guys do to me!"

I tried to calm him down. "You know that isn't true," I said. "You wouldn't be in my office if you believed that. Now, what happened? Sit down and tell me about it."

He went through the already familiar litany of his woes. "And they said they'd get me after school," he concluded. "Well, I'm not waiting for them. I'm going home."

"You can't do that," I said. "If you left the school without permission, I'd have to suspend you. I can't make special rules just for you."

"I don't care!" he insisted. "I'm not going to stay here and get killed."

"No one is going to kill you. I'll tell you what I'll do. I'll call your grandmother. If she wants to come and get you, that's all right with me. We can say you aren't feeling well. You don't look too well right now anyway."

I phoned his grandmother. As we waited for her to come, a messenger entered with a note from Harvey's teacher. She was reporting that he had run out of the room without permission and had not returned. When his grandmother arrived, I explained the situation to her and told her I would talk to the boys involved. She muttered something about my not doing my job which was, of course, to protect Harvey, and then she took him home. I informed his teacher that he had gone home with his grandmother and sent for the boys he had named as his assailants. I warned them that I would hold them responsible for any attack on Harvey. Then I called their parents and repeated my warning to them.

I now seriously considered transferring Harvey to another class and mentioned the possibility to his teacher. Although she was dissatisfied with his conduct, she was not receptive to the suggestion. She had already had several heated encounters with his grandmother. If I transferred him, she believed his grandmother would regard it as a victory. It would indicate that the teacher had failed. Personally, I had some misgivings about making the change anyhow. Our sixth-grade classes were homogeneous—that is, each on a different scholastic level. One was probably too advanced for Harvey and the other too low. Besides, I had spoken to the other teachers, and neither of them was anxious to take Harvey. I decided to leave things as they were for the time being.

There were a few more complaints from Harvey during the course of the school year, and I learned once again to appreciate the truth of an article I had read (and the title of a previous chapter), "The Principal—Man in the Middle." Harvey's grandmother was outspoken in blaming me for not doing enough to protect him. His teacher, though not so outspoken, implied that I was undermining her authority by not punishing him for his transgressions. Even my clerks evinced disapproval because I allowed a student to burst into my office without going through the proper channels (their office) first. Also, they thought I was letting him take up too much of my time. Meanwhile, Harvey was more often reproachful than grateful, and the parents of the boys I had reprimanded believed I was unfair to their children. Fortunately, I survived and so did Harvey.

The next year I did not see nearly as much of him for two reasons. I had taken pains to separate him from his chief tormentors by putting him in a different class (our seventh grade was not homogeneous), and he was now on the second floor, far away from my office. Perhaps there was a third reason. He was a year older. While he still was involved in altercations from time to time, and he still stopped by after school occasionally, now it was more as if he had found someone he could confide in. As my time was limited, and Harvey tended to be loquacious, I often had to cut him short. However, I tried to do so in a way that would not make him feel unwelcome. His grades were improving. By the time he got into eighth grade, they were above average. He had few friends. He just withdrew into his private world and pursued his hobbies. I believe he had taken up stamp collecting and was learning to play trombone.

Eventually, Harvey was ready to graduate, and there was another problem—one which I may have worried about more than he did. The high school in our neighborhood was over ninety-five percent black. Most of our white graduates avoided attending it by transferring to a Catholic high school, moving out of the neighborhood, or applying for a permissive transfer. The last was an option given to a limited number of students to transfer from the neighborhood high school, which was overcrowded, to one which had room for them. The number of requests always exceeded the number that these schools could accommodate. Consequently, a drawing would be held to select the successful applicants.

I knew that the neighborhood school was not as bad as the white parents believed—or the black parents, for that matter. (Many of the black parents were as outspoken in their condemnation of the school as the white ones were and would also apply for permissive transfers for their children.) The rumors of students being beaten up—and worse—were never substantiated by those of our graduates, black, white, or Hispanic, who came back to visit me. Nevertheless, I had heard some stories of students being "ripped off" (their money taken from them), and who would be a better target for that, or who knows what else, than Harvey? I pictured this still skinny, effeminate, naive white boy in a rough ghetto school which was almost all black. It would never work. After all, he had just barely managed to survive in our school.

I did something now that I had never done before, personally intervened in a student's decision about which high school he planned to attend. I called Harvey's grandmother, asked her to meet with me, and discovered that she knew very little about the neighborhood high school. Perhaps that is why she was not as apprehensive as the other white parents. I did not wish to alarm her. Without going into details, I asked her if she had considered sending Harvey to another school. She told me she hadn't thought much about it. She couldn't afford to move or to send him to a Catholic school. I explained the permissive transfer plan. I stopped short of specifically recommending it, as I felt that this was not a decision for me to make. However, I informed her that this was a legitimate option offered by the Board of Education and that Harvey could submit an application if he wished. He brought his application the next day. Several weeks later, I was notified of the outcome. Most of the requests had been approved. Harvey's was not.

Some of the parents whose children's requests had been denied believed that I, or someone else, could alter the results. They asked—even insisted—that I use my influence on behalf of their children. But the drawing of the names was scrupulously fair and entirely a matter of chance. It was not within my power to make any changes even if I had wished to do so. There was nothing I could do for Harvey.

A few months after Harvey started high school, he came to visit me. I believe there was a teachers' meeting at his school and classes had been dismissed early, so he stopped by on his way home. I guess I expected to see some scars or bruises. None were visible. He had brought no problems or complaints—just stopped by to say hello.

"How are you getting along?" I asked cautiously. Though I was curious, I did not want to elicit a bitter recital of grievances.

"It was hard at first, but I'm getting used to it."

Used to what, I wondered. "I hear some of the kids are pretty rough. Do they bother you much?"

"No, not much."

I wasn't convinced. "I understand that a lot of kids get 'ripped off.' Does anyone ask you for money?"

"Yeah, sometimes."

"So what do you do about it?"

"I don't bring any money. I tell them I don't have any money, and they leave me alone."

"And they believe you?"

"I show them my pockets. See?" He turned his pockets inside out, revealing that they were indeed empty.

It was hard for me to accept that this simple expedient could be effective. It had been my impression that if you had some money and handed it over, you had a better chance of escaping a beating. Yet here was Harvey, whom I had always placed very high on "the most likely to get beaten up" list, looking alive and well. Either he had finally learned to adjust, or the school wasn't as bad as I had been told.

"How do you like the school?" I inquired.

"Fair. Some of the kids aren't too smart, so we have to go pretty slow in some subjects, but I guess it's all right. I've joined the band. We've got a real good band."

"Yes, I've heard they have a good band. What instrument do you play?"

"The trombone."

"Oh, that's right. I forgot. Well, I'm glad you stopped by. I was wondering how you were getting along."

"I turned back to my desk, hinting that I had work to do. He asked and received my permission to visit some of his former teachers, and left.

I didn't see him for quite a while after that—possibly a year. Then he came in one day, resplendent in his band uniform, blue and gold with tassels and piping. I hardly recognized him.

"How do you like it?" he said proudly.

"My, aren't you something! You look like a general."

"Our band got a superior rating. We're going to play a concert tomorrow. Maybe you can come."

"I'm afraid I can't. I have a meeting. You really look great though. How are things going otherwise? What kind of grades are you getting?"

"Mostly B's. I suppose I could do better, if I wasn't so busy at the boys' club."

"Oh, what do you do there?" He had mentioned something once before about joining a boys'club, but I hadn't paid much attention.

"I'm in the photography club and the stamp club and I help the director with different things. I go there almost every night."

"I used to belong to a boys' club when I was a kid," I told him. "I enjoyed it, and it was educational too. I'm sure you'll find it worthwhile."

We talked for a while; then he left to show off his uniform to his former teachers.

He dropped by occasionally during the next two years, and each time he had something to tell me about the band, the club, and his hobbies. He had found his place, his little circle of activities which isolated him and protected him from outside interference. In a school of about three thousand students, he managed to avoid contact with all but those few whose interests were similar to his own. He actually seemed happy—quite a change from the hysterical boy who used to burst into my office screaming, "I'm not coming back to your school!"

I remember quite well the last time I saw him. It was a day or two before his high school graduation. He could hardly wait to tell me the good news. He had been offered a job at the boys' club as assistant director. What did I think of that?

I told him I thought it was great and I was very happy for him. Working in a boys' club could be a very rewarding experience and might lead to a good future. I really was happy for him. As I thought of all the counseling I had given him, all the time I had spent, I also felt a personal pride in his accomplishment. Harvey had made it—or so I thought.

A number of years later I happened to notice an item in the newspaper. The headline was, "CLUB DIRECTOR CHARGED AS BOY MOLESTER." The story went on to describe how the assistant director of a boys'club, while taking a group on a camping trip, had allegedly sexually molested one of the boys. There were other charges and other alleged incidents. I won't go into the details. They weren't very pleasant. The assistant club director was tried, found guilty, lectured by the judge on how despicable his crime was, and sentenced to four years in prison. Yes, that assistant club director was Harvey.

I do not fault the judge for his sentence or even for his remarks. I too find a crime against a child particularly loathsome. Yet, knowing Harvey as I did, it is hard for me to think of him as some kind of monster. As I look back at what I know of his childhood, I wonder what effect it had had on him. I do not offer that as an excuse for his actions, for if it is, it's an excuse we all have for any wrong we commit. All people with bad childhood experiences do not become criminals. Harvey was now a responsible adult and had to be judged accordingly. Still, I cannot help feeling sorry for him. I really thought he had made it. I wonder what went wrong. I know I sound like a broken record, but I have to say it. His reading ability, his accomplishments in school, seem insignificant now.

Well, these are isolated cases and don't prove anything. The schools cannot be expected to cure the social ills of the world. Nevertheless, I don't think that educators should ignore the fact that these problems exist and keep feeding the public platitudes about how wonderful things will be if we raise reading scores a few percentage points. Is it a drop in reading scores that is responsible for the high rate of unemployment during times of recession or for the state of the economy? By the way, according to a news release I saw recently, among the unemployed are about one hundred women with Ph.D.'s in science. I wonder if they are poor readers. But let's assume the validity of the argument that those who are the worst readers are the least employable. If we raise everyone's reading score, won't someone still be at the bottom? Of course, no parent wants his child to be that someone.

I would suggest that parents demand more and better vocational schools instead of worrying so much about reading scores. While this will not cure the problem of unemployment, it should reduce the dropout rate and give these youngsters some marketable skills. Even more important psychologically, it would give them identifiable goals, a sense of achievement (instead of their present feeling of failure) if they can achieve these goals, and improved self-esteem. All this has to be a plus. It might even reduce juvenile delinquency.

I have not lost my faith in academic education, though at times that faith gets a little shaken. I would like to see all children learn to read, and read well. It would be nice if they went to college, provided they have the desire and the aptitude. My own children have gone to college, and I'm glad they did. I told them it would broaden their horizons (and teach them to recognize cliches like that one), enhance their appreciation of art, music, and literature, make them better conversationalists and more interesting people, and provide them with options when they seek employment which they would not have otherwise. It should also make them better informed and therefore better citizens. If an education can achieve half of these things, it would be worthwhile. However, parents and teachers should stop lying to themselves and to the children by promising them that an education will yield rewards which it may never provide. A college degree does not assure one a good life, and it certainly is not a ticket to financial success. Who should be more aware of the latter than a teacher? I know very few wealthy teachers, but I have known a number of college graduates who couldn't find teaching jobs and had to seek other employment—and that number is likely to increase.

Early in my teaching career I had a conversation with a Puerto Rican girl who was a very poor reader. She was fifteen years old and had been in the United States for about two years. Because of her age, she had been promoted to seventh grade. Even so, she was still the oldest in the class. Though she had learned to speak English fairly well, she showed greater interest in some of the older boys than in her textbooks (a normal reaction), and she did not appear to care if she ever graduated. One day, when she had neglected to do her homework as usual, I kept her after school. As I started to explain to her the importance of getting an education, she interrupted me.

"Mr. Greenstein," she said, "how many buildings you own?"

I was a beginning teacher at the time earning three thousand dollars a year. Even for those days, though the cost of living was much lower than it is today, it was not a munificent sum. Supporting a wife and children on my salary was a constant struggle. The girl's question disconcerted me temporarily. I wondered if I had heard her correctly.

"Buildings?" I repeated. "You mean houses?"

"Yes," she insisted. "How many buildings you got?"

"I don't own any buildings," I admitted. At that time I often found it difficult just to manage the rent for our small four-room apartment.

"Well, my father come from Puerto Rico five years ago. [He had sent for her later.] He is a janitor. He own two buildings. And he can't read."

It took me a little while to think of an answer, but I found one. I have given it to students many times since then. I even believe it myself.

"Maria," I responded, "do you expect to get married and have children some day?"

"I think so. Sure."

"Well, I have children and they go to school. When they need help, they come to me and I can help them. They respect their father—at least I think they do. Do you think your children will respect you, or will they think you're a dummy?"

This may not be the best reason for getting an education, but it's better than promising financial success. For all I know, her father may have ten buildings by now, and he probably still can't read. All I have is my own home. (I used to own it in partnership with the bank, but my mortgage is paid off now.)

I don't want to be misunderstood. I'll say it again. I'm certainly in favor of teaching reading—what teacher isn't? Nor am I opposed to trying to improve reading scores, though I question the validity of the scores and of the tests used to measure them. What bothers me is that this new crusade, with its emphasis on "back to basics" and not letting students advance from grade to grade until they have "proved" their competence, may have other results. One consequence may be the use of methods that will make school more boring than it already is—and heaven knows it's often pretty boring now. The cure can be worse than the disease. I'm not saying that school should be all fun, fun, fun. That's unrealistic. Some drill is necessary—and certainly some studying. Multiplication tables, for example, have to be learned. Students can't master them just by osmosis. However, if you show me a teacher who can make school interesting, I'll show you a class that is learning. I suppose I should qualify that statement. I'm always accusing others of offering simplistic solutions to complex problems, and now I'm indulging in the same practice myself. Still, it should be obvious that students will learn better in an environment that stimulates their interest and participation.

As a result of the reading crusade, the teachers in our school system are now required to maintain charts indicating the progress of each student and his mastery of certain reading skills. In addition, they must keep a card for each student and upgrade it regularly by frequent testing. This "new, improved" reading program has elicited lavish praise in newspaper editorials and even on television. I wonder if the writers of these laudations have bothered to talk to the teachers. I have. They tell me that so much time is spent on testing and record-keeping that there is little left for teaching. Their morale is very low. Ah, but the program works, these writers say, and point to a very slight improvement in the scores on the standardized reading test which is administered annually. What they don't realize is that the pressure upon teachers to achieve improvement in the scores is so great that many of them coach the students specifically for the purpose of doing well on this test. Some even obtain a copy of the test and go over it item by item. (In other words, they cheat.) Statistics may not lie, but they are certainly subject to misinterpretation. Well, during the course of my educational career I have seen many innovations and cure-alls come and go. This too shall pass—I hope.

The administration contends that this accounting system will expose teachers who are incompetent. Big deal. Both principals and teachers already know who are the incompetents. As I've said before, the problem is that we have no adequate machinery for getting rid of them. In our local school system of over twenty-five thousand teachers, there have been about twenty certified (tenured) teachers dismissed for cause in the last twenty years, an average of one a year. A remarkable record, depending on which way you want to interpret it. We can't expect to have all good teachers. It may be necessary to settle for many that are mediocre. However, if we could get rid of the really bad ones, it would help immeasurably. Identifying them doesn't mean a thing unless we can do something about it.

Of course, teachers get tired of being the scapegoats for the decline in reading scores and try to find some scapegoats of their own. One of these is too much television viewing. I'm not sure I can accept that.

Too much television is not good just like too much anything else. However, I happen to have made a study way back in 1950 entitled, "Effect of Television Upon Elementary School Grades" which appeared in the November 1954 issue of the *Journal of Educational Research.* My findings were based on a sample of only sixty-seven students and can hardly be called conclusive. Nevertheless, I discovered that those students included in my sample who watched television for an average time of six hours or less per day actually got higher reading grades than the control group which did not watch television. (There were still many families in those days who had no television sets.) I also found that students who watched television for more than six hours a day had poorer grades. This is understandable. If children watch television from the time they come home from school until they go to bed (and at a late hour), they won't have time to read, do homework, or anything else. As far as I can see, these children don't even have time enough to sleep. (Perhaps they sleep in class.)

I am sure that television has cut into the reading time of many children, and that is unfortunate. I would like to see them read books. However, I doubt if a moderate amount of television viewing is harmful. I'm only discussing here its effect upon reading, not the psychological impact of the subject matter.

Teachers also attribute an increase in discipline problems and decline in scholarship to a lack of supervision by the parents. I'll have to go along with that. I have known many families with only one parent, the mother. Most of these women were on ADC and stayed home to take care of their children, but it was still a one-parent family, and the supervision was often inadequate. In some instances, the women worked to support their families. That meant that an older sibling would be entrusted with the care of the children until the mother came home, or sometimes the children would be on their own. This is not a healthy situation. Another disturbing trend, at least from the standpoint of caring for children, is the increase in the number of families in which both parents are working. When one income is insufficient to support the family, I suppose they have no choice. However, I have always believed that children, especially young children, need a parent at home to pay attention to them. And when the mother is working just so the family can have fancy furniture and a second car, I am afraid that these luxuries may turn out to be more expensive than she realizes in terms of the ultimate effect upon the children.

I would like to advance one more reason for the decline in scholarship. Many of our students don't believe that reading, or education for that matter, is really important. They see rock stars, television personalities, and prominent athletes making fortunes, while we tell them that school is the way to success. We have all heard about well-known professional athletes who go into the ghetto and talk to children about the importance of staying in school and getting an education. I don't doubt their sincerity. I think it's a nice gesture. But do the kids really buy this? The very presence of these athletes makes their statements a lie. They were not invited to speak because of their scholastic achievements. When the former heavyweight boxing champion of the world, who, by his own admission, was practically a nonreader when he went to school, lectures on the value of an education, can anyone take him seriously? I began to have doubts myself when I realized that he was paid more for one fight than I have earned in an entire lifetime. I sometimes wonder if I made the right decision. I don't think I could have succeeded in boxing, football, or basketball, but I might have made it with a guitar. While many good musicians can't make a living, I've seen some no-talent kids who have done pretty well, financially at least, with outlandish costumes, weird gimmicks, and strange noises. I'm afraid many students who do poorly in school have noticed it too. I have known some who got together to form bands. They dream of getting that big break some day. I don't want to knock it. These kids could be doing something much worse. They practice very hard and appear to enjoy it. They are quite sincere in what they are doing. So are the kids who play basketball and spend hours practicing free throws and jump shots. I guess they have dreams too. Unfortunately, I know that most of those who have visions of achieving great financial success by this means will suffer disappointment. I have tried to explain to them that their lives must be based upon something more tangible than a one-in-a-million chance. But who are they going to believe—me, or the glamorous success stories they see daily on television? No wonder they aren't turned on by reading.

13. He Didn't Get Religion

Mr. Hill, the new assistant principal, had set up an office on the second floor. Some of the students who were sent to him for disciplinary purposes were unaware of its location and would come to the main office to look for him. Therefore, when a tall youngster entered the office and stood at the door, fidgeting nervously, my clerked sensed his problem.

"Who are you looking for?" she called.

The door of my office was open, and the answer came through loud and clear. "My teacher told me to go to Hill," he replied.

One day, as we were waiting for a principals' meeting to begin, a colleague related the following anecdote which may or may not be apocryphal:

A young teacher had requested to see the elderly principal. "It's about Tommy," she explained hesitantly. "He's making it very difficult for me to teach. He won't sit still, he gets into fights, he's always talking, and he's constantly bothering his neighbors."

The principal nodded sympathetically. "He sounds like a handful. How is the rest of the class?"

"Oh, fine. They're really good kids. If only something could be done about Tommy . . . " She paused expectantly.

"Of course. We have to do something about Tommy, don't we?"

The young teacher was encouraged. Perhaps help was forthcoming.

"By the way," asked the principal, "didn't the teachers get a raise recently?"

"Yes. Last month," the teacher affirmed.

"And they deserve it," asserted the principal. "Teaching is not an easy job. Now, let's see . . . if we got Tommy out of your class, it would be much easier, wouldn't it?"

The young teacher's face brightened. This was more than she had hoped for. "Oh, yes," she agreed enthusiastically. "I could really teach if he weren't there."

The principal appeared to go off on a tangent again. "Teachers get paid pretty well now since they received that last raise. Wouldn't you agree?"

"I guess so," said the teacher, mystified. What did all this have to do with her problem?

As if answering her unspoken question, the principal continued, "You see, if there were no 'Tommy' in the class, anyone could teach. He's the one you get paid for."

A nice story—from a principal's point of view. I imagine few teachers would appreciate it or agree with its conclusions. The implication that there is only one difficult child in a class is seldom borne out by the facts. There may be two or three—or even nine or ten. I remember a class—probably the worst I ever had—whose conduct was such that, rather than count the troublemakers, I found it easier to count the number of students who behaved reasonably well, as they were the minority. What do you do with a class like that? Pray that the semester will come to an end before you do. And even if all the children in the class are well-behaved, a dream seldom realized, the good teacher still earns her salary and more. She takes advantage of the situation and tries to do a better job of teaching. She works just as hard, though with less headaches and greater satisfaction. Occasionally, however, as was the case in the principal's narrative, the teacher's problems seem to focus upon one student. Wherever he is, that's where the action is—the kind of action the teacher would gladly do without. Such a student was Jamey Hawkins.

Jamey was twelve years old when he came to our school—actually almost twelve and a half. He had a sister, Mary Jane, who was ten. I believe it was the third or fourth day of the school year when they were sent to my office for placement.

The first few days, as usual, had been sheer madness, at least for me. In a transient community such as ours, several hundred students would usually be transferring in and out. My clerks would prepare the transfers for the outgoing students. I would assign teacher-aides and teachers without homerooms (gym teacher, home economics teacher, etc.) to register the newcomers who would take numbers and wait their turn. Some of them had to wait all morning. Most of the students were with their parents, and a few of the parents would get pretty impatient and start complaining, but there was nothing we could do about it. After the registration form was completed, the student had to be assigned to a classroom. That was my job, and I would not delegate it to anyone else, for I had seen inexperienced people mess it up pretty badly. As I was the only one doing it, I never seemed to catch up. I had to interview all incoming students, check their report cards, and determine which class to put them in depending upon their level of achievement. I also had to monitor the size of the classes and try to equalize the number of boys and girls in each. While adjustments could and would be made later, I wanted to keep them at a minimum. It would be a few weeks before I would have time to get around to that. By then the students would have made friends, become adjusted to the teacher, and learned the routine of the classroom. Shifting them to another class could be a traumatic experience, especially for children in the lower grades. It wasn't so good for the teacher either as it would necessitate making changes in the attendance book and grade book.

After the first few days, when the initial rush had subsided, I was able to evaluate each student at a more leisurely pace. That was the situation when my clerk ushered a big-boned, heavy-breasted, middle-aged woman into my office. Walking behind her were two children, a boy and a girl, carrying their registration forms. As I asked each of them to take a seat, the woman smiled at me ingratiatingly. They had just come from North Carolina, she revealed. The children's parents, who had been her closest friends, were both dead. The children had nowhere to go except to an orphanage, so she had adopted them.

"Do you have their report cards?" I inquired.

"Here is Mary Jane's," she said. "She is real smart."

I looked at the grades. About average. So were her test scores. "I see she's been promoted to fifth grade. I'll put her in room 209—Mrs. Enright's class. She's a good teacher." We only had three fifth-grade classes and this was the middle one.

"Now what about the boy?"

"Jamey is a bit slow," she confided. "He was in fourth grade last year. I guess he passed, but I don't rightly know. You see, he was absent the last week of school and he didn't get his report card. I was going to pick it up before we left, but what with the packing and all, I didn't get around to it."

I checked the registration form. "I see he's twelve years old." I glanced at the boy. Big for his age—about the size of our eighth graders. On the chubby side. Regular features. Not bad looking. Ash-blond hair combed neatly to the side. Eyes a pale blue like his sister's. The girl sat beside him, prim and straight, thin arms, thin legs. She was only ten and had not yet started to develop. As they sat there, staring straight ahead, I had the feeling I was looking at a junior edition of Wood's painting, "American Gothic."

"Is there any reason why he's so far behind?" I asked.

"Well, he don't read too good, so they held him back. He's not smart like his sister, but he's a good boy."

She smiled at Jamey. He sat there impassively, as though the proceedings were not his concern. I had the impression that he didn't particularly care where I placed him. I tried to picture him in fourth grade with our nine-year-old boys. It would never do. "Suppose we try him in fifth grade and see how he does," I proposed.

The woman nodded. I could see she was pleased with my decision. Now I had another decision to make. Obviously he belonged in the lowest group, but that class was overcrowded. I had already placed a number of the incoming students in it. For some reason, the new students always seemed to belong in the lowest group.

"How does he get along with his sister?" I asked.

"They get along just fine," she assured me.

"Well, if I put them in the same room, maybe they can help each other." What I had in mind was that Mary Jane might be able to help Jamey, but I didn't want to embarrass him by saying so. "On the other hand," I continued, "putting a brother and sister in the same room doesn't always work out too well." Especially if the brother is two years older, I might have added, but didn't. "I'll leave that up to you. You know them better than I do."

"I think that'll work out fine. They were in the same room last year and didn't have no trouble."

I turned to the children. It occurred to me that I had not yet heard their voices. "How does that sound to you?"

"That's O.K.," said Mary Jane, and Jamey nodded his head in agreement. The response was not enthusiastic, but they weren't offering any objections. I completed their registration forms, directed them to room 209, and instructed my clerk to send in the next student for placement.

I saw their teacher, Mrs. Enright, a few days later and inquired how Jamey was doing.

"He can't keep up with the class," she replied. "I have to give him special work."

I had previously explained to her that I didn't have room for him in our lowest group. "Just do the best you can," I told her. She hadn't mentioned his behavior, so I assumed that did not present a problem.

It must have taken Jamey a while to get acclimated. After all, he was a stranger in a strange land. And Mrs. Enright had good control of her class. She was quick to rebuke any transgressor. So, like an experienced boxer who maneuvers cautiously in the early rounds as he sizes up his opponent and tries to figure out his weaknesses, Jamey was not too aggressive at first. If he called someone a name it would be under his breath, or he would kick his neighbor under the desk, trying to avoid getting caught. Soon he got bolder, though his actions were still sneaky, and he always blamed someone else for "starting" a fight or disruption. Although his teacher was not fooled, he was able to convince his mother that he was sinned against rather than sinning. This was not difficult as she would hear only his version of the incidents. Because of his size, he could push around anyone in the class with impunity—and he did. Evidently it did not occur to him that one of his victims might have an older brother who could avenge these attacks. For some reason—possibly because the upper grades were on a different schedule—this did not occur. However, in desperation, realizing they could not cope with him individually, the boys in the class decided to act collectively. After he had had a disagreement with a classmate, which usually took place in the cloakroom or in the hallway, and which he always settled physically, three or four of that boy's friends would stalk him after school. This was more than he could handle, and sometimes he would have to run all the way home to escape them.

Mrs. Enright was becoming concerned. She wrote me several notes to inform me that Jamey was causing trouble and upsetting the class. She was aware of his classmates' attempts at retaliation and warned them against it, but it was quite apparent to her that Jamey was the instigator. Of course, Jamey's mother interpreted these episodes differently. She came to me with a complaint that the other boys were picking on him. She implied that there was prejudice involved and reminded me that "these Mexican boys stick together." The prejudice, if any, I thought emanated from her and Jamey. I responded that the information I had received did not substantiate her charges and suggested that she talk to Jamey's teacher about it. This may not have been a good move on my part. Their divergent views of the situation provoked a heated argument. Mrs. Hawkins returned to my office to complain bitterly that the teacher also was biased against her son.

It should be remembered that no matter how many witnesses testified against Jamey, one was always on his side, his sister. Whether this was due to sibling loyalty or fear of reprisals I had no way of knowing—though I suspected the latter, especially when there was another development. Mary Jane accused Mrs. Enright of slapping her. Mrs. Enright was furious. Although, to my knowledge, she had never slapped a child, I had to investigate. I found absolutely no basis for the accusation. Actually, according to the teacher, there had been no reason—at least up till now—for her to have meted out such a punishment, as the girl was usually well-behaved. I interrogated Mary Jane and found discrepancies in her story. I suspected that the accusation was Jamey's idea, but I couldn't prove it. Although a forced apology is really meaningless, I wouldn't permit Mary Jane to return to class till she had apologized to Mrs. Enright. And now Mrs. Hawkins was more convinced than ever that the teacher was mistreating her children. She asked that they be placed in another room. I had begun to consider that possibility myself.

At this point, Mrs. Enright made an attempt to salvage the situation. Jamey had filled out an application to become a patrol boy. While I marveled at his "chutzpah," Mrs. Enright decided to approve it and sent it to the office for my signature. She had read in an educational textbook that an antisocial child's behavior often improves if he is given responsibility. (It must have been the same book that my first principal had read.) And sometimes it does. On the other hand, sometimes it doesn't—as it didn't when my first principal tried it. However, that had been a decision imposed upon me, while this was at the suggestion of the teacher. I saw no reason to object. I figured it couldn't hurt to try.

I figured wrong. It did hurt. It was obvious that Jamey had not read the textbook. He enjoyed being a patrol boy. It gave him power. He manifested that power in various ways. He would keep students waiting for his signal to cross even when no car was coming, he would report those he didn't like for real or imaginary offenses, and he would blackmail students by threatening to report them if they didn't give him candy. Some of them changed their itinerary in order to avoid crossing at his corner. Finally, when several girls came to me in tears because he had caused them to receive undeserved punishment assignments, I investigated the situation. The testimony I obtained from one student after another convinced me to terminate his services. This prompted a note from his mother complaining that the students were lying about him. Jamey countered by warning one of the girls he believed to be responsible for his dismissal that he was going to "get" her. The frightened girl reported his threat to me, and I then did some threatening of my own. I assured Jamey that he would be suspended immediately if the girl was harmed.

Whenever a student was sent to me for discipline, I recorded the offense and the action I had taken on a file card. Naturally, I had a card for Jamey. I also clipped to the card some of the notes his teacher sent me. This was one of her notes after an incident in the gym.

"Jamey claims that his finger was broken by Fred Pollack during a gym class, but the other boys say if Fred did it, it was an accident. This afternoon Jamey hit Fred, knocked him down, and hurt his knee. This happened on the way home for lunch. A number of children say they heard Jamey say that he was going to do this—that he was going to break both of Fred's legs. Fred is not here this afternoon. Jamey supposedly ran across the street against the light in order to hit this child."

I called Fred's home. His parents were working, and he was there alone. He told me he had accidentally fallen on top of Jamey while they were playing a game in the gym. Jamey would not accept his explanation that it was an accident and vowed to get him later—with the consequences that Mrs. Enright had delineated in her note. I reprimanded Fred, though rather mildly, for staying home instead of coming to me—then instructed him to tell his mother what had happened, to assure her that I would see that no further harm came to him, and to have her write a note explaining his absence. The following morning he brought the note from his mother. In it she apologized for his unauthorized absence, informed me that he had never been in trouble before (which I had already confirmed), and repeated Fred's version of the incident (which had been corroborated by seven witnesses). She realized, she continued, that this was a "mixed" school, but she was not prejudiced against anyone and trusted me to protect her son. Obviously she thought Jamey was Mexican. Funny how easy it is to imagine racial undertones where none exists. I had thought that Jamey was prejudiced against Hispanics. Well, at least he had proved his impartiality by attacking Fred and threatening several non-Hispanic girls.

I decided that the time had come to suspend Jamey for these and his other offenses. That would give Fred and Mrs. Enright a brief respite. When I notified Mrs. Hawkins of my action, she expressed her displeasure, declared that her children could not adjust to this neighborhood, and advised me that they would soon be moving. I relayed this information to Mrs. Enright, and it cheered her up considerably.

As is often the case, the effect of Jamey's suspension was transitory. In a few days he was his usual obnoxious self, but his teacher, buoyed by the prospect of his imminent departure, bore up pretty well. Not even a note from her for two weeks—except that she would inquire almost daily if I had heard anything from Mrs. Hawkins. I hadn't, but Jamey kept Mrs. Enright's hopes alive by telling her that they had already found an apartment and were waiting for the occupant to move out. As the days became weeks, however, and nothing happened, Mrs. Enright began to suspect that Mrs. Hawkins had no intention of moving. The first of the month had passed, and people don't usually move in the middle of the month. Besides, Jamey was pretty vague about such details as their new address and the proposed date of their departure.

Mrs. Enright was a conscientious teacher. While Jamey's behavior was her prime concern, I believe she was genuinely disturbed because he wasn't learning anything. She requested a conference with me to discuss this situation. He was unable to do the assignments she gave the class, she told me. Consequently, she had been preparing special lessons for him. It wasn't working too well. Furthermore, she didn't think it was fair that she should have to sustain this additional burden when we had a lower fifth-grade class in which he could be placed. I had to admit there was merit to her argument. Besides, I thought to myself, she had suffered long enough. Maybe it was time for someone else to be "challenged." It was also possible, though unlikely, that Jamey would respond better to another teacher. I agreed to transfer him to Mr. Buchanan's class with the stipulation that she would have to take one of his students in exchange.

When I conveyed my decision to Mr. Buchanan, his reaction was less than ecstatic. Although he did not know Jamey, he had frequently listened to Mrs. Enright's accounts of her prize student's exploits. He already had his share of "characters," he said, and he didn't know if he could handle another one. I assured him it would be an even trade. He could dispose of a "character" in return, though it would have to be one of his better students as it would involve an advancement to a higher level.

The exchange was duly consummated, and it provoked an immediate reaction from Jamey, as the following frantic note that I received from Mrs. Enright indicated:

"Apparently there was a terrible fight on the playground at noon. It seems that Jamey threatened the boys of our room with revenge. He thinks they have something to do with his no longer being in our room. One boy's trousers were ruined by Jamey this morning. The bearer of this note was threatened by Jamey and his friends last night. He says there was a knife involved. Another boy was threatened with a bottle at noon time also. My boys say that Jamey and some other boys are going to 'beat up' on them today after school. My class is very upset and excited."

I sent for all the boys involved and spoke to them. The situation was not as bad as it sounded. Mostly it had been a case of threats and counterthreats. The actual injuries were minor, a few bruises at most. I was more concerned about the damaged trousers. It was pretty difficult, especially in a poor community such as ours, to convince parents to pay for damages caused by their child. While I had no legal authority to request it, I had sometimes been able to persuade parents to make such a payment—providing, of course, I was able to prove to their satisfaction that their child was at fault. In the case of Mrs. Hawkins, however, I imagined that would be impossible. Fortunately, the mother of the boy whose trousers were "ruined" acknowledged that they could be repaired. Although she was upset, she did not insist upon compensation and accepted my assurance that I would talk to Jamey's mother and there would be no further trouble.

I did talk to Mrs. Hawkins and to Jamey. He responded with his usual protestations of innocence. Mrs. Hawkins, as always his staunch advocate, volunteered proof that he was the injured party.

"Show Mr. Greenstein where they hurt you," she instructed him.

He rolled up his pants leg and exhibited a scratch about an inch long. Though the skin had been broken, there was no evidence of bleeding. I concluded it was not likely to be fatal. However, I made a sympathetic noise.

"I don't want Jamey hurt and I don't want anyone else hurt," I declared. "I transferred him to put an end to the fighting. Let's get one thing cleared up first. I've heard that Jamey has been blaming some of these kids for his transfer. I'm the only one who has the authority to move a student to another class. That was my decision—and I didn't consult any of the students about it. Now if this doesn't work out, I may have to make another decision—only this time it will be to put him in fourth grade or send him to Montefiore."

Neither Jamey nor his mother showed much reaction to my threat. Time would tell if it had any effect. As far as I was concerned, there was nothing else to say. It is difficult to have effective discipline without the cooperation of the parents, and I obviously wasn't going to get it in this case. I terminated the conference and sent Jamey to his room.

I have often advised young inexperienced teachers not to make threats they cannot—or do not intend to—carry out. "Sooner or later," I warned them, "someone will call your bluff and you will be placed in an untenable position." I had just come dangerously close to ignoring my own advice. True, I could put Jamey in fourth grade. However, I didn't see that as a practical solution. While that might be closer to his academic level, I suspected that he wasn't learning mainly because he was making no effort to learn. There was no reason to believe that his attitude would change if he was put back another grade. Besides, it was likely to aggravate our problem. He was big enough to intimidate all of his present classmates and took pleasure in doing so. Putting him in with even smaller boys hardly seemed advisable. As for transferring him to Montefiore, I wasn't sure I had sufficient cause to request it, and, even if I did, it would take time to accomplish. I preferred to see how he would do in his new class first.

Mr. Buchanan, Jamey's new teacher, was a methodical individual. He believed in keeping records and immediately started a dossier of Jamey's activities. I'm not knocking this. In fact, I strongly recommend it. Though time-consuming, it can be very helpful when confronting a parent or even explaining to the principal what a particular student has done to cause the teacher to age prematurely. One's memory is not always reliable. Besides, a written chronicle is much more impressive—like corroborative evidence in a courtroom.

Mr. Buchanan, who prided himself on his sense of humor, bore up pretty well at first under the slings and arrows of Jamey's peccadillos. When I would inquire how Jamey was doing, he would reply with a grin, "Oh, he's making life interesting. I'm writing it all down."

The grin started to fade. Writing things down does not, in itself, alter the situation. Mr. Buchanan began insisting that some action be taken about Jamey, and I reluctantly agreed to initiate a case report recommending that he be sent to Montefiore. Mr. Buchanan gladly surrendered his anecdotal record to me to be used as evidence. It read as follows:

> 3-23. Choking two smaller classmates at recess.
>
> 3-23. (Same day.) Out of line and talking during fire drill.
>
> 3-24. Loitering in cloakroom in gym. Gym teacher very upset. Reported by patrol boys for cutting through yards. Patrol boys gave him a punishment assignment.
>
> 3-25. "Forgot" punishment assignment. Patrol boys say he has been given assignments before but always "forgets." Same thing happens to his schoolwork.

Took two rubber bands from my desk. Denied doing so, but I found them on his wrist.

Kicked and tripped the leader of the boys' line when they lined up.

3-28. Talking, disturbing others during silent reading lesson. A girl said he was "swearing."

3-29. I left the boys doing arithmetic lesson while I took girls to gym. When I returned, he was walking around the room. Told him to stand near me for a while. He kept talking and moving his arms and feet.

3-30. Gym teacher saw him hit a smaller boy in stomach as they went to recess.

4-5. Kicking and hitting a boy during recess. Punching another boy in line after recess while I was standing right near him.

Reported for throwing branches at girls during the lunch hour.

Fighting in line.

Playing with safety pin and rubber band during class. I took them away as I thought he intended to use them on another student.

I now began to receive frantic notes from Mr. Buchanan (often accompanied by Jamey). Here are his messages (slightly edited) in chronological order:

> 4-6. Jamey was fighting with another boy twice today while almost within arm's reach of me. The victim is a mild-mannered boy. I'm afraid Jamey is going to hurt someone. He kicked a boy during recess yesterday and was reported by a patrol boy for throwing branches at girls. I feel that he needs more help than a classroom teacher can give him.
>
> Mr. Buchanan
>
> 4-12. Yesterday Jamey was reported for throwing candy and some other things at some girls. Apparently he intends to supply his friends with candy to chew in class (as he did yesterday). I hear it clinking in his pockets. He hasn't done any work but continues to disrupt the class. I wish you would eliminate him from the class . . . please.
>
> Mr. Buchanan
>
> 5-6. Help! Jamey is getting on my nerves today. Can you find a place for him elsewhere?
>
> Buchanan
>
> 5-13. Jamey pushed a boy down while they were in line. He

chewed gum in class, then lied to me about it. I told him to stand in the hallway. A little later, when I looked out, he was gone.

He's back now. It's a shame our class has to stop while I deal with him. Please try to eliminate him from our group. At times he's unbearable!

Buchanan

5-16. Help! Jamey has been cursing all day. Bad influence. Please keep him.

Buchanan

5-23. The end again. Playing too rough. Inspiring the other boys to rough-house. He's a bad influence.

Buchanan

Well, here we have these anguished cries for help from a teacher, and what is this "gutless wonder" (an affectionate term for administrators that seems to have come into vogue lately) of a principal doing about it? Up to this point, I had had repeated conferences with Jamey and his mother. I had suspended him once. I had transferred him to another class. I had even removed him from the room several times at Mr. Buchanan's request and found some place to put him temporarily. All of this had not solved the problem, so now I was writing a case report. Why didn't I just get rid of Jamey—or as Mr. Buchanan had put it, "eliminate" him? Nice word. It doesn't propose a specific course of action—just an end result he would have liked me to achieve. It is understandable that parents are unaware of the difficulties involved in complying with such a request. What has always surprised me is that teachers, who should know better, are equally ignorant with respect to the powers and prerogatives of a principal. How does one go about "eliminating" a student? Strangle him? Shoot him? Or just tell him firmly never to come back. A principal can suspend (a temporary removal); he cannot expel (a permanent dismissal). He can recommend in a case report (as I was now engaged in doing) that the child be transferred to a correctional school. This must contain all pertinent information, must be accompanied by a report from the truant officer, and requires the signature of a parent. It may take a month or more to process. The request may also be denied.

Invariably, when I have tried to transfer a student to Montefiore, I have been informed that the school was overcrowded. On one occasion, after being told (as usual) that the student I had recommended would be placed on a waiting list, I protested so vehemently that the principal of Montefiore offered me a trade—one of his for one of mine. I was tempted to accept his proposal, then decided that it was better to "bear those ills we have than fly to others that we know not of." I recalled an unpleasant experience involving a girl, supposedly rehabilitated, who had been sent to me from a correctional institution and didn't want to risk a repetition.

The probation officer had brought the girl to see me. I had a nice talk with her, told her she was starting with a clean slate, and assured her I was available if she needed help. Then I assigned her to a classroom. She had a fight the next day—and I had an unhappy teacher. I called her probation officer. He had a talk with the girl and warned her that if there was one more complaint about her behavior he would have to take her back to the correctional school. He assured me everything would be all right. She was just having a little difficulty getting adjusted.

She had a few more little difficulties getting adjusted during which time she terrorized most of the girls in the class and persuaded a few of them to join her newly formed gang. I called the probation officer again and informed him that this girl had outlived her welcome. He said I hadn't really given her a fair chance. He would talk to her again. He knew how to handle her. After that she got into several more fights. Then, with no apparent provocation, she threw a brick at a younger girl. It barely missed her head. I had had enough. I suspended the girl, called the probation officer, and demanded that she be removed. The probation officer insisted that I give her one more chance. After all, she hadn't killed anyone—yet. I refused to take her back, called the district superintendent, wrote a strong letter to the downtown office, and finally prevailed.

I am not trying to create the impression that a student cannot be removed from a school but to indicate that it can be very difficult. The offense has to be extreme. On three occasions I have had students transferred expeditiously, and all for the same crime—attacking a teacher.

I have read that teachers live in an atmosphere of fear in some schools (mostly high schools, I imagine). I don't know if these accounts are true or exaggerated, but I was determined that such a situation would never exist at our school. I am inclined to be lenient, too lenient, I am sure some teachers will say. However, I have never tolerated an unprovoked attack upon a teacher nor permitted the guilty student to return to school even for one day. When such an incident occurred, I am glad to say that I have had the complete cooperation of the downtown office in what I considered an emergency situation.

Well, Jamey had not attacked a teacher, and his offenses, no matter how monstrous they appeared to his teachers, might not be viewed as particularly heinous by the people downtown. Besides, I didn't really believe that sending him to "Monte" was the appropriate solution. I had the uneasy feeling that the kids there would make mincemeat out of him. It is true that by this time I couldn't stand him, but I didn't hate him, and I didn't want his blood on my conscience. Meanwhile, he had to be somewhere. I wondered if I could persuade Mrs. Enright to take him again for a while. I didn't want to order her to do so as she had already had her turn. Perhaps she had someone she would like to offer in exchange. She might even consent to do it as a favor to Mr. Buchanan. It didn't look like he could take much more.

As I was contemplating the possibilities, another solution miraculously presented itself. Mrs. Hawkins came to see me. She wanted to know if I would permit her children to transfer to St. Agatha, the Catholic school in our neighborhood. I hastily explained that she did not need my permission. I had no authority to refuse such a request. All she needed was a confirmation from the Catholic school that her children would be accepted. If she had such an assurance, we would gladly (and I meant gladly) issue the transfers. It turned out that she had not yet contacted St. Agatha. I urged her to do so immediately—for the good of the children, of course. I pointed out that the Catholic school's membership was much smaller than ours and her children would probably receive more individual attention there. Also that Jamey would get away from the boys who were bothering him. (At this time I did not care to raise the issue of who was doing what to whom.) Mrs. Hawkins promised to go to St. Agatha the next morning and enroll them.

I told Mrs. Enright the good news. She was not impressed. "It doesn't mean a thing," she declared.

"Why not?"

"In the first place, I don't think St. Agatha will take them. In the second place, even if they did, they would never keep them. A Catholic school wouldn't stand for Jamey's shenanigans for one day."

"Well, we can always hope," I said.

The following day I had a call from the Mother Superior of St. Agatha. She had just had a visit from Mrs. Hawkins. After listening to her complaints, the Mother Superior had decided against enrolling

Jamey and Mary Jane. However, she thought I should know what Mrs. Hawkins had said. The Mother Superior and I were on pretty good terms, and she considered it her duty to warn me that Mrs. Hawkins did not have very friendly feelings toward me.

"This woman claims that her children are being beaten up by gangs, and that you and the teachers refuse to do anything about it. She says that the gangs control the school and you're afraid of them. I don't believe this nonsense, but I thought you should know about it."

The charges were so ludicrous I hardly knew how to reply. No use getting indignant or angry. I couldn't help wondering how gangs could control the school without my knowledge. "Well, you know how parents are," I responded. "I guess we can't please them all. The boy isn't getting along too well with some of his classmates. They're fifth graders. I'd hardly call it a gang. As for the real gangs, they haven't bothered us for quite a while now. Anyhow, we've never had gang trouble inside the school—just on the outside."

"I see your students when they come to catechism," said the Mother Superior, "and if this kind of thing were going on, I'm sure I would have heard about it. I just thought I should tell you what she said."

I thanked her for her solicitude and admitted we did have a problem with Jamey. "It isn't fair to say we haven't done anything about it. The teachers and I have spent a lot of time with the boy and his mother. I even transferred him to another class. However, he still sees the other boys at recess and after school. Maybe a fresh start in a new environment would be a good thing for him."

"Well, I'm sorry," said the Mother Superior, "but I can't take them. We're pretty crowded, and if there's one thing I don't need it's another behavior problem. We have enough of our own."

"I understand. I'm sorry for the children though. They're orphans you know. They would have been in an orphanage if Mrs. Hawkins hadn't adopted them." I paused to let this take effect, then continued. "The girl is no trouble. As for Jamey, I don't think he would be so bad if his mother didn't always take his side. You've seen her attitude. If we could get him away from our boys, she wouldn't be able to use them as an excuse. That would put the burden of proof on him—and on her. She couldn't keep blaming someone else if he got into trouble."

I waited for an answer, but she didn't respond. Was I beginning to convince her? All right, so I had understated the situation a bit, but I hadn't actually lied. I had admitted that Jamey was a problem. I just hadn't said how much. Anyhow, I was doing it for a noble cause. If I could get Jamey transferred, I might preserve the sanity of two teachers. Besides, I was beginning to believe my own argument. Who knows? A change of environment might help. And the Catholic school, with its reputation for good discipline, might be able to accomplish more than I had. All this went swiftly through my mind as I continued. "Maybe you could try them for a few days—on probation, of course. You can always send them back if it doesn't work out. You know we will have to accept them. We have no choice."

The point I was making was valid. The Catholic school really had nothing to lose. And if I was pushing a bit, well, I had done a few favors for the Mother Superior in the past. I had no intention of being so crude as to mention it, but she owed me. Possibly the same thought had entered her mind.

"All right," she said. "You can make out the transfers."

Just like that! I could hardly believe it. I hung up the phone and strutted into the outer office. "Make out a transfer for Jamey and Mary Jane Hawkins," I told my clerk jubilantly.

She beamed. "I'll do it right now. Where are they going?"

"To St. Agatha."

"Oh." Her smile faded. "I'll make it out, but it's a waste of time. They won't keep him."

My enthusiasm subsided a bit. I remembered that Mrs. Enright had made a similar comment, and she was herself a product of the Catholic schools. She should know. Oh, well, it was worth a try.

I personally handed Jamey the transfer. I wanted to be able to give him a little pep talk before he left. "Making out a transfer is a lot of work," I told him, "and I don't want them sending you back in a few days. If they do, I won't be very happy. I've still got the papers made out to send you to Montefiore. Remember, they're not going to stand for a lot of nonsense at St. Agatha. You'll be doing us both a favor if you behave yourself. It's up to you."

A few days went by. I asked Mr. Buchanan how things were going without Jamey. "A distinct improvement," he declared with a satisfied smile.

Mrs. Enright, however, was still cynical. Any rejoicing, she assured me, was premature. "He'll be back," she said darkly. "I give him a week at the most."

But one week slipped by and then another, and the memory of Jamey began to fade. In a school the size of ours, there were plenty of alternate aggravations and aggravators to break the monotony. Often I felt like Hercules in his encounter with the Hydra. It seemed that no sooner had one problem been laid to rest than two sprang up to replace it. Occasionally I did wonder how Jamey was getting along. I could have called St. Agatha to find out, but I didn't want to tempt fate. Let well enough alone.

At this juncture, I really had mixed feelings. I must confess that I have always been a little jealous of the reputation enjoyed by the Catholic schools. While I can find plenty to criticize in our school system, I get upset when I hear it compared unfavorably to theirs. I guess I'm like the sibling who fights with his brothers and sisters but always comes to their defense against any outsider. I get tired of hearing how good their discipline is and how much better their students do scholastically than ours. The comparison is unfair. A private school has a number of advantages which we don't have. As I had indicated to the Mother Superior, she could summarily expel a student. I couldn't. As a teacher, I had inherited a few Catholic school rejects from time to time. One in particular had been quite a handful, but I had to endure him for a whole year. I had no choice in the matter. As a principal, I had been obliged to accept students who were failing in the Catholic school. If their parents became dissatisfied with the progress these children were making, they could, and did, transfer them to us. We had no alternative but to accept them—so the Catholic school was losing some of its poorest students and we were getting them. This was hardly likely to improve our scholastic average while it could raise theirs.

As I see it, there are other factors in their favor. Parents who pay tuition are more likely to be concerned about their children's education and more apt to insist that they behave properly and keep up with their studies. And parent involvement is one of the most important ingredients in a student's success. Also, I doubt if the Catholic schools face the problems we do with poor attendance and truancy. I imagine that parents who are paying for the privilege would make sure that their children attend school. The public schools, on the other hand, not only have to deal with children who "ditch" school but with some parents who deliberately keep their children home (presumably to baby-sit or to do housework). And even the best of teachers can't teach a child who isn't there.

It's human nature to want to get your money's worth. It's also in the nature of things to believe that that which is free has little value. The public school student (no matter how hard we try to convince him otherwise) cannot understand that his parents are paying for his education with their taxes. If he squanders the opportunity for an education, he doesn't necessarily feel that he has wasted anything. In contrast, the Catholic school student knows that his parents are paying tuition. (I'm sure they remind him often enough.) This has to have important psychological consequences. It is reasonable to suppose that it affects his attitude toward school. (The religious aspect of the curriculum may also be a factor, but I will not attempt to evaluate it.)

I am no expert on the Catholic schools. I assume they have good teachers and bad ones just as we do. I have visited several of them briefly, have attended a few meetings with some of their teachers (both sisters and lay teachers), and have had limited contacts with some of their principals. I have never asked them about their methods of enforcing discipline. I have heard it said, admiringly, that the sisters stand for no nonsense and will administer a good slap when needed; that they know how to keep the kids in line—figuratively and literally—but I refuse to accept corporal punishment as the basic ingredient that accounts for their success. Officially, as in our school system, corporal punishment is forbidden in the Catholic schools, although I have heard that some teachers ignore this rule.

I won't belabor the issue. I am sure the Catholic school people could come up with a pretty good rebuttal. (Their teachers are paid less, so it may be harder for them to attract good teachers, and they spend far less per student than we do.) No matter. The point right now was that Jamey had not been returned to us, and, while I didn't want him back, it was beginning to bother me a little. Was I really too tolerant, too "soft," as some of the teachers believed? I had always been student-oriented. I had worked with children so long that I had come to think of them as human beings. (That's a joke, I think.) I couldn't change the way I felt, nor did I want to. I couldn't become a tyrant, a screamer, a dictator, the school bogeyman. Yet my tactics had failed with Jamey, while the Catholic school was apparently succeeding. What did they know at St. Agatha that I didn't?

A third week went by. I was sitting in my office working on a book order when my clerk knocked on the door. Mrs. Hawkins was there to see me.

"Send her in," I responded. As she entered, I put on my professional smile. "What can I do for you?" I said. "How are Jamey and Mary Jane?"

"They're just fine. But I had to take them out of St. Agatha."

"Oh, really? That's too bad. Were they having problems?"

"No, they were getting along just fine—only I couldn't afford to send them anymore. I couldn't keep up with the payments, so the Mother Superior said the children would have to leave. I asked her to transfer them back here. That's all right, isn't it?"

"Yes, of course," I replied with a decided lack of enthusiasm. I had suspected at once why she was here but had hoped I was wrong. "Just give the transfers to the clerk. She'll take care of it. You say they were getting along alright?"

She turned back and smiled sweetly. "Oh, yes. Just fine."

Well, Jamey was coming back. Where would I put him? Should I try Mrs. Enright again? The semester was almost over. She ought to be able to stand him for a few weeks. Maybe the Catholic school had taught him to behave a little better. I sat there for a while reflectively, then, acting on a sudden impulse, I picked up the phone and called St. Agatha. "May I speak to the Mother Superior?" I asked.

"I just wanted to check something out," I said when she picked up the phone. "Mrs. Hawkins came to see me."

"Oh, yes. I gave her the transfers this morning."

"She said her children had to leave because she couldn't pay for their tuition."

"That's what she told you?"

"Yes. Isn't that what happened?"

"Mr. Greenstein, you should know better than that. We don't force children out because they can't pay. We make some kind of arrangement. It got to the point where either they went or some of my teachers would. I want you to know we tried. We really did. But that boy has been absolutely impossible! He's been nothing but trouble since he came here. The poor sisters were going out of their minds. Yesterday was the last straw. He found out where the fuse box was and unscrewed all the fuses—and that's the second time he's done it. The lights were out all over the school. I'm sorry, but we've had enough. You'll have to keep him."

I thanked her and hung up. I felt a little better. At least he had never touched our fuses. But then, he probably didn't know where our fuse box was. For that matter, neither did I.

Well, there was a happy ending, at least for us. Mrs. Enright managed to put up with Jamey for the next few weeks, sustained by the knowledge that the semester was coming to an end. Possibly Jamey was behaving a little better—for Jamey, that is. And finally, the good news. Mrs. Hawkins came in to tell me that she was moving. She wanted a transfer for the children. I managed to stifle a shout of joy.

"That's too bad," I said. "I'll be sorry to see them leave."

All right, so I'm a hypocrite. It comes with the territory.

14. What's in a Name?

The little boy came into the office and diffidently approached the clerk standing behind the counter. He peered up at her.

"I lost my ball," he ventured in a small voice. "My teacher said I could ask you if someone found it."

The clerk beamed down at him as she opened the lost-and-found drawer. In it was a variety of items including several softballs and a collection of rubber balls of different sizes and colors. "What did it look like?" she asked gently.

The little boy reflected for a moment, then replied solemnly, "It was round."

My admiration for the bard, William S., is second to none. He has a way with a couplet, a simile, a metaphor that is, as some of my students might have put it, something else. However, this business of a rose smelling the same no matter what it's called bears further examination. Oh, I go along with him on the rose all right. I'm not one of those who talk to plants, and I doubt if the rose answers to its name, so I imagine it doesn't care what we call it. However, Shakespeare carries the argument further to include people, and that's where we part company. Actually, I don't believe he meant it. He was just putting words into the mouth of Romeo, a young man in love, who could hardly be expected to speak logically under the circumstances.

I have read several studies which indicate that a child's name does effect him psychologically. While I take all studies with a grain of salt, common sense or a little observation tends to support this conclusion. Certainly the naming of a child is taken pretty seriously by most parents. Personally, I endowed all of my children with middle names for one reason—so they would have an alternative if they ever became dissatisfied with their given names. For one of my children, my foresight proved fortuitous. He did indeed evince an antipathy to his first name at a very early age and has used the middle one ever since.

Occasionally I have run across boys (never a girl) who were known only by their first and middle initials. I used to be very curious about this. After solving the mystery in one such case, I have learned to let the kids alone. If they are using initials, they must have a reason. It is best to respect their privacy. I had this student who used the initials L.J. in front of his surname. That was it. He adamantly insisted that he had no other first or middle name. I happened to run across his enrollment form and learned his secret, poor kid. He had actually been named Love's Joy. Don't ask me how a parent could do this to a child. I'll never know. I have to assume it was simply ignorance and that no malice was intended.

There is a city in France where L.J. would have been protected by law from such an act by his parents. A child whose given name is not on an official list of five thousand published by the state cannot be registered there. The purpose of this regulation, a very laudable one in my opinion, is to protect children from being made ridiculous by parents giving them unusual names. In a recent case, for example, the parents of a boy whom they had named Gilou were notified that he would not be eligible for state family allowances or social security benefits unless his name was changed. A town official suggested that the boy be called Giles to remedy the situation.

Personally, I have some reservations about restricting the choice of a name to those on an official list. My experience with L.J., however, convinced me to permit students to use whatever names (barring some outlandish nicknames) they preferred. And when I became a principal, if a teacher insisted on using the child's "real name" even though he disliked it, I would arrange a compromise. His "official" name was to be entered on all records, but his request, if reasonable, would be honored, and we would refrain from calling him by a name that made him uncomfortable. I could never understand why some teachers considered the use of the student's real name so important. But then I have never understood a lot of things that some teachers do. Summing the whole thing up, a rose is a rose is a rose if that's the way you want it, but give children a break and allow them some measure of choice about what they are called.

Johnny Cash once popularized a song about a boy named Sue. Presumably the boy's father theorized that a name like that would afford him ample opportunities to defend himself, and thus he would learn how to survive in this cruel, cruel world. I used to think about the song whenever I saw one of our eighth-grade students named Chauncey. How he felt about that name I don't know. According to his teacher, he had never requested that he be called anything else.

Perhaps he was accustomed to it by now. And at the time I knew him, no kid in his right mind was likely to make fun of Chauncey's name.

I doubt if his parents intended to make a fighter of him. They probably thought the name had a mellifluous, aristocratic quality which would offset the prosaic surname of Walker. That he became very handy with his fists may have been coincidental. A more likely cause was that he grew up in a rough neighborhood. We also had some pretty tough customers with ordinary names like Bill and Dick and George, so I don't want to jump to any conclusions. Nevertheless, there is no doubt that Chauncey became quite a scrapper. Though he was not the biggest, he had a reputation as the toughest boy in his class, perhaps even in the entire eighth grade. Everyone knew that it wasn't wise to "mess around" with Chauncey. Yet he wasn't considered a bully. In fact, he was generally well-liked by his fellow students and only dangerous when he lost his temper. This, unfortunately, he was prone to do quite easily.

I never knew Chauncey very well. He came to us in seventh grade and managed to stay out of serious trouble that year. If he was in any fights, they were not called to my attention. After he entered eighth grade, however, I became aware of his reputation. Several teachers were upset about his fighting and reported him to me. I spoke to his homeroom teacher, and she assured me she would take care of the matter herself—for which I was grateful. I only hoped her attitude was contagious. He was really a "sweet" boy, she informed me, except for his terrible temper. Normally he didn't give her much trouble. She believed she could straighten him out. She had a sort of missionary zeal, and she would talk to him when he got into scrapes. I am not saying this in a derogatory sense. A teacher should have this zeal—a desire to help—a conviction that what she is doing is important. The teacher who doesn't have it, who is only there to collect a paycheck every two weeks, would be doing the kids a favor if she quit. However, one should be aware of one's limitations and not get carried away with playing God. To the teacher who comes to these "benighted little savages" with a heart full of love, I can only say this: "They may just spit in your eye. They don't have to accept your love or return it. From their point of view, they didn't ask to be in school nor did they invite your concern. You'll have to learn how to control them and earn their trust the hard way." Perhaps the best advice I can give a new teacher (or a new parent) is contained in the title of Bruno Bettleheim's book, *Love Is Not Enough*. That title says it very well.

Maybe I should have spoken to Chauncey myself instead of relying upon his teacher, though I have no assurance that I could have done any better. It was not benign neglect on my part; I had plenty of other discipline problems to take care of. And as to what happened later, there was no way I could have anticipated it.

It was a warm, breezy spring morning. A cascade of sunlight poured under the half-drawn green window shades and flooded my office, stopping short of the large wooden desk at which I sat. The upper-grade recess bell had just rung, and I listened instinctively for the noise which signaled the approach of the third-floor classes. I heard shouting and loud laughter emanating from the north stairway. That would probably be Mrs. Hinckley's students, I surmised. She seldom accompanied her class downstairs as she was supposed to. Considering the excess weight she had to carry, perhaps that was understandable—and she wasn't getting any younger. I realized that walking her class all the way down and to the door, then walking all the way up again, might be difficult for her. Still, she should be able to accompany the kids to the second floor and then watch them as they went the rest of the way. If she had good control of her students—which she didn't—that might have sufficed, and I would have overlooked the fact that she wasn't obeying the rules to the letter. As it was, the commotion was too loud to ignore. I had received a number of complaints from the first-floor teachers whose rooms were near that stairway that the noise was "impossible." (That's a favorite word with teachers, especially when they are referring to some of their students.) When our school was built, air conditioning had not yet been invented. Consequently, the warm weather necessitated keeping the doors open, and they insisted that it was impossible to teach with all that racket.

I had reviewed the problem at our last teachers' meeting. Students were running down the stairs, taking two or three steps at a time. Some were sliding down the banisters (as kids have done since banisters were invented). This could be dangerous. I therefore reiterated, for this had been the established policy, that teachers should accompany their students to the exit, not only to reduce the noise level but to prevent accidents. Although I didn't mention any names, everyone—with the possible exception of the teachers for whom my remarks were intended, for Mrs. Hinckley wasn't the only one—knew which classes I was talking about.

Now, as the cacophony of voices swept through the corridor, I reluctantly went to investigate. I was trying to complete my furniture and equipment order which would be due in a few days, and I was annoyed at the interruption. But I wanted to see if Mrs. Hinckley's class was responsible for the disturbance. I had decided to speak to her privately about the complaints, and I liked to deal with facts, not rumors.

By the time I reached the stairway, her class, if it had indeed been hers, was gone. As I looked up, I observed Mr. Murdock turning the corner at the second-floor landing with his class right behind him.

"I don't want to hear a sound," he said brusquely. The command was superfluous as there wasn't any. Maybe it was just a habit on his part. "All right, let's keep in line," he continued automatically.

A student saw me and broke the silence with a very audible stage whisper. "There's Mr. Greenstein," he warned.

"Quiet!" said Mr. Murdock. "Face the front!" This was addressed to several students who glanced furtively in my direction. The students complied, and the class continued in silence and in step.

I realized that Mr. Murdock was aware of my presence and probably expected a comment. "You have a very nice class," I said approvingly. This brought a satisfied smile to his face and he mumbled a reply. The faces of the students brightened too.

"A compliment never hurts," I thought to myself, though I couldn't avoid a feeling of guilt. Was I selling out? Was I becoming the kind of principal who was impressed by a straight line? Was this really the criterion of a good teacher? I knew that it impressed visitors—even the superintendent. I didn't want them coming down like a mob as Mrs. Hinckley's class did. That was indicative of what went on in her classroom too. There couldn't be much learning going on there. And everyone agreed that Mr. Murdock was a good teacher—even the kids—most of them, anyway. But I hadn't done so badly as a teacher myself, and I had never expected my class to march like an ROTC unit. There had to be more to teaching than that.

Oh, well, back to my furniture and equipment order. I returned to my desk. A few minutes later, as I was trying to decide which we needed more, another record player or another overhead projector, a student ran up the steps that led from the corridor to my office. I had left the door open to take advantage of whatever air was circulating, and he burst in, breathing hard, his brown skin wet with perspiration.

"Mr. Vezak's been hurt!" he yelled.

"Where is he? What happened?"

"Someone threw a brick at him. He's on the boys' playground."

"Is he badly hurt?"

"I don't know. His head is bleeding. Mr. Murdock is with him."

I got up quickly. "Show me where he is," I said.

I started running down the stairs, the boy tagging along at my side. As we trotted toward the playground, I was thinking to myself, "Oh no, not this," as if I could somehow wish it away. A teacher attacked and injured at our school! For his sake, I hoped Mr. Vezak's injury was not serious. For my sake too. This would really create consternation among the teachers. It would reflect upon me as well. I knew that. I could hear some of them now. "Nothing like this ever happened before Mr. Greenstein came. That's what happens when you're too lenient with the children." Somehow, no matter what the facts were, I would be held responsible. Well, never mind all that. I should be worrying about Mr. Vezak. Hit by a brick! That sounded bad. But Mr. Murdock was with him. He impressed me as the kind of person who could be counted on in an emergency. If an ambulance were needed, he would have sent someone to the office by now to notify the clerk.

Still running, I turned to the boy again. "Was he bleeding much?"

"No, just a little."

Well, that was a relief. "Did you see who did it?"

"No. I don't think it was anyone from our school. I saw two big boys running outside the fence after it happened."

That explained it. High school students—or dropouts. A few of them were always hanging around our school. They had even robbed some of our students.

By this time we were at the boys' playground. As we went through the open gate, I could see a crowd of students milling around near the school wall. Obviously something was going on there. I pushed my way through. In the center was Mr. Vezak, with Mr. Murdock holding him by the arm, more for emotional support, it seemed, than because he needed to be sustained physically.

Mr. Vezak was applying a handkerchief to the side of his forehead. There was a red stain on it. As he removed the handkerchief, I saw a small crimson blotch, but the bleeding appeared to have stopped. "Are you all right?" I asked.

"Just a little dizzy, but I'm O.K."

I wasn't so sure. His eyes had a glazed look. "We'll get you to a doctor," I said. "Mr. Murdock, maybe you can take him."

"Sure. I'll take him in my car. Do you have someone to cover my class?"

"I'll find somebody. First let's get the kids into the building."

I turned to the boy who had accompanied me. He was still at my side. "What's your name?" I asked.

"Maurice. Maurice Adams."

"All right, Maurice. Listen carefully. I want you to go to the office and tell the clerk to ring the recess bell right away. Tell her I gave the order. Hurry up, now. Run!"

As he took off, I turned back to the two teachers. "Any idea who did it?"

Mr. Vezak shook his head. "I didn't even see what hit me. It felt like a rock. It just grazed me. I think it came over the fence."

"I was on the other side of the playground when it happened," said Mr. Murdock. "We were both on recess duty. One of the boys told me Vezak was hurt and I came right over."

"That boy Maurice said someone threw a brick. Did you find it?"

Mr. Murdock held up a weathered piece of two-by-four about a foot long. "I think this is what did it. A boy brought it to me."

"I'd better take that. You get him to the doctor and I'll call the police."

Just then the bell rang. Mr. Murdock and I started ushering the boys toward the entrances. Gradually other teachers arrived on the scene to pick up their charges. At first some of them appeared disgruntled at having their recess interrupted, but the word quickly spread that Mr. Vezak had been injured, and everyone cooperated to conduct the students into the building.

I still had plenty to do. "You go ahead," I told Mr. Murdock. "I have to see about covering your classrooms. Ask the clerk what doctor to take him to. She has an approved list from the board. Have her call first to make sure he's in."

"I don't think I need a doctor," protested Mr. Vezak feebly.

"Yes, you do. He'll probably take X-rays to make sure you're all right. Besides, I have no choice in the matter. The board will require a medical report."

As they left, I considered the next item on my agenda. Two classrooms had to be covered, and it had to be done quickly. Once the students discovered they had no teacher, there would be bedlam. As it happened, we had two extra teachers at the time as our large membership entitled us to two more teachers than there were classrooms. From an administrative standpoint, this was sometimes a blessing in disguise. That meant they were available in case of an emergency—such as this one. One of them was teaching a special reading class in the lunchroom. Those kids could be returned to their rooms. The other, unfortunately, was already in a classroom. Several teachers were absent and, as was often the case, "sub" center had been unable to furnish us with enough substitutes. I'd have to use our librarian. The teachers whose library periods were canceled would be very unhappy. Hell hath no fury like a teacher who loses her free period. Well, I'd explain to them later. Once they understood the reason, I knew they wouldn't complain.

There was no time to write a note. I ran upstairs to the library, briefly explained the situation to the librarian, and instructed her to return her students to their homeroom and to proceed to Mr. Vezak's class. Then I rushed to the basement, repeated the explanation to the reading teacher, sent him to Mr. Murdock's room, and personally escorted his students to their respective classrooms. After that I proceeded, at a more leisurely pace, back to my office.

I checked with my clerk. She had contacted the doctor, and Mr. Vezak and Mr. Murdock were on their way. What next? I'd better call the police. The culprit or culprits might still be in the vicinity. I contacted the station and was assured that a squad car would be at the school shortly. The police would want a description. Time to start some detective work. Someone on the playground must have seen who threw that two-by-four. I decided to begin with my original contact, Maurice, and sent for him. He reiterated that he had noticed two big boys near the fence which bordered the playground and that's all he knew. He couldn't remember what they wore or what they looked like.

"Was there anyone else who might have seen them?" I asked.

"Alvin and Julio were playing catch near the fence. Maybe they did."

I dismissed Maurice and sent for the boys he had named. When I asked if they had seen who threw the two-by-four, each waited for the other to answer. Finally Alvin spoke up. "It happened real fast. I saw someone running, but I couldn't tell who it was."

I turned to Julio. "How about you? What did you see?"

"Well, like he said, it happened fast. I saw this stick flying in the air and I didn't even know where it came from."

I sensed something wrong. "Alvin, wait in the outer office for a minute. I want to talk to Julio," I said.

Alvin left, and I sat there for a while without speaking—employing one of those pauses I've observed prosecuting attorneys use to good advantage in the movies. Then I turned, looked right at Julio, and said deliberately, "All right, who threw that piece of wood?"

"Honest, I don't know," he insisted plaintively.

"But you did see someone out there, didn't you? Who was it?"

"I'm not sure."

"Julio, you were right there near the fence. You saw someone there. Who was it?"

He lowered his head. "Well, it looked like Chauncey. But I didn't see him throw anything," he added quickly.

"Was anyone with him?"

"I don't know. I didn't see anyone else."

"All right, you can go back to your room." (For the benefit of the purists, I know the proper word is "may." When I was conducting an investigation, I sometimes ignored the grammatical niceties.)

I conducted him through the front door, the one facing the hallway, so he wouldn't come into contact with Alvin. Then I opened the door to the outer office where Alvin was seated. "You can come in now," I said.

He entered diffidently, obviously uncomfortable. "You're not in any trouble," I said soothingly. "All I want to know is what you saw. Now you know a teacher was hurt. I think he'll be all right, but he could have been seriously injured. Do you want to go to a school where we let things like that happen?"

"No, sir."

"Do you think you would be safe in a school like that?"

"I guess not."

"All right, who threw that piece of wood?"

"I don't know," he insisted.

"O.K. I'll ask you something else. You saw someone on the other side of the fence. Who was it?"

He didn't reply. I tried one of my other routines. I never used force or threats or outright lies to get information, but I wasn't above being a bit tricky.

"Alvin, I know who was out there and so do you. I just want to make sure."

"Did Julio tell you?" he demanded suspiciously.

"What makes you think you and Julio were the only ones I talked to? There were lots of other kids out there, you know. [I always tried to protect my informants.] I'll make it simple. Did you see Chauncey during recess?"

"Yes, sir."

"Did you see him outside the fence?"

"I—I think so."

"O.K. I already knew he was out there. I just wanted to make sure. You can go back to your room now."

As I dismissed him, my clerk informed me that two police officers were waiting to see me. I asked them to come into my office. "Have a seat," I said. "I'll be with you in a minute. There's something I want to check first."

I penned a note to Chauncey's teacher, called the messenger who was on duty in the hallway, and instructed him to bring me an answer immediately. I then turned to the officers and briefed them on the circumstances as I knew them of the attack on Mr. Vezak.

"Any idea who did it?" asked one of the officers.

"I'm not sure yet. I'll tell you as soon as I get an answer to my note."

While we waited, one officer started to make out his report. He wanted to know the name and address of the school, my name, my age (which I gave grudgingly), my home address (which I refused to give—just as a matter of principle—we had been advised by our legal department that we didn't have to disclose it), who was injured, where, at what time, how, and other pertinent and impertinent information. By the time he had recorded my responses, the messenger had returned. I had my answer.

"Chauncey did not come back from recess," his teacher had written.

I take a legalistic approach. Stick to the facts without embellishment. Innocent until proven guilty. Some teachers have found this attitude very exasperating. As far as they were concerned, when they "knew" a student was guilty, that should be sufficient. Proof was unnecessary. Contrary testimony would be brushed aside as lies. I have to acknowledge that their assumptions were usually correct. However, I can remember instances where the teachers' vehement, positive, unequivocal accusations turned out to be wrong. So I was not going to jump to conclusions. I just gave the officer the facts.

1. Mr. Vezak had been hit by some object, apparently a piece of wood. I offered the two-by-four as evidence to the officers. I assumed they would put it in a plastic bag so they could check it for fingerprints, blood type, and who knows what else, but they exhibited little interest in it. They just told me to hold on to it for the time being.

2. At least one boy, tentatively identified as Chauncey, had been

observed at the approximate place from which the object that injured Mr. Vezak presumably had been thrown.

3. Chauncey had not returned to his class from recess. Damaging, but circumstantial.

At their request, I provided the officers with Chauncey's address, though I conjectured that if he was indeed responsible they weren't likely to find him there. If they did locate him I hoped he could come up with a logical explanation. I remembered that his teacher had always been able to perceive compensating good qualities to balance his faults. He had great leadership potential, she claimed. Maybe someone else had thrown the piece of wood and he had run because he thought he would be blamed. (Maurice had said there were two boys.) Maybe he had thrown it but hadn't meant to hit anyone. (I realized he could use that as an alibi even it it weren't true.)

About a half hour later I received a call from the police station. They had picked up Chauncey at his home. He had made no attempt to run or hide and had readily admitted that he had thrown the two-by-four. It was no accident. He had done it deliberately. Why? Because he was "mad" at Mr. Vezak. That was all he would say. He was being charged with assault, or aggravated assault, or battery, I didn't know which. A date would be set for a hearing in Juvenile Court. I asked how long he would be held at the station. Probably just till his mother came to pick him up, I was told. As he was a juvenile, he would be released in her custody until the date of the trial. They had contacted her at work, and she was on her way right now.

Well, that was that. I was a little disappointed, though hardly surprised, at these developments. I had hoped they would discover that someone else—perhaps a high school student as I had originally conjectured—was responsible. Now I had to accept the fact that it was Chauncey.

Under the circumstances, I obviously couldn't allow him to come back to our school. I had to buy time while I figured out what to do. A ten-day suspension would serve that purpose. I completed the form and instructed my clerk to type it and put it in the mail. There remained the unpleasant task of notifying his mother by phone to make sure she wouldn't send him to school the next day. That would have to wait till she returned from the police station.

It was almost lunchtime. I often dropped into the teachers' room during the lunch hour just to keep in touch, but I wasn't in the mood to answer a lot of questions right now. They would get the news soon enough. At this point, my clerk knew about as much as I did. She ate lunch with some of the teachers, and I was sure she would fill them in on the developments. I had brought a sandwich. I ate half of it, decided I wasn't hungry and went back to work.

Mr. Vezak and Mr. Murdock walked in at about one-thirty. The doctor hadn't bothered to take X-rays. The injury was superficial. A small bandage had sufficed. They had had lunch and were now ready to return to their classrooms. I dispatched a note to the teachers whose library classes had been canceled informing them that those classes would now be resumed. At least I would make somebody happy.

The next morning Chauncey's teacher asked if she could speak to me. She didn't have much to say—just that she was sorry about Chauncey, he really wasn't a bad boy, and that one of her students had requested to see me. He had refused to tell her what it was about, but it had to do with Chauncey. I told her to send the boy down.

The boy's name was Cleotus. He was a thin, amber-skinned kid with an Afro, but almost all the black kids had Afros then.

"I wanted to tell you about Chauncey," he said. He hesitated as if he was not sure he was doing the right thing and was trying to gauge my reaction before he continued.

"Go ahead. I'm listening," I replied.

He looked at me for some sign of encouragement, inspected the floor as if that might offer some help, then blurted out, "They beat him up. That's why he did it."

"Who beat him up?"

"Mr. Vezak and Mr. Murdock."

"Did you see them beat him up?"

"No, but he told me about it."

"I don't understand. Did they beat him up right there on the playground?"

"No, not on the playground. In the building."

"All right, tell me what happened."

"It started when we were going downstairs for recess. Chauncey was at the end of our line and he was talking. I guess he was talking kinda loud. Mr. Vezak's class was right in back of us, and Mr. Vezak, he was walking in front. He told Chauncey to shut up, and then Chauncey said something back."

"What did he say?"

"I don't know. I wasn't near him, but it got Mr. Vezak mad and he said something back and then we got outside. I was standing out on the playground with Chauncey, and I saw Mr. Vezak talking to Mr.

Murdock. Then they came up to me and Chauncey, and Mr. Murdock says he wants to talk to him, and they took him inside the building."

"You mean they forced him to go with them?"

"No, they just said to come with them, and he went. Well, I was waiting outside, and in a couple of minutes he came out and he was real mad. He told me they took him underneath the stairway and said they would teach him not to be a smart aleck. Then Mr. Murdock held him and Mr. Vezak started punching him."

"Did anybody see this?"

"I don't think so. Chauncey said nobody was there except them."

"Then all you know is what Chauncey told you. You didn't see any of this yourself—except that they took him inside the building. Was he bleeding when he came out, or did you notice any bruises?"

"No, but he said Mr. Vezak kept hitting him. Then they told him he better learn to behave, and they let him go. He was real mad. He said he was going to get even with Mr. Vezak. That's when he ran in the alley and found that piece of wood. Then, the next thing I know, he threw it at Mr. Vezak."

"Was anyone with you when he told you all this or were you the only one?"

"Just me. He told me what happened and then he ran in the alley."

"I don't think it would be a good idea to spread this around. After all, you didn't actually see anyone hit Chauncey. All you know is what he told you. If he or his mother want to talk to me about it, that's different. If what you say is true, it would explain why he did it—though I don't really know that it's true. I'm not saying Chauncey was lying—but there were no witnesses, and it could turn out to be his word against theirs. Besides, he wasn't badly hurt when you saw him, while if had hit Mr. Vezak square on the head with that two-by-four, Mr. Vezak could have been killed. Do you think that was the right thing to do?"

"I guess not—but he was awful mad."

"That's no excuse. I'm not saying that what the teachers did was right. Still, he could have come to me and told me about it. Haven't I always listened to the kids when they came to see me?"

"I guess he didn't think about that. He's got a real bad temper."

"That's still no excuse. We've all got tempers, and we have to learn to control them. If he didn't want to talk to me, he could have told his mother. I'm always ready to talk to a parent. I want you to remember that if you ever get in trouble. I happen to like Chauncey, but after what happened yesterday, I don't see any way that I can let him come back to this school. He attacked and injured a teacher. I can't allow that. If kids could do that and get away with it, this wouldn't be much of a school. Anyway, I want to thank you for telling me about this."

I dismissed Cleotus and began to ponder this new development. I shouldn't jump to conclusions—students had lied to me before—but this story had the ring of truth. Chauncey had been hit and he had hit back. Naturally, I had told Cleotus that Chauncey's action was wrong. But didn't another wrong precipitate it? One could almost call it self-defense. No, that wasn't true. It wasn't self-defense. He had waited till he got outside. He wasn't being attacked then. What I had said to Cleotus still held good. Considering his temper and his mood at the moment, maybe it was unrealistic to expect Chauncey to act otherwise. Nevertheless, the alternatives I had mentioned had been available to him.

That night I didn't sleep too well. (Insomnia is one of the occupational hazards of the job.) I had problems. Should I confront Mr. Vezak and Mr. Murdock with the information provided by Cleotus? What if they denied it? I had no proof. I didn't even have the story from Chauncey himself—just a second-hand version from his friend. This was a sticky situation. The teachers should be given an opportunity to defend themselves against this accusation. On the other hand, I didn't want to place them in a situation in which they would probably lie to me. Of course they might not. They might even come to me voluntarily and tell me about it. That was wishful thinking and I knew it. My firm stand against corporal punishment had not been too well received by some of the teachers. Nor had it eradicated the practice. It had just made them more cautious. These were not bad people—nor were they brutal. Most of them were good, hardworking teachers. However, they were convinced that when a child was insolent, a well-aimed slap was the quickest and most effective method of punishment and that a principal should know when to look the other way. Yet here, in effect, was proof that I was right. By hitting Chauncey, the teachers had driven him to retaliate, and one of them could have been severely injured. It was unlikely, however, that they would see it that way. Ironically, things might work out in their favor. I couldn't very well permit Chauncey to return to our school, so they would get rid of an offending student. Was this fair to Chauncey? What if he were punished—suspended—and then permitted to return? I would probably have a revolution on my hands. I had grave doubts about my popularity quotient as it was. If Gallup conducted a poll of the staff right now, I wasn't at all sure how I'd make out. If I let Chauncey return, I might as well ask for a transfer. Even if I received some support for my action (Chauncey's teacher might approve, for one), it would cause dissension in the faculty, and I didn't want to be responsible for that. Most of the teachers would probably back their colleagues, especially Mr. Murdock. He had been there a long time and was very popular with the teachers, particularly with the older ones who were the backbone of the staff. Should I get rid of Chauncey? Make him the scapegoat—a sacrifice to my career? Then I'd have another problem—that pesky conscience of mine. It was gnawing at me already. Well, I didn't have to make an immediate decision. Certainly the ten-day suspension I had given Chauncey was not unwarranted, and it would give me time to deliberate further.

The next day I went about my work as usual and tried to put the matter out of my mind, to forget I'd ever seen Cleotus. I hadn't heard from Chauncey or his mother, so technically there were no charges against the teachers. Meanwhile, I had been notified of the date of Chauncey's hearing. I relayed the information to Mr. Vezak and advised him that he, as the injured party, would be expected to attend. Several days later, during the lunch hour, I happened to be sitting opposite Mr. Murdock and Mr. Vezak in the teachers' room. I wasn't consciously eavesdropping, and I don't believe they were aware that I could hear their conversation. This is what I heard:

> MR. MURDOCK: So next Wednesday is Chauncey's hearing. Do you know what you're going to say?
>
> MR. VEZAK: Yes, I'm ready. I've talked to my attorney.
>
> MR. MURDOCK: What if they ask if you— [here he lowered his voice and I couldn't make out the rest of the sentence, but I heard Mr. Vezak's reply distinctly].
>
> "I'll deny it," he said.

I can't say that I heard a confesson or admission of anything, but, considering what I already knew, I didn't see any other way to interpret it. And what if I were called upon to testify? What would I say? Well, I was pretty sure of one thing. I wouldn't lie.

However, if Chauncey were released, as I thought he would be (I had seen juveniles get away with plenty), what would I do then? Still wrestling with the problem, I decided to seek some enlightenment from Chauncey's past. I sent a note to the adjustment teacher requesting his folder. The messenger returned with a large manila envelope securely sealed with masking tape. (The adjustment teacher and I were both very fussy about the secrecy of school records, something I haven't always found to be the case with others.) I removed the folder from the envelope and checked through its contents. There were two "blue slips" (records of psychological examinations) for antisocial behavior. There were comments from some of his former teachers—mostly unflattering, reports of fighting, of insolence in the classroom, and records of conferences with his mother. The picture was much worse than I had expected. In my own brief encounters with him, he had been respectful, even friendly, and possibly his present teacher's defense of him had influenced me. Now, after reviewing the data in his folder, I was forced to conclude that he had had plenty of chances. That settled it. If the judge released him, I would insist that he be transferred to Montefiore.

Now that I had come to a decision, I felt better. Then I began to feel guilty about feeling better—we all have our masochistic moments. I reflected that I had no business feeling good about sending a boy to Montefiore. Didn't this prove that I was more concerned about my conscience than about Chauncey? Not necessarily. I just wanted to be fair. It's not as if he were innocent by any means. Not only had he attacked a teacher, but, to put things in proper perspective, he had apparently initiated the entire incident with some smart-aleck remarks. What had been bothering me was that, in view of the extenuating circumstances, I didn't want to punish him more severely than the crime warranted. Well, I had my answer. He was hardly a first offender, or even a second. Besides, I wasn't sending him to Siberia. After all, kids did survive "Monte," and some even came out the better for it. And Chauncey would be in no danger from his fellow students there. He could take care of himself. If all this sounds like an elaborate attempt at rationalization, so be it. Analyzing one's motivation is always tricky. It doesn't pay to delve too deeply. If we do, every good deed would be suspect, and we wouldn't have a saint or a hero left. Why should I let conscience become a dirty word? It would help a lot if people paid more attention to it. Too often it has been replaced by "Everyone does it."

A few days later we appeared in Juvenile Court—Chauncey, his mother, Mr. Vezak, and myself. I glanced at Chauncey, not really wanting to meet his eyes. He probably considered me in the enemy camp, I reflected—and I wasn't quite sure on which side I was. His eyes, dark brown and luminous, were staring straight ahead. He didn't look very menacing. Maybe it was the neat, dark blue suit, the white shirt, and the tightly knotted tie, all of which his mother had probably insisted that he wear to make a good impression. He seemed to have shrunk a little—or was it because the white shirt, contrasting sharply with his chocolate-brown skin, was a size too large? His mother sat in the row behind me. Middle-aged, or perhaps prematurely so. Fleshy brown arms and a plump body encased in a neat print dress. She too was looking straight ahead, though not with with the wooden stare of her son but respectfully, as if she were attending a church meeting.

I don't know what I expected, but the proceedings were nothing like a courtroom scene on TV. No prosecutor, no defense attorney, no string of witnesses being examined and cross-examined, no objections, no speeches. The whole thing only took a few minutes. The judge, white-haired, dignified, sat behind his desk quietly for a while as he studied some documents the clerks had handed him. Then he turned to Chauncey and addressed him softly, almost kindly. "Come here, son."

Chauncey came forward and sat as he was directed. His face was impassive. The judge looked at the papers again, then at Chauncey. "It says here that you attacked a teacher. You threw something at him—a big piece of wood—and injured him. Is that true?

"Yes, sir," Chauncey responded clearly.

"Why did you do it?"

"I was mad because he hit me." There was no anger in his tone now. Just an unemotional statement of fact.

"Did he hit you very hard?"

"No, sir."

"Were you hurt?"

"No, sir."

I had to be sorry for him. He had blown the whole defense right there. But I had respect for him too. No attempt to lie, to explain, to alibi—maybe he didn't know how. And he had no attorney. He was on his own.

In a few minutes it was all over. My worry about what to say had been needless. I wasn't called. And Mr. Vezak, if he had intended to perjure himself, was denied the opportunity. His testimony was not requested either. From a legal point of view it wasn't pertinent. The laws of our state—and I believe this is true in most states—do not prohibit corporal punishment. Mr. Vezak had broken no law. If he had disobeyed a board rule, that was not the business of the court. The case being heard here was Chauncey's attack upon a teacher. The fact that the teacher had struck him first, especially since Chauncey had admitted that he hadn't been hit hard, did not constitute a legal justification. At best, it might be considered an extenuating circumstance.

The judge was ready to pronounce the verdict. Though he addressed Chauncey, he seemed to be speaking to a larger audience. His voice was even, firm, not overly dramatic.

"There have been too many attacks upon teachers in recent years," he declared somberly. "This kind of crime must not go unpunished. It is the duty of this court to protect the schools and its personnel. You assaulted a teacher with what could be considered a dangerous if not a lethal weapon. It is fortunate that the injury was not more serious. I sentence you to be committed to the juvenile correctional facility at St. Charles, where you are to remain until such time as the authorities there consider you fit to return to the public schools."

That was it. Chauncey was taken to wherever it was they were going to keep him, and the rest of us prepared to leave. No one said anything. I glanced at Mr. Vezak. There was a slight smile on his lips. He was obviously satisfied and relieved. I approached Chauncey's mother and murmured, "I'm sorry." She nodded to acknowledge that she had heard, but did not reply. I couldn't think of anything else to say, so I left.

The next day, as the word circulated among the teachers, I could denote a general sense of approval. Justice had been done. No one seemed a bit sorry for Chauncey. He got what he deserved! (His teacher did come to my office later and privately expressed her sympathy for him. She probably didn't consider it prudent to do so publicly.)

Maybe he had gotten what he deserved—and even if he had had an attorney and a better defense, the outcome might have been the same—though I had my doubts about that. One thing stuck in my mind—it always has. This tough young boy from the ghetto, so prone to anger, had told the truth unequivocally, with no attempt at excuse or evasion. And the teacher—maybe I had no right to prejudge, but I was convinced that if he had been called to testify he would have lied.

I felt that someone ought to talk to Chauncey, give him a word of encouragement, but who would be likely to do that? Except for his mother, probably no one, I decided—unless I did. Why not? Certainly I could do that much. I learned that he was being detained temporarily at the Audy Home and would be leaving for St. Charles in a few days. The Audy Home wasn't very far. I could drive there after school. I didn't have to announce my intention, but I purposely mentioned it to my clerk under the guise of asking for directions on how to get there. I didn't care if she told the teachers. If this be treason, let them make the most of it!

As I parked my car around the corner of the Audy Home, I was still wondering what I would say to Chauncey. Maybe I could make him feel that someone still cared about him. Surely that would be something. Would he suspect an ulterior motive and reject my solicitude? But what ulterior motive could I have? At any rate, I didn't see how my visit could do any harm.

I walked in, introduced myself, and was given permission to see Chauncey. A guard escorted me to a small room and instructed me to wait. I heard a gate snapping shut somewhere, and Chauncey entered. He looked straight ahead without expression just as he had at the trial. If he was wondering why I had come, he didn't show it.

"I just dropped by to see how you were getting along," I said. "Are you all right?"

"Yes, sir," he replied in a loud voice, with emphasis on the "sir." He sounded like a West Point cadet, and was standing stiffly as if at attention. For a minute, I thought he was mocking me, but I carried on.

"How are they treating you?" I inquired.

"All right, sir." Still the peculiar, monotonous tone and the emphasis on the last word.

"What do you do here?" I persisted. "Do they send you to school?"

"Yes, sir. We have classes every day." His face was impassive.

"Listen, Chauncey, I'd like to give you a little advice. I don't know anything about St. Charles, but I imagine it's a pretty rough place. You've got to try to stay out of trouble. No matter what they do to you, don't lose your temper. That's what got you in trouble in the first place. Remember?"

"Yes, sir." His expression was unchanged. I wasn't even sure he heard me.

"It probably won't be easy—and don't expect everyone to treat you fairly. You won't get anywhere by fighting them. Whatever they dish out, you have to learn to take it. That way maybe you'll get out sooner."

"I understand, sir." That same tone again with the loud upbeat on the "sir." It was disconcerting. I didn't know what to make of it.

"Well, they said I could only see you for a few minutes. I have to be going now. Take care of yourself."

"Yes, sir."

I knocked on the door. The guard entered, unlocked the outside door, and waited for me to leave. I looked back at Chauncey. "Well, good luck," I said.

"Thank you, sir."

I was glad I had come, though I didn't know if I had accomplished anything. Maybe my visit, or something I had said, would have a positive effect later. I hoped so. I certainly couldn't tell anything from his response.

Several years passed. It was the time of our annual Fun Fair, an event of which I was very proud, although I was only marginally involved in its planning or execution. While I did make a few suggestions, some of which were actually adopted, the real work was done by our Parents Club. Nevertheless, as the titular head of the school, I was not above accepting the compliments for its success, much as a high school principal does for a winning football team of which he is neither a coach nor a player.

The turnout always amazed me. Our gymnasium, the site of these festivities, was jammed to capacity. There was hardly room to move around. Admission was free, but tickets, which were being sold at a table near the north wall, entitled one to participate in the games or partake of the refreshments. These were ten cents each. A number of booths were screened off in carnival fashion, monitored by perspiring parents intent on collecting as many tickets as possible to raise money for the school. In an integrated school like ours, where racial tensions occasionally surfaced and their consequences usually blown out of proportion, it was refreshing to see the students—black, brown, and white—come together in a relaxed atmosphere, all having a good time. Equally satisfying to me was the sight of the parents (some of whom may not have been as tolerant as they pretended) cooperating selflessly and harmoniously to make the evening a success.

A policeman had been promised to us for the evening but had not yet shown up. Fortunately, a number of our male teachers were on hand to offer moral and (what was more important) physical support. I assigned one of them to stand at the entrance. His mission was to keep out high school students or others in that age group. Most of these were our own former students and I knew them well—some only too well. Others were complete strangers. To let them in was to invite trouble.

For a few minutes I observed the teacher, a veteran of many years, as he parried their verbal assaults with a breezy equanimity. Occasionally someone would try to sneak in by pretending he was part of a family group, but he thwarted the attempt with a minimum of fuss and argument. Satisfied that he was quite capable of handling the situation, I returned to the gym.

A little while later I checked to see if he needed any help. He didn't, but he was getting impatient. It was chilly outdoors, the job was a thankless one, and I knew he would much prefer to be inside with his colleagues. I placated him with the assurance that the police officer was probably on his way and that he would be relieved momentarily. Then I hurried to my office and called the police station. I spoke to the deputy commander, and he promised that an officer would be there in about fifteen minutes. I returned to the entrance and relayed this information to the teacher. The news did not appear to buoy his spirits. He implied that he was sacrificing himself above and beyond the call of duty. Well, maybe he had been out there long enough.

"I'll take over for a while," I offered. I thanked him for his cooperation, but I'm not sure he heard me. He was already inside.

It was getting colder, quite a contrast to the sweltering heat inside. I retreated to the doorway, stuck my hands in my pockets, and ruefully reflected upon my situation. When I was attending college, I had worked part-time as a doorman for a large shoe store. Now here I was, many years later, back to being a doorman again. Was this what my education had prepared me for? And it seemed that I was always thanking everyone—the police, the parents, the teachers, and the engineer and janitors (who were getting time-and-a-half for their services). While the parents and teachers were exhibiting their unselfish cooperation, it was understood that I was just doing my job. My labors were taken for granted.

My immersion into self-pity was interrupted by the clamor of some of the teenagers. "Come on, let us in. We won't make any trouble. You know us."

It was precisely because I did know them that I considered their pledge questionable. "Sorry," I said. "You know the rules. This is only for our students and their parents."

A long half hour dragged by, and finally a police car pulled up. An officer emerged. "I've been assigned here," he said. "What's the problem?"

"No problem," I said. "I just need someone at the door. Don't let anyone in except our students and their parents. We don't want any high school students."

"Do your kids have any identification?" he asked.

"No they don't, but you can tell by their size. Of course, we have some pretty big kids too. Just do the best you can. The main thing is to keep things cool. You know—avoid confrontations if you possibly can. They'll pester you a bit, but they aren't really bad. If you just sort of kid them along, they shouldn't give you any trouble."

"Not to worry," he assured me confidently. "I can handle it."

I went inside and was almost swept up by the movement of the crowd. I stopped at the table in the rear where three women were busy selling tickets, making change, and counting the money. On the next table was a small portable television set and the other prizes which were to be awarded at the close of the evening to the holders of the winning raffle tickets. The president of the Parents Club, agitated and perspiring, was guarding a cigar box overflowing with dollar bills. Beside her was a canvas bag which contained the proceeds that had already been counted and tabulated.

"How is it going?" I asked.

"Fine. We're already ahead of last year. Can't you do something about the heat?"

"I'll check with the engineer."

I found the engineer in his office, a floor fan whirring beside him. He was resting leisurely at his desk and talking to one of the janitors. He looked serene and comfortable. "And they're getting paid for this," I reflected enviously. At this point, I suppose I could interject a few caustic remarks about the custodial employees. Their relationship with teachers and principals is not always harmonious. I have known janitors whose primary duty seemed to be to collect their paychecks. However, I have known others who were hardworking and unfailingly cooperative. As for the engineers, most of those with whom I have been associated were pretty good and a few were not. Our present engineer was the best of the lot. He didn't just supervise but worked right along with the janitors. He took a personal pride in keeping the school, old as it was, in good condition.

"It's awfully hot in the gym," I observed. "Can you turn the heat down?"

"That won't help. It would take too long for it to cool off."

"How about opening a few windows?"

"They're stuck. They've been that way ever since the last time they were painted." He thought it over. "Well, we might be able to open one or two." He turned to the janitor. "Frank, let's see if we can pry open a couple of windows."

The janitor nodded, and I followed both of them back to the gym. They located a long pole in the corner and attacked one of the windows. After a struggle, they pried it open. There was a refreshing surge of cool air. As they prepared to tackle another window, I glanced around the hall and noticed a group of Mexican youths—at least of high school age—in fact, one of them had a small mustache and another sported a scraggly beard. They obviously didn't belong here. While I was contemplating what course of action to take, I heard my name called. I turned and saw the president of the Parents Club gesticulating wildly and trying to attract my attention. I pushed my way through the crowd and approached her.

"Anything the matter?" I inquired.

"Two of the prizes for the raffle are missing," she whispered. "There are a lot of big kids around. I think one of them is responsible."

"Do you have any idea who did it?"

"No, but a couple of big girls have been giving us a hard time. And some big boys have been around here too."

I looked around and observed that a number of high school age youngsters had infiltrated the crowd. They must have outsmarted the officer somehow. "We can't accuse anyone without proof," I said. "We'll just have to replace the prizes out of the profits. Don't say anything. It won't do any good to create a disturbance. I'll see if I can get rid of those who don't belong here."

Reluctantly I approached the Mexican group I had previously noticed. "I'm sorry, but you'll have to leave," I said. "This is only for our students and their parents."

"I'm here with my little brother," responded the one with the mustache. "My mother couldn't come."

"Yeah, and I'm with my little sister," said one of the others with a slight grin.

I turned to the first youth. "What's your brother's name?"

"Pedro," he replied.

"What room is he in?"

He hesitated a moment, then responded, "Room 210."

"What's his teacher's name?" I persisted.

"I'm not sure. I think it's Miss Brown."

Not a bad try, I thought. If he had to take a guess, it was reasonable to suppose we had a teacher named Brown. "Sorry," I repeated, "but I'm afraid you'll have to leave. In the first place, there is no room 210. In the second place, we have no Miss Brown. And besides, this is only for our kids and their parents. No big brothers."

"How about those guys over there?" demanded the one with the beard. "How come they can stay and we can't?" He was pointing to three black youths across the room, each over six feet tall. They obviously weren't our students.

"They'll have to leave too," I replied.

"Well, when they go, we go," said the one with the mustache tendentiously. I could sense a little racial undertone. For all I knew, these were Latin Kings prepared to defend their "turf" against the black intruders. If I could get one group out, I probably would have no trouble with the other, but which do I get out first?

"I'll be back," I said shortly, and approached the three black youths.

"I'm afraid you can't stay," I said, trying to sound firm but not antagonistic.

"Why not?" one of them demanded. He was big, broad-shouldered, hostile. His voice was not friendly. I repeated the ground rules, but he didn't seem to be impressed.

"Hell," he said. "They been takin' our money." He reached into his pocket and pulled out some tickets which he waved at me. "And now you say we can't stay. If we go, we want the money we spent."

"I'm certainly not going to return the money you spent, but I'll redeem the tickets you have left. How many do you have?"

"Six," he said.

"O.K." I pulled out some change from my pocket. "Here's sixty cents."

He took the money and relinquished the tickets, but he clearly wasn't ready to leave. "I don't see anyone else going," he declared. "What about those dudes over there?" Naturally he was indicating the Mexican contingent.

"They'll be going too," I said evenly. "They're next."

The second member of the trio spoke up. "I bought me some raffle tickets," he announced, "and I ain't leaving till after the drawing. I want that TV set."

"All right," I said wearily. "How many tickets do you have?"

"Five."

I dug into my pocket again and pulled out two quarters. "Here's your fifty cents. Give me the tickets."

"I don't want my money back," he insisted. "I want to win that TV set."

The situation was becoming difficult. As I looked at the three youths, I could swear they had grown a few inches taller since we had started the conversation. Maybe I'd better recruit some help—but if I did, it might create a disturbance. I wanted to avoid that. By now, I was perspiring freely, and it wasn't just from the heat in the building. "Don't do anything foolish," I thought to myself. However, I decided to give it one more try.

"Look, you weren't supposed to be here in the first place. I'm returning your money, and that's the best I can do. Let's not have any trouble."

They did not appear in the least intimidated, and I was considering whether it was time for a strategic retreat when the third member of the trio spoke up.

"Take the money," he said to the one with the raffle tickets, almost as if it were a command. Then, as if to explain his position, "Come on, let's split. This place ain't that much fun anyway."

I quickly exchanged the money for the tickets, and they started for the door. I could hardly believe they were really going. I had done it—and without any help. Three big, tough kids—young men, in fact, and I had successfully confronted them. I was pretty proud of myself. It just showed what a calm, firm, resolute attitude could accomplish. With renewed self-confidence, I prepared to engage the other group. They should be easier. Meanwhile, the three black youths, whom I kept watching out of the corner of one eye, were almost at the door. Suddenly, the one who had commanded or persuaded the two others to leave turned and called to me, "Hey, Mr. Greenstein. I bet you don't remember me."

Hesitantly I reversed my steps and approached him. He looked entirely unfamiliar. "Were you a student here?" I asked.

"Yeah, I used to go here."

"It must have been a long time ago," I said. "What's your first name?"

"If I tell you my first name, you'll know," he asserted, almost scowling.

That didn't make too much sense, but I persisted. "Just tell me your first name, and I'm sure I'll remember you. I remember most of our students."

He hesitated, then looked straight at me. "Chauncey," he declared.

Reacting instinctively, perhaps as much with relief as surprise, I threw my arms around him. "Chauncey! Well, for heaven's sake! How have you been?"

Slowly his face relaxed into a smile. "I'm O.K.," he said, a little embarrassed, though evidently pleased by my warm reception.

I could hardly believe it. He had grown much taller and heavier—nothing like my last recollection of him. "I'm glad to see you," I said. "How have you been getting along?"

"Oh, pretty good."

I was preparing to ask some more questions, when I heard an insistent voice calling me. It was the president of the Parents Club again and she sounded unhappy.

"I have to go now," I said. "I have to get those other guys out." I shook his hand warmly. "Take care of yourself," I said.

I watched as he and his friends departed. So it had not been my forceful personality that had prevailed, I mused. Lucky for me it had been someone who knew me.

I walked back to the table to see what was the matter. The women were obviously very upset. "A couple of little kids are crying," said one. "They say some big kids took their prizes. Some of the parents are complaining too. Maybe we'd better close up. We can announce the winners of the raffle on Monday."

I looked at my watch. The fair was supposed to end at 10:30. Only about twenty minutes to go. But a lot can happen in twenty minutes. Why risk further trouble? I decided that I'd had enough valor for one day. Maybe it was time for a little discretion.

"All right," I agreed. "I'll make the announcement and we'll start getting everyone out."

I quickly rounded up the teachers and enlisted their aid. They had no objection to quitting a little early. It had been a long day for them. After shouting repeatedly above the noise, I managed to convey my decision to the assemblage. There were some scattered boos and assorted protests. However, slowly and persistently, the teachers and I steered the straggling crowd toward the exit. The Fun Fair had come to an end.

There is one more episode to report in this unfolding saga. It occurred several years later during one of our perennial gang skirmishes. As usual, some minor incident, I forget what, had touched off a gathering of the clans. After the dismissal bell rang, the Kings began congregating at one corner, and, across the street, kitty-corner from them, the Deuces stood watch. Resignedly I embarked upon my familiar task. I went to one group and then the other, cajoling, exhorting, ordering, and gradually persuading them to disperse. Fortunately, the older gang members were not in attendance. These were mostly our own upper-grade students, although a few of our recent graduates were on hand to lend their support. As all of them knew me and I knew them, I was able to keep the opposing forces apart. When things don't get worse, they usually get better. The smoldering flames would probably have subsided if the Deuces had not received a stalwart reinforcement in the person of Dexter Malone.

Dexter was a very tall, very thin, light-brown, pockmarked youth who had graduated the previous year. He had been only mildly obnoxious while he was in seventh grade but had become increasingly difficult and pugnacious as he matured, and the teachers were not sorry to see him go. On the second day of the present confrontation, he had appeared on the scene and had established himself as a leader. Each time I dispersed the group, he would call them back.

"Hey, you guys chicken?" he would demand scathingly. "Stay where you are!" Then he would turn to me. "We ain't goin' till they do," he insisted. Despite my remonstrations, he would then hurl insults at the group across the street, which didn't help matters at all. This went on for several days. I concluded that if I could get rid of Dexter the hostilities would soon come to an end, but if he stayed around the situation could easily deteriorate.

I thought of eliciting the help of his mother and checked our "out" file for his phone number. No phone. I contacted the high school to see if I could get any assistance there. He hadn't been in school for two weeks and the truant officer was unable to locate him. Searching for a solution, I sent for an eighth-grade boy who, although he had stood on the corner with Dexter, had usually obeyed my instructions when I told him to move along.

"Who's the leader of the Deuces?" I asked him.

"I don't know," he said. "They really don't have a leader anymore, not since Chauncey left."

"Chauncey?" I repeated in surprise. "Are you telling me that Chauncey Walker was the leader of the Deuces?" (It was hardly likely that there was another Chauncey.)

"Yah, but I think he tried to break them up. He made them turn in their guns."

"Guns! That's pretty heavy. How many of them had guns?"

"Some of them did. He said to get rid of them. He said it would only get them in trouble."

"That's pretty good advice. Does Chauncey still hang around with the Deuces?"

"Naw, he's too old. He's got a job now."

"Do you ever see him?"

"Once in a while."

"If he talked to Dexter, do you suppose he could get Dexter to stay away from the school?"

The boy smiled. "I guess he'd listen to Chauncey all right," he said.

"You know if this gang business doesn't stop, someone is going to get hurt. If it's a gang member, maybe he deserves it—and that includes you. But it will probably be some innocent kid."

"I'm not in the gang," he protested.

"Then why do I see you on the corner with Dexter?"

"We're just trying to protect the black kids when they're going home. I got a sister in seventh grade and my momma wants me to take care of her."

"And does your mother know you're out there with the Deuces? Do you really think that's the way she wants you to protect your sister?"

"No, sir," he admitted.

"I'll tell you how to protect your sister. By helping me to put an end to this gang fight. The black kids, especially the younger ones, are the ones most likely to be injured. You know they have to go through the Latin King's territory to go home. If I can get Dexter out of the way, I'm pretty sure things would cool off. I want you to take a message from me to Chauncey. He's a friend of mine—at least I think he is. Tell him I'd like him to keep Dexter away from the school. Can you do that?"

"Maybe. If I see him."

"Well, you do it—for both of us. And I don't want to see you out there with Dexter anymore. He's a troublemaker."

The next day, when I checked the corners after school, both groups were still there, but Dexter was conspicuous by his absence. I convinced them to leave without too much difficulty. Dexter did not show up again, and in a few days things were back to normal. Did Chauncey talk to him? I have no idea. But I like to think he did, that he had become an influence for good, and that this, coupled with a friendly feeling for me, had caused him to intercede and effect Dexter's departure.

15. The Case against Corporal Punishment

Although I had mimeographed a set of instructions for substitutes, I knew they didn't always read them, so sometimes, if I wasn't too busy, I would give them a few verbal suggestions. "Above all," I would caution, "don't lay a hand on a child."

One day, shortly after I had briefed a new substitute, a boy came into the office and complained that the teacher had hit him. Naturally I was upset. I sent a note to the teacher asking him to see me at recess. When he entered my office, I looked at him sternly. "Do you remember my telling you that I didn't want you to lay a hand on a student?" I asked.

"I certainly do," he responded.

"Well, a boy came in to see me, and he claims that you hit him!"

"I didn't lay a hand on him," insisted the teacher. "I hit him on the head with a book."

"What this kid needs is a good slap!" How many times have I heard teachers say that? And on some occasions I have been tempted to agree. All too often, however, I have observed the negative consequences of corporal punishment. Therefore, while my opposition to its use in the schools is based chiefly upon moral and ethical values, I am firmly convinced that my position is a pragmatic one.

Having never taken a poll on the subject nor seen one, I don't know how the majority of parents feel about it, though I am sure that many of them do not share my sentiments. Quite a few to whom I have spoken, especially the fathers, have confided to me that they favored a strong, no-nonsense approach. If a kid misbehaves, give him a whack. It worked very well, they maintained, when they went to school, and it would undoubtedly have a salutary effect upon the present crop of troublemakers. The troublemakers, of course, were always someone else's children. Their own had been taught to behave (usually, they boasted, by the use of a strap), and consequently had become paragons of virtue. From my observation, and from the reports of their teachers, I was aware that the behavior of many of these children was far from exemplary. Actually, the child who is frequently beaten at home is very likely to be a discipline problem at school. Perhaps he has been conditioned to respond only to the strap and is not deterred by our more orthodox methods of control. Or he may have become so accustomed to punishment that he is no longer intimidated by it.

It was not uncommon for a parent, while enrolling a boy, to give me or the child's teacher permission to slap him, paddle him, or "take a strap" to him if he didn't behave. (I've had similar instructions with regard to girls, though this did not occur as frequently.) These statements were almost always made in the student's presence, probably in the hope that the implied threat would have the desired effect and make such a punishment unnecessary. Perhaps these parents were also trying to impress me with their staunch support of our educational system and their sincere interest in their children's conduct. I interpreted such instructions a little differently. In effect, they seemed to be saying, "I can't control my child, so I want you to do it for me." I would explain, politely and firmly, that such actions on my part, their permission notwithstanding, would be contrary to the rules of the Board of Education and could subject me to official censure or worse. Surely they did not expect me to risk losing my job. These measures, I suggested, were within the parent's domain, not mine.

The approval of corporal punishment by many teachers and parents can be construed as an unconscious acceptance of the doctrine of "in loco parentis," which recognizes that the teacher is really acting as an agent of the parent and as such should have comparable prerogatives in establishing his or her authority. However, as the parent can usually be contacted if necessary, this should not be taken too literally.

Certainly teachers and principals have a right to expect the support and cooperation of the home—though they don't always get it. Some parents feel that when the child is at school he is no longer their responsibility. I remember an irate father who expressed this attitude very bluntly and graphically. When I called to inform him about his son's repeated transgressions, he replied contentiously, "I take care of him at home. When he's at school, he's your job. That's what we pay you for! You do whatever you have to with him, and don't bother me about it." I mentally started counting to ten. When I felt that I had regained my composure, I responded that it was his son I was calling about and that, while we certainly had an obligation in the matter, he could not conveniently disclaim responsibility. "There isn't much we can do if the parent doesn't help us," I told him. "Just remember one thing. Whether we do or don't succeed in controlling him, he'll be out of here in a year or two. But he's still going to be your son. I think you'd better pay attention to what he's doing before it's too late. Besides, if I decide to suspend him, you'll have to take care of him at home whether you want to or not." This threat had the desired effect, and I was able to proceed more calmly to discuss what "we" should do about the problem. I have a feeling that this father vented his wrath physically upon his son when the boy got home that day. Whether corporal punishment is an appropriate form of discipline when administered by parents is not relevant to this discussion. I will say, however, that when a parent employs a strap, a stick, or some other instrument, the line between legitimate discipline and child abuse can become very tenuous.

Many parents and teachers are not interested in debating the moral implications of corporal punishment. They contend that a timely slap or a judicious paddling is effective, and that's all that counts. After all, look how much better kids behaved in the good old days than they do now. They will give you chapter and verse about teachers they remember who would straighten kids out in a hurry with a swift crack in the mouth. I can only say that memories of my own school days cause me to doubt the efficacy of such tactics.

As a rule I was reasonably well-behaved in school. (Let's say I wasn't caught too often.) Consequently, although some of my teachers were not averse to slapping an offending child, I was seldom the recipient of such dispensations. I know that on the rare occasions when it did happen to me, I would dream about ways to get even—and if I found an opportunity to misbehave without getting caught, I would take advantage of it. I don't think this attitude is unique. If anything, I find it even stronger today (when most children are well aware that a teacher is not supposed to strike them) than it was in my time.

Struggling young teachers have sometimes tried to justify to me their use of corporal punishment by claiming, "Nothing else seems to work." As their problems usually continued (at least until they gained experience), this evidently didn't work too well either. Nevertheless, it may have mitigated their feeling of helplessness. If we consider it as a form of therapy for teachers, I suppose it can serve as a means of releasing their aggressions. I doubt, however, if any psychiatrist would recommend using children as punching bags to alleviate the anxieties of teachers. Besides it never affected me that way. When I tried it, very early in my teaching career, its principal result was to give me feelings of guilt. Once I had decided that this method was not for me, I not only felt better but I began to experiment with more acceptable methods of maintaining order.

When one student hits another, it might be deemed appropriate to physically chastise the offender so "he will know how it feels." Or if a student hurls insults and obscenities at a teacher in front of the whole class (I have never had this experience, but I know it does happen), the teacher may consider it obligatory that he retaliate immediately and forcefully. Otherwise, as he sees it, the class will lose all respect for him. I have contended that there are better ways of dealing with the offender and that it is a teacher's obligation to exhibit self-control and always behave in a professional manner. On the whole, the reaction to my views was decidedly lukewarm. Though they may not be willing to admit it publicly, many teachers believe that a violent physical response to this kind of provocation is justified. ("After all, we're only human!")

Having experienced some stressful moments myself, I know there are circumstances in which it is not easy to retain one's self-control. I am not unmindful of or unsympathetic to the teachers' problems. I have found, however, that such a response often triggered a visit to my office from an angry parent, and I have naturally resented being placed in a difficult position for which I was in no way responsible. I considered it manifestly unfair that I should be forced to defend an act which I have publicly condemned. (A very personal reason for my bias against corporal punishment.) Nevertheless, like the attorney who, though he may doubt his client's innocence, is prepared to defend him to the best of his ability, I would try to persuade the parent that there were extenuating circumstances. I had an established policy—to present the teacher's side of the story as favorably as the facts permitted, to emphasize the provocation which had led to his action, and sometimes even to invoke the teachers' favorite excuse, "After all, he's only human,"—but never to condone the act itself.

Over the years, I developed a technique which worked pretty well in these situations. After listening to the parent's grievance, I would usually ask him to wait in the outer office while I went to the teacher's room and heard his version of the incident. Assuming that he admitted hitting the student—subsequent to what he considered extreme provocation—I would return to the office to face his accuser and begin, "I can understand why you're upset. I have talked to the teacher about this, and I assure you it won't happen again. I want to make it clear that I don't approve of this kind of punishment. But we have to consider how this whole thing started. What would you do if you were a teacher and a student swore at you (or talked back to you) right in front of the whole class? If your son or some other kid talked that way to you, how do you think you'd feel? And remember we're talking about a teacher in a classroom who is certainly entitled to some respect. I don't see how he can be expected to teach without it. I'm not saying he did the right thing. But before we blame him, let's remember that it was your son's action that really caused this to happen. Maybe you should have a good talk with your son about his conduct. I'm sure that isn't the way you've taught him to behave."

With this line of reasoning I have been able to defuse practically every threatening situation. Then, when I was satisfied that the parent's wrath had subsided, I permitted him to see the teacher—usually in my presence. More often than not, the parent would discover that the teacher was not the brutal, insensitive ogre his child had described. (Sometimes he was, but he managed to conceal it.) In fact, after one such conference with a penitent teacher who, to my knowledge, had never struck a child before, the father confided to me, "You know, he's really a nice guy." Considering that this man had been threatening all kinds of mayhem a few minutes earlier while avowing his intention to sue me, the teacher, the school, and the Board of Education, I regarded this dénouement as both gratifying and amusing.

After pacifying the irate parent, I would meet with the teacher the following day and indicate that these encounters were not only time-consuming but embarrassing to me. I would make it clear that I did not appreciate the position in which the teacher's act had placed me and that I wanted no repetition of it.

It is true that sometimes there was a beneficial effect. The parent often heeded my advice and talked to the child at home (or possibly took some stronger measures). The teacher might then report an improvement (usually temporary) in the child's behavior. Nevertheless, I was acutely aware of the potential dangers of the situation.

What if the parent should decide to attack the teacher? I have read of cases where this has happened, and the teacher was injured, and the whole mess ended up in court.

There was one confrontation in my office that could easily have precipitated such a disastrous consequence. A father had come to protest that the teacher had paddled his son. I knew the teacher kept a paddle in the room and I had previously questioned him about it, but he had assured me that he didn't use it. While I found it difficult to believe that the paddle was there merely for ornamental purposes, I had no hard evidence to the contrary (although I had heard rumors), and was reluctant to make an issue of it. I assumed that my mention of it and my obvious disapproval would be a sufficient deterrent. Apparently it wasn't. Still, an accusation was not proof. As I was trying to calm the father by promising that I would investigate the matter, we were interrupted by a knock on the door.

"Come in," I called. It was the boy's teacher. Had I known, I would have kept him out. I wasn't ready for him. Unfortunately, one of his students had informed him that the boy's father was in the office and he had come to defend his action. He admitted that he had used the paddle and cited the boy's insolence and disobedience as a justification. Almost immediately a shouting match ensued.

The father leaped out of his chair. "You lay a hand on my son again and I'll hit you right in the mouth!" he yelled. He was a stocky, powerfully built man, but the teacher, a former athlete who was still in good physical condition, was not intimidated.

"Why don't you try it right now?" he retorted.

I got between them and, with all the authority I could muster, cried out, "Stop it! There's not going to be any fighting in my office."

I ordered the teacher to leave, which he did with obvious reluctance. Finally, the parent also left, still muttering threats. Under the circumstances, and with the issue unresolved, I thought it best to transfer the boy to another class. I did not want to risk another confrontation. I also confiscated the teacher's paddle.

Aside from the danger from the parent, there is the very real possibility, especially in the upper grades, that the student will strike back if he is hit. We have all read of attacks upon teachers by students. In most cases I am sure they are unjustified. I have no doubt, however, that some are the result of corporal punishment. I remember reading an item in the newspaper that illustrates this all too well. The headline was, "Paddled Student Shoots Principal." The article revealed that a seventh-grade student, after receiving a disciplinary paddling from the principal, stated, "I'm going to get you for this." He returned a short time later with a pistol which he fired. The bullet grazed the principal's skull. Fortunately the wound was not fatal.

During my ten years as a principal, four attacks upon teachers were reported to me. The first was the assault by Chauncey which I have previously recounted. I have no doubt that it was provoked by the teacher's attack upon him.

The second incident was actually the result of a mistake. A very pugnacious sixth grader with a record of violent behavior ran into our librarian and almost knocked her down. She put out her hands to protect herself, and the boy, misinterpreting her gesture as an attempt to hit him, started to punch her. It was later well-documented by a number of witnesses that she was only attempting to grab his hands in self-defense, but he kept flailing away at her. Fortunately, three male teachers were in the hallway at the time as it was between periods and they were escorting their respective classes to their rooms. They hurried to the rescue and managed, with great difficulty, to subdue the boy. Then two of them dragged him, kicking and screaming, to my office. The sight of two grown men holding tightly to the skinny arms of a rather small sixth grader struck me as incongruous. I instructed them to release him—which they did, very gingerly.

"Sit down," I ordered. To the teachers' surprise (and my own) he obeyed meekly. I listened to the teachers' story and then told them, "You may go back to your classes now. Thanks for your help."

It was evident, from their hesitation, that they thought I was being foolhardy. They had seen this boy in action. However, I was intrigued with the idea that while it took two big, strong men to drag the boy to my office, I could handle him without violence. "He'll be all right," I said confidently. "I can take care of him."

This was a calculated bit of bravado on my part, and I hoped it wouldn't boomerang. The boy wasn't very big. Should he decide to attack me, I was sure I could defend myself, but, judging from the teachers' report, subduing him would be another matter. Yet, as the teachers backed slowly out of the office, Derek (that was the boy's name) remained docile. I could see the bewilderment on the faces of the teachers. While enjoying their discomfiture, I was puzzled by this turn of events myself. The victory had been too easily won. Perhaps his vigorous struggle had resulted from their very physical efforts to restrain him. I carefully avoided touching him.

As we sat there facing each other, I tried to preserve the calm atmosphere by asking questions entirely unrelated to the incident that had precipitated his onslaught. I pretended that I was only concerned with the report I was writing and requested his name, age, address, the names of his parents, and similar innocuous information. My tactics appeared to be succeeding. There was no evidence of his previous agitation. Then, a victim of my own curiosity, I chanced a more provocative question.

"Just a few minutes ago you were fighting with three teachers. How come you're not trying to hit me?"

"I never fight with principals," he responded simply.

Evidently it was my title rather than my forceful personality which had brought about such a favorable change of attitude. I was properly chastened, although I could see the humor of the situation. I sent for his records. They revealed that his previous history was none too savory. And now his unwarranted assault upon a teacher—actually upon four teachers, for his violent resistance to the three who had tried to subdue him could also be construed as an assault—left me with no alternative. I called for someone to take him home—I think an older sister came for him—and then immediately arranged for an emergency transfer to Montefiore. He remained there for two years, after which he was returned to us, just as pugnacious but several sizes larger, and he continued to plague us until he graduated. (His reading and math skills were questionable. However, he was over fifteen years old, and my assistant principal, who was in charge of discipline at the time, was very anxious to get rid of him.)

The third attack upon a teacher was definitely the result of his own action. The teacher, an inept individual who had only been with us for one semester, very unwisely struck one of our big eighth graders. The student retaliated. He was taller and heavier than the teacher and evidently a more accomplished boxer. The teacher emerged from the brief encounter with a superficial but humiliating injury—a varicolored eye. I suspended the boy for his defiance of authority, but, considering the extenuating circumstances and his previous good record, decided that a transfer to Montefiore was not justified. I anticipated a demand from the faculty for a more severe punishment but none materialized. The teacher involved was an FTB (a substitute assigned on a full-time basis). He had no close friends among the teachers, and many of them were aware of his inability to control the class (which no doubt accounted for his action). Actually, I was tempted to dismiss him at the time. As he had no tenure, it was within my authority to do so. However, I knew it would be difficult to find a replacement in mid-term. Besides, regardless of the provocation, he had been struck by a student, and it seemed inappropriate that he should be dismissed as a result. Instead, I contented myself with cautioning him that I would not countenance another such incident.

Subsequent developments caused me to regret my decision. A parent came to me a few months later with a disturbing report. As the teacher's attempt at corporal punishment had miscarried, and as I had made it clear that he was not to hit a student again, he had devised an alternate plan. He had appointed the largest boy in the class to act as sergeant at arms with full authority to pummel unruly students—either those designated by the teacher or those he himself elected to punish. Though the parent assured me that this was happening (his son, who was in the class, had provided the information), I could scarcely believe it. I summoned the boy who allegedly served as the dispenser of justice, and he admitted his role without hesitation. After all, he had only followed the teacher's orders. Armed with this corroborative testimony, I confronted the teacher. In the face of this evidence, he acknowledged the truth of the allegation. That was his last day at our school. His parting request, which I considered the height of "chuzpah," was for a letter of recommendation from me.

I must report that the fourth assault upon a teacher was completely unjustified. The teacher involved did not even know the student. The boy, Danny, had come late, and his class had left on a field trip without him. Consequently, Danny was placed in another room for the day. He was unhappy with this arrangement and demanded that he be allowed to go home. Naturally the teacher could not permit this, so Danny, after sitting moodily for a while, seized a map from the wall (the kind that rolls up on a wooden shaft like a window shade) and, using it as a club, hit the unsuspecting teacher from behind. As the injury to the teacher was slight, I was almost glad the attack had occurred. It gave me an excuse to transfer Danny to Montefiore. This was something I had wanted to do for a long time but had been unable to accomplish due to insufficient evidence, particularly about his gang activities, and a fiercely protective mother. Danny had been a gang member since the age of eight and a school problem even before that. Actually, when he was eight years old he was the leader of a "midget" branch of an established neighborhood gang. When this was reported to me, I couldn't believe it and checked it out personally. I managed to break up this midget gang, but when Danny got older he became one of the leaders of the real gang. Yet, whenever he got in trouble and I called his mother, she would claim that we were "picking on him."

"I'm sure he is not the only one who misbehaves. Why do you always call me?" she would respond. An illogical and not uncommon attitude to which I could only reply that no, he was not the only student who misbehaved, and that I did call other parents as well. Even now, despite the gravity of his offense, she asked if I would give him one more chance. I asserted emphatically that under no circumstances would I permit him back in class and reminded her that we could charge him with assault. Faced with this alternative, she finally agreed to sign his transfer to Montefiore. When I reproached her for always defending him, she responded tearfully, "He hasn't got a father. I'm his mother. If I don't stick up for him, who will?"

"Taking his side when he's wrong is not the answer," I said. "You can see that he's been getting into more and more trouble. I've already suspended him twice, but it hasn't helped because you never cooperated with us. It's time he learned that he can't keep getting away with everything or he may end up in jail."

So far, I have tried to establish that (1) corporal punishment can result in an attack upon the teacher by a parent, and (2) it may trigger an assault by a student. Here are some other points to consider:

3. It puts a premium upon the physical or fistic prowess of the teacher, an attribute not covered in our teacher examination, and sometimes places female teachers in a subordinate position where they may have to enlist the aid of a physically more powerful colleague to chastise an offending student. Obviously, if the students are bigger and stronger than the teacher (not uncommon in our seventh and eighth grades), the teacher is at a disadvantage. As a consequence, the teacher might hit the smaller students but be afraid to administer a similar punishment to the larger ones—hardly an equitable situation. I'm all for physical fitness, but I hope that expertise in karate does not come to be considered a teaching prerequisite.

4. It is degrading to both student and teacher. When we should be teaching the use of reason and logic, resorting to force is hardly compatible with such instruction.

5. Vandalism is a major and continuing problem in our schools. While there is no single cause, I am aware of instances where a student's motive in vandalizing a classroom was to "get even" with the teacher. I firmly believe that a student is more likely to retaliate in this manner if he has been hit by a teacher.

6. It sets an example to the students and indicates that the use of force is an appropriate method of punishment. Here is an instance to illustrate this point. On days when we had indoor recess, it was customary for some of our upper-grade students, usually chosen for their exemplary conduct, to serve as monitors in the lower grades while the teachers took their recess break. (Contrary to the belief of many students, teachers do have to go to the bathroom.) I was shocked to learn that some of the monitors habitually walked around the room with yardsticks in their hands and sometimes used them upon their charges. I put a stop to this and had several of them relieved from duty. However, considering their excuse, I had to wonder to what extent they were really at fault. They told me they were only doing what the teachers did. I explained to them, with debatable logic, that they were not teachers, that the teachers were adults, and that at no time did they, as students, have the right to hit another student. I conveniently evaded the issue of the teachers' culpability, but I'm not sure I fooled anyone.

7. Corporal punishment makes the student resentful toward the teacher and the school. An elderly principal of my acquaintance was obviously aware of this. He would tell parents who gave him "permission" to spank their children, "I can't do that. If you spank your child, he will still love you. After all, he knows all the good things you do for him and he will accept it from you. But if I spank him, he will hate me—and I don't want him to hate me."

8. Children can be injured, sometimes inadvertently, when corporal punishment is sanctioned. A substitute once came into my office to report that she had hurt a child. She was contrite and very upset. She explained that while she was walking through the aisle with a yardstick in her hand she had accidentally hit a student in the face. Fortunately, the stick just missed his eye. Although there were a few drops of blood, the wound was little more than a scratch. The teacher insisted that she had had no intention of using the yardstick upon anyone. She was only carrying it to "scare" the students. The boy in question was entirely innocent of any wrongdoing. In fact, the whole class had been behaving pretty well. So why carry a yardstick? Obviously as an implement for or an implied threat of corporal punishment.

9. More important are the injuries that can be caused by teachers who overreact to a situation and lose their self-control. I can recall quite vividly such an occurrence at our school.

I was sitting in my office one rather quiet morning when a student burst in and yelled excitedly, "Come quick! Mr. Barnett is killing a kid in his class."

As I hastily followed him up the stairs, he amplified, "He's got him out in the hall on the second floor and he's choking him."

I accelerated my pace apprehensively. When we reached the top of the stairs, I saw Mr. Barnett, very red-faced and breathing heavily. Facing him was a disheveled and obviously frightened student, his shirt unbuttoned at the top and the flap sticking out over his pants, his hair matted with sweat, and his chest heaving as he gasped for breath. Two teachers, one male and one female, were standing between them. They were noticeably agitated but attempted to regain their composure as they saw me approaching.

"It's all right. Everything is all right, Mr. Greenstein," said the female teacher, Mrs. Hartmann. Well-groomed and personable, she was normally poised and self-assured, one of the veterans of the staff and a recognized faculty leader. Though still visibly shaken, she came toward me and spoke in a soft, controlled voice. "I can take care of this," she said almost in a whisper, "Why don't you just go back to the office? I'll be down to see you in a few minutes. It's my free period."

As whatever had been going on was evidently over, I decided to comply with her suggestion. She entered my office a short time later and carefully closed the door. Obviously she did not want to be overheard by the clerks in the outer office. In a barely audible voice she related what had happened.

"It was sickening," she confided, "just sickening. I talked to one of the boys in Mr. Barnett's class, and according to him Mr. Barnett gave Dominick—that's the boy you saw in the hall—a punishment to write and Dominick refused to do it. When Mr. Barnett threatened to take him to the office, Dominick talked back and used some bad language. Well, Mr. Barnett grabbed Dominick, practically threw him out into the hall, and started choking him. I heard the noise and went out to see what was going on. He was actually banging the boy's head against the wall when Mr. Hunt and I stopped him. If we hadn't, I don't know what would have happened. Dominick's all right—he's more scared than anything else. He must have a hard head. I know Dominick. I had him last year. He's pretty obnoxious, but still—." She shook her head in disbelief. "I don't want to see anything like that again."

I reminded her that she was one of the teachers who had not been particularly impressed by my lectures to the faculty condemning the use of corporal punishment, and had even admitted to me that she sometimes slapped a student "when he really needed it."

"Oh, I've slapped a kid occasionally," she conceded, "but never anything like this. This is different. I'd never hurt a student."

"So what you are telling me is that when you hit a kid it's all right because you don't lose control the way Mr. Barnett did. But teachers are human and they do lose their tempers. Mr. Barnett is not the only one. And if something like this can happen even though the teacher knows it's against the rules, what would happen if the board sanctioned corporal punishment? How many more incidents would there be like the one you just witnessed? How many teachers would overreact? Or should we say it's all right for you to hit a kid because we know you'll use the privilege wisely, but we won't let Mr. Barnett do it? That doesn't make much sense, does it? If you have that right, then so does Mr. Barnett and so do other teachers who may not have the self-discipline that you do. Sooner or later some kid is going to be injured."

Mrs. Hartmann pursed her lips thoughtfully. "After what I saw today, I suppose I have to admit that you're right. I never want to see anything like that again. It made me ashamed that something like that could happen at our school. I promise you I won't lay a hand on a student again."

"Are you sure the boy is all right? I assume I can expect a visit from his parents."

"Oh, he's all right. A little bump on the back of his head, but that's all. And I know his father. I don't think Dominick will say a word when he gets home. His father would kill him."

"I'd better talk to the boy anyway. Would you mind sending him down when you get upstairs?"

She left, and Dominick came in a few minutes later. His shirt was torn and he still looked a little frightened. Other than that, he appeared to be unhurt.

"I've just been talking to Mrs. Hartmann about you," I said. "She tells me you've got a big mouth. It looks like it got you into trouble."

"A teacher isn't supposed to hit you," he whined defensively. "He almost killed me. He's a man and I'm just a kid."

"No, he's not supposed to hit you," I agreed, "and you're not supposed to swear at a teacher. You did, didn't you?"

"I wasn't swearing at him," he muttered. "It just slipped out."

"What do you think your father would say if I told him you talked back to a teacher and you swore at him or in front of him—whichever it was?"

He hung his head and didn't answer.

"Well, I won't tell him," I said magnanimously. "I guess you've suffered enough." I was suggesting, though I didn't want to make it too obvious, that I wouldn't say anything if he didn't. I could do without another angry parent. "I'll let you go back to your room now. But remember, the next time you talk to a teacher like that, I'll suspend you."

It was really lucky that Dominick wasn't hurt. Now I had to talk to Mr. Barnett. I couldn't just ignore his part in the incident. On second thought, I'd let it go till tomorrow. It was a rule I had, and it worked pretty well. Wait one day to give the emotions, both mine and the other person's, time to subside. I left a note in Mr. Barnett's mailbox requesting that he see me in the morning.

A very contrite Mr. Barnett was waiting for me when I arrived the next morning. "You don't have to say a word," he declared. "I know I was way out of line. You have my word it won't happen again. But when that kid swore at me, I just saw red. You know, I'm not used to this. I went to a parochial school and if a kid did that he'd get a whack right across the mouth. I've got six kids of my own, and they wouldn't dare talk to me like that. I don't have any trouble with my class. I like my class, but that Dominick—well, anyhow it won't happen again."

His apology seemed to be sincere and made most of what I had to say superfluous, but I couldn't let him off that easily. "You know, if that boy's father comes to complain, you could be in a lot of trouble," I said. No sense telling him that such a development was unlikely. "I won't report it, but if he wants to go over my head to the superintendent, there's nothing I can do about it. There's no way I can defend that kind of action."

"I understand," he said. "Believe me, I've learned my lesson."

Well, he was a good teacher. And this episode had probably taught him more than any rebuke from me could possibly accomplish. There was no sense in prolonging the agony. As I saw it, we had both "lucked out"—this time. However, this strengthened my opposition to corporal punishment. And perhaps I had also made two converts.

10. Many people are convinced that corporal punishment is effective, and I suppose nothing I can say will change their minds. Sometimes their logic puzzles me. I have spoken to teachers who have

been transferred to our school from one in which corporal punishment, usually administered by the assistant principal, was sanctioned and openly practiced despite the Board of Education rule to the contrary. Apparently no one complained to the district superintendent, or perhaps he chose to ignore it.

The teachers assured me that the children at that school, especially the upper graders, were so hard to manage that they could only be controlled by physical punishment. Despite these measures, discipline was a constant problem, and these teachers were glad to have escaped to the relative tranquility of our school. Now our upper-grade classes have never been regarded as rest havens for timorous teachers. In fact, we have sometimes had substitutes who, after a calamitous experience in one of these classes, have vowed never to return. Yet, according to the teachers from the other school, our discipline problems were not nearly as severe as the ones they had encountered. (We also had less vandalism.) Their interpretation, and the one generally accepted, was that the situation at the other school would be even worse if physical force was not used to "keep the kids in line." I know of no evidence to support their conclusion. My own assessment of the situation is that this is an example of the failure of corporal punishment. As far as I know, the discipline at that school, and at others in which its use is prevalent, is not any better, perhaps even worse, than at those schools where it is not practiced.

11. Let us go from the pragmatic to the ethical. We certainly want teachers to be good role models for the students to emulate. As authority figures they symbolize the establishment; and a student's perception of the society as a whole could very well be colored by his opinion of them. If a student knows his teacher is lying, it is not likely to enhance that teacher's image. Yet, when teachers hit children, they will sometimes deny doing so, especially if there are no witnesses. (The situation with Chauncy is a case in point.)

I find it exceedingly strange that many well-meaning teachers blithely disregard the rules they are supposed to observe and even deny their transgressions without a twinge of conscience. Meanwhile, they exhort their students to obey the rules and are furious if they catch one of them lying. Are we to assume that the students are unaware of or unaffected by this contradictory attitude? I don't believe it.

I don't want to leave the wrong impression. The fact is that few of our teachers punished the children physically and even fewer did so with any degree of regularity. Some teachers, even if they approve of the practice, do not resort to it for fear of being discharged. Unless the teacher's action is extreme, however, the usual penalty for such a violation is a reprimand—and sometimes not even that. The parents can, of course, take the matter to court. But unless they can prove that the child was injured, the teacher (or the board) will not be found liable as state law permits corporal punishment, and its use has been upheld by the United States Supreme Court.

16. Crime and Punishment

One day a teacher informed me that a boy in her class had been accosted in the alley by a man who wanted to kiss him. This sounded so bizarre that I was sure the allegation would turn out to have no basis in fact. Nevertheless, as she was very upset about the matter, I instructed her to send the boy in question to the office. He was a European immigrant, about twelve years old, nice-looking, and intelligent. I had temporarily placed him in a lower grade until his English improved.

"All right," I said, "tell me what happened."

"I go home for lunch like always," he said. "I walk in alley and a man come up and ask me for kees."

I was beginning to be concerned. Possibly we were dealing with an attempted homosexual assault. Before calling the police, however, I wanted more facts. "Did he grab you or try to do anything to you?"

"No, he don't grab. He just ask for kees."

"Well, what did you do?"

"I don't give him," he responded cooly.

"You mean you refused to kiss him and he didn't force you. Is that it?"

The boy shook his head impatiently. "No, he don't want to kees me. He ask me for kees—kees to house. I tell him I don't have kees and he go away."

Vandalism! Needless, senseless, wanton, wasteful destruction! It is a very aggravating problem. After a while, one learns to accept, with a sigh of resignation, an occasional broken window, especially if it is the result of an accident. Ball playing is probably the most common cause of broken windows. For that reason, most schools prohibit playing ball in the playground, though the rule is not always enforced and is unenforceable after school hours. There are also the semiaccidents resulting from students throwing stones or snowballs. If apprehended, the perpetrator would have you believe that his target was something else entirely or that he didn't know glass was breakable. Assuming one is naive enough to accept such an excuse, one can attribute the accident to poor aim or poor judgment. Some of the breakage, however—it is hard to estimate the percentage—is undoubtedly deliberate. If the culprit was apprehended, I would consult with the engineer as to the cost of replacement and charge him accordingly, though usually a little less if I really thought it was an accident.

Occasionally, a student would ask to see me, acknowledge voluntarily that he had broken a window, and even offer to pay for the damage. Upon recovering from the shock, I would chide him for his carelessness, compliment him for his honesty, and accept his offer. However, I would give him a discount as a reward for such a sterling display of virtue. My clerks, who were inclined to be sentimental, thought I shouldn't charge at all in such circumstances. I couldn't agree. The window still had to be replaced, and I didn't believe I had the right to donate the taxpayers' money. Besides, I reasoned in my cynical fashion that some student might be smart enough and sneaky enough to figure out that he could break a window and avoid the consequences of his act by simply admitting his guilt—and even receive plaudits for his honesty. Just because it worked for George Washington didn't mean that I was going to let some kid pull that trick on me.

There are two items which I have often wished had remained uninvented—the marking pen and the spray paint can. The former was frequently employed in decorating the hallways, especially after they had just been painted. Something about the lure of a clean canvas, I suppose. The latter facilitated the adornment of the exterior with names, gang slogans, and certain other words which bothered me more than they did the students. I had a remedy for the interior markings providing the guilty party was identified. The culprit would be supplied with cleaning fluid and some cheese cloth, courtesy of the engineer. I would then instruct the student to remove not only his artistic efforts but all the graffiti in the area. Unfortunately, as I didn't have time to supervise the work, the punishment lost some of its effectiveness, especially if the student didn't mind missing class. Some students apparently preferred this activity to sitting in the classroom. (Not exactly a tribute to their teacher or the curriculum.) Consequently, I tried to schedule the task during the student's gym period or even during part of his lunch hour.

The spray paint on the outside of the building was another matter. As it was usually applied after school, those responsible were seldom apprehended. If the language was too lurid, one of the janitors would paint over it. Otherwise, as it was impossible to remove from the ridged gray stone by ordinary means, it would remain there until the building received its scheduled rejuvenation by sandblasting, which occurred about every five years.

Even so, the harm this caused was minor compared to the destruction which often accompanied a nocturnal break-in. To come into a classroom the next morning and survey the aftermath of such a visitation—this is a chilling and frustrating experience for a teacher or principal. A burglary, though its consequences can be equally expensive, at least makes some sense, and there is always the hope of recovery if the thief is apprehended. There is no recovery from vandalism. Oh, yes, the mess can be cleaned up. Some of the books and papers may be salvaged. But the students often have to be moved to another room or, of none is available, to the hallway or the basement while several janitors are taken away from their regular duties to do the work. (The next day I was sure to receive indignant complaints from teachers whose wastebaskets weren't emptied.)

Sometimes the damage is not as bad as it looks. Sometimes it is worse. Students' records may have been destroyed. Then the distraught teacher has to try to replace them—to rewrite them somehow, frequently with important information missing. I have walked gingerly through the rubble trying to rescue various items before the custodial staff began its operations. Some janitors will pick up books and papers before sweeping, but they may overlook valuable records. Others will just sweep everything into a heap and shovel it into large garbage cans. It's easier that way.

The causes of vandalism? A student may be angry at the teacher or the principal or society in general. Or it may just be something to do, perhaps out of boredom and a lack of more constructive activities. He may even be showing off, his way of getting recognition from his peers. If none of these reasons apply, I would have to ascribe it to pure orneriness. Not very scientific, but there were times when it was the only reason I could find.

If one can instill a sense of pride and belonging in the students and make them feel it is "their" school, perhaps the incidence of vandalism can be reduced. Easier said than done, though some principals have reported considerable success in reducing vandalism by involving all the students in a beautification project to improve the appearance of the school. Of course students should not be so alienated by teachers and principals that they want to get revenge. Perhaps this is also easier said than done. However, I have always believed that it is possible to maintain discipline and yet have the students feel that they are being treated fairly.

Another factor in prevention is security. Unfortunately, schools are very vulnerable. In our school, for example, a would-be vandal could pull down the fire escape, scale it to the first floor, break a window just above the landing, unfasten the latch, and enter directly into a classroom. He could then wreak havoc upon that room or roam the school unhampered and devastate other classrooms. I had asked the engineer if protective wire could be placed behind that vulnerable window or if it could be replaced with unbreakable plastic. He said that fire department regulations precluded such measures. The window leading to the fire escape had to be operational as an exit in case of fire.

I had also requested that a burglar alarm be installed in our school. I was assured by the person in charge of considering such requests that this would be done—eventually. Maybe in four or five years. As this was an expensive project, the budget would permit only a few schools to be accommodated each year, and there were about thirty schools ahead of us whose need was more pressing than ours. After we had had several break-ins during a comparatively short time, however, I was able to persuade him to assign a night watchman to our school. Then, when a few months went by with no intrusions, he was transferred, without my knowledge, to another school that presumably had a greater need for his presence. In other words, no break-in, no watchman. At a later date, after two more break-ins had occurred, I was again rewarded with a watchman. And after a period of tranquility he was again removed. A classic case of the barn door continually being locked after the horse was gone. Some time later, we were the victims of a costly burglary, but my petition for the watchman's reinstatement was denied on the grounds that one break-in was not enough to warrant his services. I was tempted (not too seriously) to stage another one so my request would be granted.

My record in solving burglaries, was not impressive. According to the police, they could have been the work of professionals, or at least of older boys with previous experience. In cases of vandalism, I was more successful. Devising an appropriate punishment, however, was another matter. A suspension was automatic, but how would that compensate for hundreds of dollars of damage? On one occasion, after a second offense by an unrepentent student, the police attempted to cooperate by directing his mother to pay five dollars a week for a total of fifty dollars. This, they told me, would at least provide partial restitution for the loss we had incurred. I didn't realize it at the time, but their order had no legal basis. Only a judge can impose such a penalty, and even he cannot do so unless the state has a parental liability law. Nevertheless, the boy's mother agreed. My gratitude to the police for their support was somewhat diminished when I learned that they had designated me to collect the payments. I was aware that the mother was on ADC. She made four payments, though not in consecutive weeks, and then pleaded for an extension. She convinced me that her meager income was barely sufficient for her family's basic needs. After wrestling with the uncomfortable feeling that I was literally depriving her children of food, I informed her that I would consider the account closed. It made little sense to punish the family while the guilty boy, who was beyond his mother's control, appeared to suffer no inconvenience. The only discernable effect upon him was to convince him, for some reason, that he had been mistreated. Actually, I believe he resented having been caught. Consequently, according to information I received from one of his classmates, he was planning another break-in to get "revenge." I sent for him and let him know that I was aware of his intentions. Of course he assured me that such a thought had never entered his mind. I countered with the assertion that I would have him transferred to a juvenile correctional institution if he made the attempt. (I wasn't sure I could accomplish this, but then neither was he.) As there was no break-in, I assume he abandoned the plan.

At a later date, I devised a rehabilitation project which was moderately successful. When a student was found guilty of vandalism, I ordered him (with the consent of his parents) to come to school a half hour early each morning for a period of two weeks. He was instructed to report to the engineer who would assign various clean-up duties in and around the school for him to perform. While the concept may have been a good one, I ran into a snag in its implementation. At first, the engineer was quite willing to cooperate. He soon discovered, however, that he had contracted for more than he had bargained. He had to check the student's arrival, find work for him to do, verify that it was performed satisfactorily, and keep track of his attendance until the student had completed his sentence. After a while, the engineer let me know that he had lost his enthusiasm for the plan. There was no one else to whom I could assign this task and I was too busy to do it myself, so I had to abandon the idea.

As I said, my track record in the apprehension of vandals was pretty good. I sometimes even succeeded in teaching them the error of their ways. One case, though typical in some respects, was quite unusual in its outcome.

I had arrived at school a little early one morning and was greeted immediately by my clerk with the announcement that there had been a break-in in room 104.

"How bad was it?" I asked.

"Pretty bad," she responded grimly. "You'd better see for yourself."

"Have the police been notified?"

"Yes. They're on their way."

"I don't suppose anyone knows who did it."

"No, not that I know of."

Years of practice had made me fatalistic. What was done couldn't be undone. I calmly walked across the hall to survey the damage. The clerk had not exaggerated. It was bad. The room looked as if it had been in the path of a tornado. The drawers of the teacher's desk had been pulled out and their contents strewn all around. Packages of art paper and manuscript paper had been broken open and scattered. The latter, in particular, would be difficult to replace as it was in short supply. It had been on order for months and we still hadn't received any. The students' desks were toppled over and formed incongruous geometric patterns on the floor. Some, though on their sides, still retained their contents. Others had been completely emptied. Little mounds of books, workbooks, papers, and pencils dotted the floor. If this had been the total damage, it might not have been so bad. These objects could be picked up and sorted out. But two large jars of tempera paint, one red and one orange, had been splashed indiscriminately on books and papers, on report cards and "cum" cards. Some paint had splattered on the walls forming bright blotches of color against the gray background. I picked my way through the debris toward the window. There, amid splinters of shattered glass, I found a large stone about four inches in diameter. Obviously this was the instrument which had been employed to break the glass, after which it had been a simple matter to release the latch and open the window.

I contemplated the destruction for a minute, then, realizing there were things I had to do, I returned to the office. "See if you can get hold of the engineer," I instructed the clerk. "There are books and records that can be salvaged. I don't want them swept out till Mrs. Monaghan has a chance to go through them. Better send her to me when she comes in."

The students would be arriving in about twenty minutes. It was evident that they would be unable to occupy the room that morning—probably not for the entire day. I retreated to my office to prepare a schedule for them. I checked the shop and home economics schedule. When the boys were in shop and the girls in home economics, there would be an empty room. These were seventh- and eighth-grade classes, while room 104 was first grade. However, it was probably better than putting them in the basement. They might even enjoy the new experience, though I was sure the teacher wouldn't. Unfortunately, they would only be able to stay in one room for two periods. Then that class would be returning. But when the next class went to shop and home economics, another empty room would be available. As I finished preparing the students' itinerary for the morning, their teacher, Mrs. Monaghan, walked in.

"You wanted to see me?" she asked.

Apparently the clerk hadn't told her anything. Why did I always have to be the disseminator of bad news? "Well, that's what you get paid for," I told myself philosophically.

In as matter-of-fact a tone as I could muster, I said, "Your room has been broken into. I'm afraid it's pretty bad. There's stuff all over the floor, but I think most of it can be salvaged. I hope so, anyway. Your 'cum' cards and report cards are on the floor. You'd better pick them up right away. A lot of the students' desks have been emptied. When the kids come in, they can try to sort out their books and things. As soon as they've finished, you can take them to an empty seventh-grade room so the janitors can start cleaning up. I've prepared a schedule for you for the morning. I'll see that you get one for the afternoon later. The seats will be too big for your kids, but it's the best I can do. It will only be for one day. Here's your schedule."

"I understand," she said quietly. "I'll start right away."

She left without saying anything further. I didn't know whether she was taking it calmly or was in a state of shock. It shouldn't have been a total surprise. That room had been broken into before—though not like this. If she wasn't in a state of shock now, she would be when she saw the room. I didn't want to be there when she did.

A few minutes later, two police officers walked in. I briefly explained the situation and took them to room 104. Mrs. Monaghan was on the floor picking up report cards, a forlorn expression on her face. I nodded and tried to look sympathetic, but I didn't say anything. What was there to say?

The officers didn't appear to be overly impressed. I imagine they had seen worse sights. I showed them the broken window and the stone that had caused it. Then we returned to my office and one of them started to write his report. After completing the preliminary information, he asked, "Any idea who did it?"

"No, but I'll see what I can find out."

"O.K. Let us know if you come up with anything, and we'll work on it."

They left. I knew there wasn't much they could do unless I supplied them with some leads. Well, when classes started, I would begin my investigation. As such an act was often spontaneous and not carefully planned, it was possible that I would find a witness. Also, since it was not done for material gain, the perpetrator was quite likely to boast about his "accomplishment" to his friends to advance his status or gain some emotional satisfaction. Or he might have left a telltale clue which would turn up later.

I recalled a previous case of vandalism in which the culprit had painted the name "Rafael" on the blackboard. The teacher, a very emotional individual, had demanded that I call the police immediately and have them pick up a boy in her class named Rafael.

"I can't do that," I told her. "There could be more than one Rafael. Besides, just because his name is on the blackboard doesn't prove he's guilty. I would say it's a good indication that he's innocent. He would have to be pretty stupid to commit a crime and then write his name on the board."

"Well, he is pretty stupid," she retorted. "and he's mad at me because he had a bad report card. This is his way of getting even."

"I'm sorry," I said. "I'll talk to Rafael, but I'll need more proof than that before I have him arrested. Do you have any other evidence?"

"I don't need evidence!" she insisted shrilly. "I know he did it, and I want him arrested."

I tried to explain to her, with very little success, that our system of justice required more than her intuitive cognition and that even a student had rights. I might also have to deal with a very angry parent if it turned out that he was innocent. She refused to be placated, muttered something about teachers not being able to maintain discipline if I insisted on protecting guilty students, and left in a huff.

I sent for Rafael and questioned him. He disclaimed any knowledge of the crime and could give no explanation for his name being on the board except to protest vehemently that he hadn't done it. I don't pretend that I always know when a student is lying. I'm not that clever. And when someone boasts to me that he has this ability, I am convinced that I am talking to a fool. Nevertheless, I was inclined to accept the boy's statement.

"If you didn't do it," I said, "it could be someone who wants to get you in trouble. Is there anyone in your room who might want to do that?"

"No, not in my room, but there's this kid in 310 that I had a fight with last week. His name is Fernando."

I continued my investigation by interrogating Fernando and his friends and eventually obtained sufficient evidence to enable me to exact a confession from Fernando. Naturally I couldn't resist pointing out to Rafael's teacher that she had been entirely wrong about him. She exhibited no remorse and refused to admit that she had been mistaken. "Well, he could have done it," she contended. "I still think he had something to do with it." That kind of logic is not easily refuted. I let the matter drop.

I began my current investigation by dispatching a note to all the classrooms requesting that the teachers send to the office any student who had knowledge of the break-in or had witnessed anybody on or near the fire escape the previous evening. The initial response was encouraging. About ten students soon trickled into the outer office. I interviewed them one at a time. Most of them had nothing of value to disclose. Several reported seeing someone trying to climb the fire escape a few days ago or even the previous week, which was not particularly relevant to what had happened last night. A few of these public-spirited citizens, whose testimony was exceedingly vague, probably came down just to get out of class for a while. Some students will go to great lengths to avoid getting an education. There were two boys, however, who had pertinent information. I questioned them separately, and their stories were identical. One of their classmates had boasted to them that he knew who was responsible for the break-in, though he hadn't told them who it was. That was the extent of their knowledge, but it was a start. I thanked the boys for their cooperation, assured them that the information they had given me would remain confidential, and dismissed them. Then I sent for their classmate, a boy named Terry.

I have had a lot of experience in interrogating students, and I will say, with no pretense of humility, that I think I'm quite good at it. I'm not sure the justice department would have approved of my methods. I didn't read the students their rights, warn them that anything they said could be used against them, or advise them that they could consult an attorney. But, come to think of it, I wasn't a police officer, and they weren't under arrest. And on the other hand, I didn't abuse them verbally or physically.

When Terry entered, I instructed him to sit down. "Do you know why I sent for you?" I asked.

"No, I don't," he replied.

"There was some trouble here last night. What do you know about it?"

"Nothing. The teacher said someone broke into the school. That's all I know."

"Were you in the playground last night? Don't lie to me because I have witnesses." (I didn't say witnesses to what, so I wasn't lying.)

"Yeah, for a little while. Then I went home." (A lucky guess on my part. I didn't know he had been on the playground.)

"Who else was there?"

"Let's see." He mentioned several names and I wrote them down.

"Did any of them go near the fire escape?" I asked.

"I dunno. They might have. I wasn't watching them. I was playing."

"And that's all you saw?"

He hesitated. "Yeah, that's all."

I had noticed the hesitation, and it made me suspicious. "You're not telling me the truth," I said. "I'll tell you what happened. Someone climbed up on the fire escape, broke a window, got into the building, and did an awful lot of damage. A lot of books and school supplies were ruined, and two janitors will have to work all day to clean up the mess. Of course they have to get paid. All this is going to cost a lot of money. Who do you suppose is going to pay for it all?"

"I guess you will," he replied.

I smiled at his naiveté, but it didn't surprise me. Some of the students actually believed that I owned the school. In fact, a boy once asked me if I owned just this school or all the schools in the city.

"Not directly," I replied, "though I will pay part of it, and so will you."

"Me?" he said in surprise. "Why should I pay for it?"

"I didn't say you should, but you're going to. The Board of Education gives us a certain amount of money each year for books and supplies. We'll have to use some of that money to replace what was destroyed. That means we may not have enough money to buy some of the books you'll need next year. But that's not all. Does your father pay taxes?"

"I suppose so."

"I'm sure he does. We all pay taxes—even you. Every time you buy something you pay sales tax. The money to run the schools comes from taxes, so you see in a way we're all going to have to pay for what this boy did last night. Do you think that's fair?"

"I guess not."

"Do you think your father should have to pay for what this boy and others do to our schools?"

"No."

(Most of the money to run the schools comes from property taxes, but some is from other sources. There was no reason to get technical. As far as I'm concerned, taxes are taxes and come out of all our pockets one way or another.)

"I want you to tell me who that boy is," I said, "the boy who is responsible for all that damage."

"What makes you think I know?"

"Because some boys heard you say so."

"Who said that?"

"It doesn't matter who said it. You know who went up the fire escape—and I know you know it. Now who was it?"

"I don't know who did it, and even if I did, I'm not going to snitch on anybody."

"I'm not asking you to snitch. Snitching is when you tell your teacher that someone threw a spit ball or shot a rubber band or something like that. We're talking about a boy who committed a crime—a crime that will cost your school hundreds of dollars. Whoever helps me find him is just being a good citizen."

I paused for a reply, but he didn't answer. Time to try something else. "Look, either you tell me, or I'll call the police and you'll have to tell them."

"Why do I have to talk to the police?"

"Because there was a crime committed and you were a witness. There's one thing I can do for you. If you tell me who did it, I promise not to give the police your name. All I want is the information. No one has to know who told me."

"I never said I knew who did it," he declared stubbornly, though I could see he was a little frightened.

"You don't have to say it. I know. You'd better make up your mind. I haven't got all day. Do you want to tell me, or should I call the police?"

He didn't reply, and I picked up the phone. "Do you have to call the police?" he pleaded.

"That's up to you. If you tell me the truth, I can give them the information and I won't say where I got it. In fact, I promise you that I won't tell anyone. If you know anything about me, you should know that I always keep my word. This is your last chance. Who was it?"

He looked down at the floor. "It was Arnold Zalenga," he muttered.

"Did you see him go into the building?"

"He was on the fire escape. Then I heard a noise like a window breaking, and then I didn't see him. I guess he went in through the window."

"Did you see him come out?"

"No, I didn't stick around. I thought there might be trouble, and I didn't want to get blamed for anything."

"Did anyone go in with Arnold, or was he by himself?"

"Yeah, he was by himself."

"How about you? You said you were playing. Who was with you while all this was going on?"

"George Perez."

"Then he saw Arnold too, didn't he?"

"Yeah, he saw him."

I thanked Terry for his cooperation, reluctant though it had been, and again assured him that I wouldn't mention his name. Then I dismissed him and sent for George. Armed with the information I had received from Terry, I was able to persuade him, with a little prodding, to tell me what he had seen. He corroborated Terry's story. Now that I had two witnesses, I was ready to confront Arnold.

Arnold was in the sixth grade. Though he had not, at least up till now, been involved in any major transgressions, I knew him by reputation. He had been reported to me several times for insolence and for causing some minor disturbances. In particular, his teacher had expressed her concern that he was in danger of failing, not for lack of ability but because he seldom bothered to complete his assignments. He was a good-looking boy, a little on the chubby side, with very fair skin and blond, curly hair. As he sat facing me, with a look of complete innocence, he reminded me of one of Botticelli's cherubs.

I wasted no time in coming to the point. "Why did you break into the school last night?" I asked sternly.

His eyes widened. "Who, me?" he asked as if in disbelief.

I looked around in mock seriousness. "Do you see anyone else here? Of course I mean you."

"I didn't break into the school. Why would I do that?"

"I don't know. That's what I'm asking you—not that it really matters. It's no use denying it because I know you did it. I've got plenty of witnesses." (I did have two witnesses, and as far as I was concerned two were plenty.)

"Maybe they saw someone else who looked like me," he said.

"He not only looked like you—he had your name. Do you think I would send for you if I wasn't sure? I'm going to call the police, and it might be a little better for you if I told them you admitted it." (It would also make it easier for me, but I didn't think it was necessary to mention that.)

His milk-white skin began to show a touch of pink. His eyes dropped. "Maybe they saw me on the fire escape, but I didn't go in."

"Then what were you doing on the fire escape? You know you're not supposed to be there."

"I was just fooling around."

"That was some fooling around. Look, I'm tired of wasting time. I have witnesses who saw you. You broke the window, unlocked it, and went in—and you know what you did after that. Now either you tell me, or you tell it to the police. I'm waiting."

"Yeah, I did it," he said sullenly.

It had been easier than I had expected. Perhaps he had hoped that if he confessed I wouldn't turn him over to the police, but I certainly hadn't made such a commitment. "All right," I said, "we've got that settled. Is your mother home?"

"No, she's at work."

"How about your father?"

"He's working too."

"Well, I'm not going to bother them at work. You can wait in the outer office. I'll take care of you later."

Maybe I should have pursued the matter further and found out why he did it. I've wondered about that since then. At the moment, however, I was anxious to get this over with. It had been a long morning.

I called the police station and requested that the officer who made out the report be sent over. He showed up in a little while. I provided him with the information I had uncovered and gave him Arnold's name and address.

"I'll take him in now," he said. "Where is he?"

"I'm afraid I can't turn him over to you. His parents are at work, and I can't release a student without the consent of a parent. That's the law. As long as he's at school, he's in my custody and I'm responsible for him."

"Why don't you call his parents at work?"

"I suppose I could do that, but I'd rather not. Look, he's not going anywhere. You can pick him up after school when he's out of my jurisdiction. Don't forget that I solved the case for you."

Some police officers are not aware of the legal ramifications involved. Once, when I refused to turn a student over to him, an officer became very abusive and threatened that he would take me in as well for obstruction of justice. I called in several teachers as witnesses, warned him that he'd be in a lot of trouble if I sued for false arrest, and advised him to call his sergeant for a ruling on the matter. He cooled off sufficiently to accept my suggestion. The sergeant, whom I happened to know, resolved the conflict amicably (in my favor) with admirable composure and restraint.

In the present instance, the officer did not argue the point. "I guess I can go along with that," he said. He left, and I resumed my work—including the preparation of an afternoon schedule for Mrs. Monaghan's class and a suspension notice for Arnold.

The next morning I called the police station and asked for the officer who had handled the case. He was out on the street, and I left a message for him to call me. He called back in a few minutes.

"Hi, how are you," he said jovially. "I picked up your boy. It's all been taken care of."

"What does that mean?" I asked.

"Well, we kept him here till we got hold of his parents, and then we made a station adjustment."

"A station adjustment! In other words, you released him to his parents, and that's the end of it."

"I guess that's about it. We couldn't hold him, you know. He's a juvenile."

"I didn't expect you to hold him. I don't want the kid in jail. But this is too easy. This boy did an awful lot of damage. You saw it. I can't just let it go with a station adjustment."

"I'm sorry. I know how you feel about it, but there's nothing else we can do. Why don't you punish him at school?"

"I already did. I suspended him for five days. Big deal. Considering the kind of student he is, I don't think that's going to bother him much."

"Well, I'd like to help you, but it's out of my hands. The case is closed."

"Can't this kid be brought before a judge in juvenile court? I'll sign a complaint myself if necessary. We can charge him with aggravated vandalism or malicious mischief or something. How about that?"

"I suppose that's a possibility, but it's too late now."

"What do you mean it's too late?"

"The case is closed. I've made out my report and the lieutenant signed it. Disposition of the case was a station adjustment. That's it."

"No, that's not it," I insisted angrily. "I want this case reopened and this boy brought to trial!"

"That's not going to accomplish anything. It's his first offense. All the judge will do is put him on probation."

"Fine. At least he and his parents will have to appear in court. That's something."

"If I knew you felt that way, maybe I could have recommended it, but as I said, it's too late. My report has been signed by the lieutenant and filed. I can't change it now."

"Well, someone has to be able to do something. Let me talk to the lieutenant."

"He isn't in. He comes on duty in the afternoon."

"Then have him call me. Tell him it's important. If I don't hear from him, I'll contact the board's legal department."

"All right," he said resignedly, "but it won't do any good."

That afternoon I received a call from the lieutenant. "Hello, are you the principal?" he said amiably. "I hear you have a problem."

"Yes, I have a problem," I responded. "You had one of our students, a boy named Arnold Zalenga, picked up yesterday for vandalism. He practically destroyed a classroom and all he got was a station adjustment. I want him brought before a judge in juvenile court."

"Yes, I remember the case. Nice-looking boy. Nice parents too. I'm afraid I can't help you. That's the normal procedure—a station adjustment. I've already signed the officer's report and it's been filed."

"So get it out of the files. I want the case reopened," I said doggedly.

"I can't do that. And even if I could, all he'd get is probation," pointed out the lieutenant.

"I've heard that before. He's a juvenile and no one can do anything to him. I still want him in court. If you can't help me, you're going to hear from the board attorney. I know you were just doing your job. I'm not trying to give you a hard time, but this boy shouldn't get off that easily—for his own good. I intend to get some action on this case one way or another."

"All right, I'll see what I can do. I'll get back to you in a little while."

He called in about a half hour. "Your boy has a court date," he said shortly.

Magnanimous in victory, I thanked him warmly for his cooperation and assured him I appreciated his efforts.

Several days later my clerk entered my office to inform me that Mr. and Mrs. Zalenga wanted to see me.

"Send them in," I said. I assumed they had come to express their regret for Arnold's behavior and possibly to inquire about his suspension. It was soon apparent that that was not their purpose. In response to my invitation, they both sat down in a stiff, formal manner and stared at the wall. Somehow, I was not getting what the younger generation calls "good vibes." I had never met them before. As they were not facing me, I was able to scrutinize them without appearing rude.

Mrs. Zalenga, though no longer young, was still pretty. Her well-formed features, blond hair, and very fair, smooth skin were obviously the genetic source of Arnold's facial characteristics and coloring. It was difficult to evaluate Mr. Zalenga's contribution to Arnold's appearance. He was a handsome man with a strong, athletic build, but his skin, though smooth, was much darker than Arnold's, and his hair was black. For a moment I wondered if he might be Arnold's stepfather, then decided that, despite the differences, Arnold did resemble this man in some way. Perhaps it was a similarity in the eyes. Mr. Zalenga was conservatively dressed in a white shirt, a red and blue striped tie, and a neat, dark blue suit. It looked a little tight in the shoulders, somehow giving the impression that this was not his usual attire. Mrs. Zalenga was farther from me. I had a vague impression of a small, light-colored hat just partially concealing her wavy blond hair and a stylish tan coat concealing the rest of her attire.

Although they had requested to see me, apparently they were waiting for me to begin the conversation. "What can I do for you?" I said.

Mr. Zalenga turned toward me, though he still wasn't facing me directly. He appeared to be choosing his words carefully. "I know Arnold got into trouble. We had to go to the police station to pick him up, and you suspended him. All right. But at the police station they said they were all finished with him, and now we get a letter saying that we have to appear in court with Arnold." Now he looked straight at me. "What I want to know, Mr. Greenstein," he said, his voice rising, "is whose idea that was."

It sounded more like an accusation than a question. I surmised that he already knew whose idea it was and just wanted confirmation.

As I was trying to decide how to answer, I temporized. "You don't know?" I asked.

"No, I don't," he responded angrily, "but I sure intend to find out!"

He seemed to be controlling his indignation with some difficulty. I could see a rush of color coming to his face and penetrating his dark skin. I didn't think he was lying. Perhaps he suspected that I was involved in some way but not directly responsible. If he had thought I was, I felt sure that he would be attacking me verbally, maybe even physically. He was not very tall, but I could easily visualize him as a football player or possibly a wrestler when he was younger. Though the width of my desk was between us, he could reach me in an instant if he decided to do so. I wondered if I could hold him off long enough for my clerk to call the police. It wouldn't be easy. Besides, how was I going to alert my clerk? I wished that I had left my office door open.

"So you really want to know who was responsible," I repeated as I considered how to extricate myself from this predicament. I could lie. That was it. I could say I didn't know, then call him at home and admit my involvement at a safe distance. It would only be a temporary lie, and in a good cause—the preservation of my health. But then he would know that I had lied. Perhaps I could answer in some indirect fashion. I would minimize my participation and imply that the police had initiated this action. The more I considered such a craven solution, the angrier I got at myself. What was I thinking of? What would happen to my self-respect if I did that? If I couldn't accept responsibility, I had no business being here. What was I so afraid of anyway? So he might try to attack me, and I would defend myself. I was sure he didn't have a knife or gun. At worst I would probably suffer a few bruises.

"All right, I'll tell you who did it," I said resolutely. "I did."

"You did this?" he said incredulously. He half got out of his chair, then hesitated, as if my admission had caught him by surprise.

"Yes, I did it," I repeated, and added quickly, "and I did it for you."

This response really caused him to suspend whatever action he had intended to take. "How did you do it for me?" he demanded.

"Sit down and I'll tell you," I said firmly. He slowly settled back into his chair. "Yes, I requested that the police reopen the case. I did it for you and for your son. I am a father. I have two sons. If either one of my boys was involved in a crime like that, I would do everything within my power to make sure it never happened again. Have you any idea how much damage your son did? This was no childish prank. He left a classroom in shambles. Paint spilled all over, books destroyed, school records damaged, desks turned over. The students couldn't use that room for a whole day. And don't forget he broke a window to get in. After all that, Arnold was taken to the police station and you took him home. You haven't even been asked to pay for the damage and neither has he. Maybe you gave him a lecture, and that's it. Do you know what that means? It means he has learned he can commit a crime and get away with it, with just a slap on the wrist. In my opinion, that's how juvenile delinquents get started. And most criminals probably start as juvenile delinquents. When he gets a little older, maybe he'll steal a car. If he's still under seventeen, he may get away with that too. And when he's over seventeen, he might decide to rob a bank. And then, if he's caught, he'll be thrown in jail. Is that the kind of future you want for your son? It could happen, you know. I've seen how bad kids get started. After a serious offense like this, all they get is a lecture. Then they do something else and get another lecture, and pretty soon they begin to think that no one can do anything to them. I suspend them, the police pick them up and let them go, and that's all that happens. I'm not saying I know the answer, but that's not good enough. Our courts have to do more, and parents have to do more. I know that you and your wife are both working. Maybe you don't have much time for Arnold. Well, in my opinion, you'd better start spending some time with him before it's too late. What I've done is to see that Arnold has to go to court and face a judge. He won't go to jail or anything like that. He'll probably be put on probation. But maybe that will teach him something. I hope so. After that, it will be up to you."

There was silence for a moment. Mr. Zalenga was slumped back in his chair, his broad shoulders drooping a little. The anger seemed to have gone out of him. His wife, who had not said anything, looked at me through moist, glistening eyes as if about to burst into tears. Then he spoke up hesitantly. "Won't this give him a criminal record? He's only twelve years old."

"No, not a criminal record. He'll have a juvenile record. It will be erased when he is seventeen. The police have assured me of that. Look, I'm not trying to tell you that your son is a criminal. He's not the first boy to get in trouble. I haven't done this just to punish him. I think he should be punished, but I'm honestly trying to help him. I'm not talking to you just as a principal. I'm talking to you as a father who knows how hard it is to raise children these days. I hope it will never be necessary for me to have this kind of conference about your son again."

Mr. Zalenga rose slowly, started toward the door, then turned to me and put out his hand. "Thank you, Mr. Greenstein," he said quietly. His wife, who was right behind him, also offered her hand. "Good-bye," she said softly, "and thank you."

As they left, I felt good. They had thanked me, actually thanked me! I had turned away their wrath and changed it to gratitude.

And what was the outcome? Well, in a Hollywood movie the boy turns over a new leaf, becomes a model citizen, and even gets on the honor roll. But this wasn't Hollywood. It was real life. And in real life, as the boy gets older he often gets into more trouble. Then he goes to high school and gets even worse. Then he probably drops out of school, and then—who knows? I've learned that I don't. I've seen them go both ways. Some grow up to become solid, respectable citizens despite the dire predictions of their teachers—and some don't.

So what happened to Arnold? Hollywood! I could hardly believe it, but it's true, every word of it. He turned over a new leaf and became a model citizen—well, almost, anyway. His teacher informed me that not only was his behavior much better, but there was a marked improvement in his schoolwork. By the time the last marking period came around, he actually did make the honor roll—just barely, but he made it.

Would all this have happened without my intervention? Of course, I have no way of knowing. I had little contact with Arnold after seeing his parents, except for the lecture (I prefer to call it "sage counsel") that I gave him when he returned from his suspension. Eloquent though that was, I can't believe it caused this tranformation all by itself. Perhaps I had influenced his father, and he had done the rest. I don't think that Arnold was beaten and severely punished. In the few times I saw him after that, Arnold did not give me the impression of a boy who was behaving himself because he was afraid. Rather, he seemed to be actually proud of the improvement he had achieved in his conduct and his grades. I guess the compliments he received from me and from his teacher didn't hurt either.

Gratifying as was this turn of events, it did not signal an end to vandalism at our school. The problem remained, and it is prevalent throughout the school system. While the home and the school may not be doing as well as they should to improve the situation, I place a great deal of the blame upon our juvenile court system. Here's a recent statistic from our city records. Of 528 juvenile delinquency cases, more than sixty percent were not prosecuted. When juvenile offenders learn that their crimes go unpunished, they lose respect for the law and are very likely to commit further and more serious crimes. Obviously we can't put them in jail with adult criminals. And from what I have read, placing them in juvenile correctional institutions has not proven to be too effective either. There is a very real danger that the young and inexperienced offender will learn all the wrong things from the older inmates in either institution.

I have an alternative proposal—that those juveniles found guilty of vandalism, or other crimes for that matter, be placed under court supervision and be sentenced to do some constructive work to compensate for the harm they have caused, and that a parole officer be assigned to supervise the work and see that it is done. This may sound expensive, but I'm sure it would be cheaper than maintaining correctional institutions, and if it were effective in deterring future delinquency and crime, it would indeed be a bargain.

17. All the World's a Stage

Our Parents Club had sponsored a collection of winter clothes for needy families. One boy, whom I had personally outfitted from this depository, returned a week later to request additional clothing. I asked him to bring a note from his mother stating his needs. Although I had specified that a note written in Spanish would be acceptable, his mother, in her rather dubious English, tried to explain that he needed warm pants for the winter. She wrote, "If you have pants he need pants. He has much shirt but no hot pants."

We had a young teacher named Mr. Langfelder, willing, industrious, punctual, conscientious, always trying to please—but, unfortunately, not very able, especially in controlling a class. I kept hoping he would improve as he gained experience. After a while, as I saw that my hopes weren't being realized, I tried to keep him out of a classroom whenever possible.

He was one of three auxiliary teachers with no classrooms of their own. I had set up a schedule for them to assist other teachers by grading papers, taking small groups for tutoring, and making themselves generally useful in whatever way the classroom teacher desired. When we were short of substitutes, which was often, I would have one of the auxiliary teachers fill the vacancy. Mr. Langfelder was always the last one I would utilize for this purpose. Above all, I avoided placing him in an upper-grade classroom as I knew our seventh and eighth graders would tear him apart—figuratively, of course. He was singularly unsuccessful even with the small groups of primary students he tutored. I would sometimes visit the lunchroom, where he took his students, to see how he was getting along. It was not a pleasant sight—at least not to a principal. He would be perspiring, shouting, and trying to explain the lesson to whoever would listen. Unfortunately, no one seemed to be listening. Apparently oblivious to the fact that the youngsters were paying more attention to each other than to him, Mr. Langfelder continued doggedly with his exposition.

In all fairness, I should mention that he did not have a degree in education and had had no previous teaching experience. This was the time of a teacher shortage, and the board was forced to hire as substitutes any college graduates regardless of their course of study.

As Mr. Langfelder seemed anxious to improve, I often spent time with him after school, trying to give him some helpful hints on how to control a class. He listened attentively, and usually, at least when I observed him, endeavored to implement some of my suggestions. Yet the tactics which I had found successful never appeared to work for him. I suggested that his practice of attempting to drown out the noise of the class by shouting above it was obviously ineffective.

"You'd do better," I said, "if you just stopped the lesson till they quieted down. You might try writing the names of the troublemakers on the blackboard. You don't have to tell them what you're going to do with the names. Let them think about it. And try to show some self-confidence. Act as if you're in control even if you don't feel that way. It's like a poker game. You have to outbluff them."

"You mean you want me to be an actor?" he protested. "I'm sorry, but I don't think I can do that. I can't pretend to be something I'm not. If I wanted to be an actor, I'd go on the stage."

"Yes, I want you to be an actor," I retorted. "Every successful teacher is really an actor in a way. When a kid misbehaves, he's often acting too. He's putting on a show for his friends. When you get right down to it, we're all playing a role. Here at school I have to act like a principal. That's not the way I am at home or with my friends."

"I'm afraid I'm not like that," he said. "I'm basically an honest person. I can only be myself."

I saw that my meaning was lost on him and gave up. At the end of the school year, his teaching career was terminated by mutual consent.

Several years later an incident occurred which reminded me of my conversation with Mr. Langfelder. I believe it demonstrated that one can achieve a favorable outcome with a good script and a convincing performance. The fact that I was personally very successful in effecting this outcome has, of course, nothing to do with why I tell this story.

Shortly before graduation Mr. Rasmussen, an eighth-grade teacher, came to see me during the lunch hour. He was obviously worried.

"I don't think you can help me," he said soberly, "but I decided I should report this anyway. One of my students has threatened to slash all of the tires on my car right after graduation."

"Did someone hear him say it?"

"No, he told me so himself."

"Well, kids say a lot of things. Do you really think he was serious?"

"Oh, he was serious all right. I don't really understand it. I've never had much trouble with him. I even thought he liked me. I reprimanded him a few days ago for not doing his homework, but we didn't get into an argument or anything like that. And now he tells me that he'll slash my tires. And he means it too."

"If he really intends to do it, why should he tell you about it? Doesn't he realize that you'd report it to me?"

"He doesn't care. He figures that once he graduates there's nothing we can do to him. I thought of calling the police, but I don't know how one can report a crime that hasn't been committed yet. Maybe you could hold up his diploma."

"I could, but I don't think that would be very effective. I'd have to explain it to his mother, and since, as you say, he hasn't done anything yet, he'd probably deny the whole thing. Parents are sometimes hard to convince. Graduation is very important to them, you know. Besides, unless I fail him, I'll have to give him the diploma sooner or later, and if I kept him out of the graduation, he'd really want to get revenge. How are his grades?"

"Good enough to pass. I guess there's nothing to do except wait and see what happens."

"Of course there's something I can do. As a matter of fact, I could call the police, but I'd rather take care of it myself. I'll put a good scare into him."

"That won't work," said Mr. Rasmussen. "He's a big, tough kid. He doesn't scare easily. He practically told me that he's not afraid of me or the principal."

I resented the implication that I couldn't intimidate an eighth-grade student. "We'll see about that," I said. "Just let me take care of it. There's something I've got to get straight first. As far as you're concerned, this is a serious threat. Is that right?"

"Yes. Certainly."

"In that case, I'll have to make an official report to the superintendent. A threat to a teacher is considered an assault. Of course, it's your car he threatened and not you personally. Still, I'd better play safe and report it anyway. And don't worry. Nothing's going to happen."

"I hope so. I'd sure hate to have to buy four new tires." He shook his head despairingly and left.

I called the district office. The superintendent was out, so I reported the matter to the head clerk. She said she would give him the message, and she agreed that this constituted a verbal assault. "You'll have to make a written report to the general superintendent," she said.

"I know."

"In triplicate."

"I know."

"And an accident report."

"An accident report? How can I do that? Nothing happened."

"I'm sorry, but that's the rule. Any assault on a teacher must be reported to the general superintendent and must be accompanied by an accident report."

Rules are rules. I went to work on my report to the general superintendent. By the time I had completed it, I was getting quite angry at this boy whom I didn't even know who had made all this necessary. I became even angrier as I began the accident report. I called the district office again.

"About this accident report," I said to the head clerk, "how am I supposed to fill it out? It says here, 'Was first aid given?' and 'Was the injured person directed to see a doctor?' All that happened is that a kid threatened to damage a teacher's car. Now how am I supposed to answer all this garbage?"

"Do the best you can," she replied unsympathetically.

The report form has since been revised and now states that the symbol N/A may be substituted if the required information is not applicable to the accident. At that time, however, the instructions clearly stated that all questions must be answered. It wasn't easy to frame sensible responses to items requesting immediate cause of accident, underlying cause of accident, physical condition of injured person prior to time of injury, and how this accident could have been prevented. I don't remember what I wrote, but I know I got a little tired of explaining that the injured person was not a person but a car and that it hadn't been injured, at least not yet. Well, this boy was going to pay for what he had put me through, I resolved.

After completing the paper work, I called his mother and asked her to see me right after school. I then notified Mr. Rasmussen that I wanted to see him and the boy in my office after he dismissed his class.

While I awaited their arrival, I reflected upon the newspaper articles which periodically revealed the number of assaults upon teachers that occurred each year. These statistics were obtained from the records of the Board of Education. An editorial comment usually followed. It insinuated that, although many teachers are in constant fear of bodily harm, many assaults probably go unreported because some principals, concerned about protecting their own image, intimidate teachers and persuade them not to publicize these incidents. As I have never discussed this matter with other principals, I cannot comment on the validity of these charges. However, let me go on record to state that in this particular year the number of reported assaults was augmented by one in which the threat of bodily harm was to a teacher's car, and that the teacher himself was at no time in any personal danger. Statistics can lie both ways.

At the appointed time, they were all in my office. Mr. Rasmussen introduced the student, whom I didn't recall having seen before. "This is Clayton, the young man I spoke to you about," he said.

I looked at Clayton curiously. He was tall, well-developed, of medium-brown complexion, his dark-brown eyes unblinking as he stared at me impassively. I turned to his mother who was standing there nervously and invited her to sit down.

"What's he done?" she inquired apprehensively.

"We'll get to that in a minute," I said. I indicated to Mr. Rasmussen that he also should take a seat but left Clayton standing.

"So you're the young man who intends to damage Mr. Rasmussen's car. Is that right?"

"I didn't say I was going to do it. I said someone was going to do it."

"That's not true," interrupted Mr. Rasmussen dispassionately. "He told me he would do it."

"I see. Well, just for the sake of argument, if you didn't intend to do it, who was the 'someone'?"

He didn't reply. He glanced at his mother, then looked away. I could see that her presence was making him uncomfortable. I didn't mind that at all.

"I think it's pretty obvious that you were the 'someone.' There's no one else involved as far as you know, is there, Mr. Rasmussen?" Mr. Rasmussen shook his head. "So the fact is that you planned to slash all of his tires. That could cost a lot of money to replace."

His mother spoke up. "He wouldn't do a thing like that. He's not a bad boy. Maybe he was only joking."

"It doesn't sound very funny to me. Were you joking, Clayton?"

"I guess so," he replied unconvincingly.

I turned to the teacher. "Did you think he was joking, Mr. Rasmussen?"

"No, I didn't," he responded.

"Did you hear that, Clayton? Your teacher didn't think you were joking. Maybe you should have laughed when you said it. Let me tell you something about joking. If you got on an airplane and said you had a bomb in your pocket—just a joke—do you know what would happen?"

"No," said Clayton.

"They would take you right off that plane and to the police station. That's what would happen. There are some things we don't joke about. Now, I don't believe you were joking, but let's just suppose you were. Mr. Rasmussen took it very seriously. He came to me and reported it as a threat. The Board of Education takes things like that very seriously. Any threat to a teacher must be reported. I had to call my superintendent. I had to notify our legal department. I had to write a letter to the general superintendent. That's a lot of work. I don't like doing a lot of extra work just because someone makes a bad joke. I'm just mad enough to call the police and have you taken down to the station." (Though I had no intention of doing so, this was not really a bluff. I was sure if I called them, the police would cooperate. Of course he would then be released in the custody of his mother.)

"Please don't call the police," pleaded his mother. "I'm sure he didn't mean it."

Clayton's composure had dissolved. "No, I didn't mean it," he echoed. "I was mad, and it just came out that way. I wasn't really going to do anything to his car."

"It doesn't matter whether you meant it. You said it, and that's what counts. Mr. Rasmussen can testify to that, and you've admitted it to me. I'm sure you won't do anything to his car, because I can guarantee that you'd be in big trouble if you did. Let me tell you a little story, Clayton—a true story. About five or six years ago—I think that's before you were here, Mr. Rasmussen—a boy threatened me right here on our playground. He wasn't one of our students. He didn't touch me, didn't harm me in any way, but he was arrested and prosecuted by the lawyers of the Board of Education. He went to prison for three months." (This was the truth, though not the whole truth. I didn't bother to mention that Limpy, the boy to whom I was referring, was over seventeen years old and was therefore tried as an adult, and that Clayton couldn't possibly suffer a similar fate.)

I let this sink in for a minute and then continued, "I want to make one thing very clear to you. If anything happens to Mr. Rasmussen's car—even if you don't do it—you'll be held responsible."

"How could I be responsible if I didn't do it? What if someone else damages his car? I couldn't be blamed for that."

"Oh, yes, you could. And you would be. You're the only suspect we've got." I turned to the teacher. "Has anybody else made any threats to you, Mr. Rasmussen?"

"No, they haven't," he responded dutifully.

"There's your answer. If I were you, Clayton, I'd keep an eye on that car and make sure nothing happens to it, because if anything does, you'll be picked up by the police immediately. I'll see to that."

"He won't touch that car," his mother assured me. "Please let me take him home. I'll talk to him."

"No, honest—I won't do anything. I wasn't going to anyway." said Clayton. He seemed almost ready to beg. He didn't look nearly as formidable as when he came in.

I was satisfied that I had accomplished my purpose. However, I had one more thing to add. "By the way, Mr. Rasmussen told me that you had the idea that once you graduated we couldn't do anything to you. Well, I suppose you're going to the high school in this neighborhood. The principal happens to be a good friend of mine, and if you think I can't get you there, you're very much mistaken. Is that clear?"

"Yes, sir," he said softly.

I turned to his mother. "I know you've been looking forward to his graduation, so I'm going to let him graduate on stage—though I really shouldn't." I hadn't intended to deprive him of that privilege, and I didn't think Mr. Rasmussen would request it, but it didn't hurt to establish my generosity.

"Thank you," said his mother, obviously relieved.

"Thank you," mumbled Clayton.

"Thank you," said Mr. Rasmussen.

I felt pretty good.

18. Race Riot

We had acquired our first teacher aide. She was young, attractive, and efficient, and I had many requests for her services. It became a standing joke among faculty members that some of the male teachers were more interested in her physical attributes than her assistance in the classroom. A note from our most eligible bachelor struck me as substantiating that allegation. It read, "May I use Miss Sanchez for a few minutes?"

Having attended integrated schools, having taught in one, and having been the principal of one, it isn't suprising that I have often expressed some opinions on the subject. After all, I know a lot of people who, though they have had none of these experiences, are more than ready to give their views on this controversial issue at great length and with great vehemence. It is not difficult to make a case either way. All one has to do is to select those incidents which reinforce one's particular bias and ignore those which support a contrary position. And that, I have noticed, is what most people do. As I also have a bias, I don't know if I'll be able to present a balanced statement, but I'll try.

To begin with, the question can be considered from two separate viewpoints, as a moral issue and as a practical problem in education. Morally it seems simple enough—or it was until it was complicated by the advent of busing for integration—especially forced busing. I, for one, can see no justification for denying a child the right to attend a school because of his race or color, or for maintaining segregated schools by gerrymandering school districts. However, when children are bused (voluntarily) to schools in other neighborhoods, we have to examine the purpose a little more closely. If it will relieve overcrowding in certain schools and at the same time restore the membership of underutilized schools, it can be justified both educationally and on economic grounds. I have seen teachers struggle with large classes, sometimes with as many as fifty students. They often came to me in despair protesting that it was almost impossible for them to teach.

About all I was able to give them was sympathy. Unfortunately, most of the neighboring schools were also overcrowded. At one time, I managed to persuade our superintendent to permit voluntary transfers to an adjacent school whose membership had been declining. It didn't help too much. Most of our students didn't want to leave as it meant a much longer walk for them. Busing children out of the neighborhood was not even considered. Eventually we did have an addition built, but that took years. In the meantime, both the teachers and the students suffered.

On the other hand, if the purpose of busing (and I'm still talking about voluntary busing) is purely and simply to integrate schools, it still may be morally justifiable though economically it becomes questionable. In a broader context, from the standpoint of giving children an opportunity to learn to live together in our pluralistic society, it can also be considered educational. However, if the goal is to improve the skills of minority students in reading and arithmetic, I doubt very much that integration per se will achieve that result. The studies I have seen which attempted to determine the effect of integration upon students' achievement have not convinced me that any improvement occurred which could not be attributed to other factors. I am hardly prepared to tell a black parent that his child will learn more if he sits next to a white child. This is an insulting inference, and he is not likely to accept it—nor do I. The reason a black parent wants his child transferred is that he is convinced the other school has better facilities, better teachers, better discipline, or a better educational program. Sometimes that is the case and sometimes it isn't, but he believes it anyway.

Now what about forced busing? Well, that's a different story altogether. It may be the law of the land, but that doesn't make it right. I am quite ready to compliment the boy scout for taking the little old lady across the street, but not when he drags her across even though she doesn't want to go. I have heard black leaders speak out strongly in favor of forced busing as the only way to successfully integrate our schools. I wonder whom they are leading. It is not only white parents who oppose forced busing. Hispanics are vehemently opposed, and none of the black parents to whom I have spoken (and I've spoken to a fair number) favored it. Some of them want the right to send their child to what they consider a better school, but even they would like to have a say in the matter. Others are satisfied with the school their children are attending or, even if they aren't, don't want them traveling halfway across the city to an unfamiliar environment. The neighborhood school concept is not merely a buzzword for white bigots.

When I purchased a home, a prime consideration was its proximity to a school. In fact, while making my decision as to which of three available homes to purchase, I reflected that my children would have to make their way to and from school twice daily during severe winter weather, and I deliberately selected the one that was within easiest walking distance.

There is another aspect of forced busing which bothers me. It seems to imply that our nation consists of only two groups, black and white. Yet we also have Mexicans, Puerto Ricans, Chinese, Japanese, Indians, and many distinct European nationalities. Most of them live in their own communities by choice. They are comfortable with people who share a common culture and sometimes even the common language of their origin. Forced integration would involve splitting up the children of these groups too. We will be taking them out of their own neighborhoods where their parents want them to remain. The moral issue here becomes the use of force to deny these people their individual rights.

It is true that blacks have often been segregated by design rather than by choice, though the situation is no longer as prevalent as it once was. Where open housing is still not a reality, that is the area in which the law should concentrate its efforts rather than attacking those schools in which segregation is de facto rather than de jure. Besides, if each school is to have a quota of black and white students, it seems logical that it should also be required to have a certain number of Mexicans, Chinese, Poles, Lithuanians, and so on. If this sound ludicrous, I submit that forcing black or white students to attend schools far from their own neighborhoods regardless of their wishes is equally so.

I am sure there are inequities in our school system. However, to inflict a cure that is worse than the disease is a questionable solution. I am not one to expound on motherhood and the American flag, but I have to be concerned when our government dictates where children—especially little children—attend school regardless of their place of residence, their individual needs, or the wishes of the children themselves. (Does anyone ever ask them what they want?) I wonder if this is really so far different from the wholesale movement and redistribution of workers and their families which we are told takes place in communist countries.

My opposition to forced busing does not alter my belief that children who attend an integrated school are more likely to shed the prejudices which they may have acquired from their parents and learn to coexist in our multiethnic society. A nice theory, one might concede, but does it actually happen? As the principal of an integrated school, I was provided with a real-life opportunity to study the matter. When I had time, I tried to observe our seventh and eighth graders on the playground as these were the only grades that were really integrated. While I did see some white, Hispanic, and black students play together, I had the impression that the majority stayed with members of their own group. On the other hand, they did not noticeably draw apart and ignore each other. There appeared to be a general acceptance of the fact that they all belonged there, and I seldom observed any real friction. Of course there were occasional fights—these happen at any school—though when the combatants were sent to me for discipline, I noticed that they were usually both black, both white, or both Latino. The interracial fight was the exception rather than the rule. When one did occur, it was naturally more noticeable and potentially more dangerous. Parental reactions were likely to be more violent, other students might enter the conflict, and, as I've previously mentioned, the gangs sometimes became involved.

How did the students really feel about each other? I wasn't sure, and I wanted to find out. Therefore, I prepared a questionnaire for our seventh and eighth grades. I personally distributed copies to each class, instructed the students to complete them honestly without identifying themselves by name, and collected them myself so that none of the teachers would be able to influence the results in any way. These were the questions:

1. How do you feel about attending an integrated (mixed races and nationalities) school?
2. How do your parents feel about it?
3. Has your opinion about children of a different race or color changed since you have attended this school? (Explain your answer.)
4. If you had a choice, would you prefer to attend an integrated school or one that is not integrated? (Explain your answer.)
5. Give any additional comments or opinions.

There were 190 responses. In the answer to the first question, 157 students expressed a positive or good feeling, 23 said they didn't know or didn't care, and only 10 gave negative replies. This means that 86 percent responded favorably while only 5 percent indicated dissatisfaction, a pretty impressive confirmation and much greater than I had anticipated. Some of the answers are worth repeating. Where necessary, I have corrected the spelling and grammar:

> I like it very much. All the kids are nice to me and kind. I think if I would move out of this neighborhood and away from this school, I would miss my friends very much.
>
> I think it is a privilege to attend a school that has so many people from different countries. In a way you are learning more than just what is required.
>
> I think it is a good experience because your parents may fill your head with ideas about white, black, Mexican, Indian, Jew, and you may be all against them. But when you go and mix with people of other races you may think different. All my life I was taught to hate white people. I never went to an integrated school before. I had heard lies about people of all races. But now most of my friends are white.
>
> I feel if kids with different skin want to come to a school to get a good education why can't they get it? After all, people with different color of skin are my best friends.
>
> I feel it's my pleasure to go to this school and to meet different kinds of people to go to school with. It's a big world and you can't live in it without meeting these people.
>
> It is a good feeling to know that you go to a school that is of all nationalities. It means that if we go to school together, we can live together.

In the interest of fair play, I would give equal time (or space) to the negative replies, but that isn't possible. As I said, there were only ten, and only half of them offered an explanation. Of those that did have a comment, these were the most comprehensible:

> I feel that there should be a school for whites and a school for blacks.
>
> I don't like it because it seems as though the white teachers like the white children the most.
>
> I do not hardly like it. Some are nice and some are mean.

I was also surprised to learn that most of the students believed their parents approved of their attendance at an integrated school. From my contact with the parents, I would not have thought so. I should have realized that the ones I usually saw were those I sent for or those who came to me with complaints. They were not necessarily typical. At any rate, 97 or 51 percent of the students thought their parents' attitude was favorable, 48 (25 percent) did not know their parents' opinion, 25 (13 percent) believed their parents didn't care one way or the other, and only 20 (11 percent) thought their parents disapproved of an integrated school. Here are a few of the replies:

> They think like me that all persons are equal and each has a right to learn. And different kinds of people can work and get along with each other.
>
> My parents feel the same way because I asked them and they said we're all the same and are equal. They tell me when I ask, "Do unto others as you would have others do unto you. If you don't learn to like different people, they won't learn to like you."
>
> They like me to go to an integrated school so that I do not grow up to hate any person.

These are some of the negative responses:

> My parents don't like it at all. My father said it would be better if they put all the black children in a different school.
>
> My parents don't want me to go to an integrated school because they say white people don't want us to go to school with their children.
>
> My parents don't really feel exactly the way I do. They're against certain races.

I was particularly interested in the responses to the third question, did attendance at our school cause a change in the students' attitude? While their answers indicated approval of integration, 93 students (49 percent) stated that their opinions had not undergone any change either because they had previously attended an integrated school, or because they had "always felt this way." However, in many instances their replies showed that there had been a reinforcement of their positive attitude. I categorized 35 of the answers as "not clear" because, though generally positive in nature, they did not specify whether any change had taken place. Two students did not answer the question at all. (If I omitted this information, someone would be sure to notice that the total number of replies did not add up to 190.) However, 55 students (29 percent) affirmed that a favorable change had indeed taken place. I also thought it was significant that the races were about equally represented in this group, and there was a similarity in the responses regardless of the student's race. Here are some of the answers:

> Yes. When I came to this school, I put labels on some races. Now I know it was wrong. I found out all the people are the same, no one inferior or superior.
>
> Yes, because I've found out that some of the white people are friendly and not prejudiced and I like that kind.
>
> Yes, my opinion has changed. When I came to this school I thought black people were mean, but I found that some of every race is good at times and bad at times including myself.
>
> I'm proud to say my opinions have changed for the better. I think everybody's opinions have changed. After being in contact with different people and different races they're bound to change their opinion.

Only five students (less than 3 percent) indicated that a negative change of attitude had taken place. Here are some of their replies:

> Yes, it has gotten a little out of hand and not just by the Negro race either. It is all the races.
>
> Yes, because too much has happened at this school, all fights and everything."

In response to the fourth question, whether the student would select an integrated school if given the choice, 130 students (68 percent) said they would, 37 (19 percent) indicated they would choose a nonintegrated school, and the rest either expressed no preference or did not answer clearly. It should be noted that a number of those who opted for the nonintegrated school affirmed that they liked their present school but wanted to try what would be, for them, a new experience. As the comments, on the whole, were similar in nature to the ones I've already quoted, I'll only select one which best expressed the general attitude:

> I would like an integrated school. I don't want to grow up ignorant about other races. I want to learn to cope, live with,

> and understand other races, nationalities, and people of different religions.

The fifth question which invited additional comments or opinions was left blank by most of the students. The sentiments expressed by those who did reply were mainly repetitious. One student, however, summarized the situation in words I would not try to improve upon. The student wrote:

> Your color do not get you nowhere. I do not judge nobody by their color. I like people of any race. Some people do not like blacks and some do not like whites. I like them all. It is a part of growing up in life.

So much for a long introduction to a short story: I was seated in my office during the lunch hour, munching a sandwich, when Mrs. Berta, one of our sixth-grade teachers, rushed in. "There's been some trouble," she said. "Some of my girls were beaten up by a group of high school students."

"Near the school?"

"About a block north of the school. It happened just a few minutes ago. One of my girls ran back and told me about it. They were on their way home for lunch when some black girls attacked them."

"Where is the girl now?"

"She went home. She said her mother is expecting her. She was pretty upset, but I don't think she was injured."

"Send her to the office when she gets back from lunch. I'll go outside and take a look." I put down my sandwich and hurried into the street. It seemed pretty quiet. I walked a block, and then another at a quick pace. No sign of any students. It was fifteen minutes into the lunch hour, and those who were going home (some ate lunch at school) had already reached their destination—at least I hoped they had. I turned around and went back to the school. As I entered the door, a teacher approached me.

"Did you hear what happened? Some of our white kids got beat up by a group of black high school students."

"Yes, I heard. I was just outside to check, but I didn't see them. I believe they're gone now."

I returned to my office and picked up my unfinished sandwich. I had taken two bites when the phone rang.

"It's for you, Mr. Greenstein," said the clerk.

I picked up the phone. "I heard there's been some racial trouble at the school," a woman's voice said.

"Where did you hear that?" I said cautiously.

"One of my neighbors told me that a bunch of high school students have been going around the school and beating up our kids."

"Who is this speaking?" I asked.

"Mrs. Hernandez. I've got three kids in school."

"I was just outside, Mrs. Hernandez, and there was no sign of any trouble. I did get a report of something happening, but I can't check it out till after lunch. I assure you I'll look into it."

"Well, I know what I heard, and I'm not taking any chances. I've got three little kids. They're staying home this afternoon."

"That's up to you. Be sure they have notes explaining their absence when they come back."

Two minutes later there was another call. "What's this about a race riot at the school?" inquired a male voice.

"I don't know anything about a race riot. I had a report that there was a little trouble and I'm looking into it."

"I want to know if I should send my boy to school this afternoon."

"That's up to you. As far as I know, whatever happened is over now."

"Well, maybe I'll keep him home anyway. He'll be back in school in the morning."

There were three or four more calls of a similar nature. My answers, as before, were noncommittal. As yet, I really didn't know what had occurred. I thought of calling the police, but I needed more information. I prepared three copies of a note to send to all the classrooms at the beginning of the afternoon session: It read: "I have been informed that some of our students were assaulted by some high school students during the lunch hour. Please send to the office immediately any student who was the victim of such an attack."

I left my half-eaten sandwich and walked onto the playground. A number of students were already there. Everything looked normal. I didn't see any strangers.

As I returned to my office, another teacher stopped me in the hallway. "I thought you should know. A gang of black kids were beating up our kids during the lunch hour not far from the school."

"Yes, I heard about it," I said wearily. "Thank you."

The phone was ringing when I entered the office. The clerk answered. "For me?" I asked.

"Yes. A woman wants to know if there's school this afternoon."

"Of course there's school this afternoon," I said shortly. I picked up the phone and repeated my assertion in a more diplomatic tone.

"I want to know if I should send my kids. Do you think it's safe?"

"As far as I know it is."

"Well—O.K. I guess I'll send them. I don't like them to miss school."

"That's fine," I said. I felt like telling her that I really didn't care one way or another if she sent her children. At the moment, I had other things to worry about. Not a very charitable thought, but I was not in a happy frame of mind.

The admission bell finally rang. As the children started to come in, I recruited three messengers from the room across the hall, instructed them each to take one floor, and to deliver my note to the teachers right away.

"There's a girl waiting to see you," said my clerk when I returned.

"Send her in."

The girl entered. She was thin, not very tall, fair-skinned, with greenish-brown eyes and long auburn hair that reached to her shoulders. "Mrs. Berta said you wanted to see me," she said.

"Oh, are you one of the girls that was beat up during lunch?"

"Yes."

"What's your name?"

"Loretta."

"All right, Loretta. Tell me exactly what happened." Finally I was going to get some facts.

"My girl friend Nancy and I were walking home with my little brother Timmy."

As she spoke, I saw a small boy enter the outer office. "That wouldn't be Timmy, would it?"

She turned around to look. "Yes, that's him," she said.

"Timmy, come in here," I called. "Go on with your story," I said after I had shown him to a seat.

"Well, we were walking, and these three big girls started coming toward us, and one of them says, 'What are you looking at?' and I said I wasn't looking at anything. I had a big comb in my hand and another girl says, 'What are you doing with that comb?' Then the first girl says, 'Here, give me that comb,' and I said, 'It's my comb. Why should I give it to you?' So she grabbed the comb out of my hand and slapped me."

"These three girls—were they black?"

"Yes."

"Are you sure you didn't say anything to insult them or get them mad?"

"No, honest. I wouldn't do that. Besides, I was too scared."

"All right, what happened next?"

"Well, Nancy said, 'Why don't you give her back her comb?' so she slapped Nancy. She said, 'Mind your own business,' and she slapped her hard, and Nancy's nose started bleeding."

At this point we were interrupted by my clerk. She knocked softly on the open door. "There's a parent in the office. She heard there was some trouble and she wants to take her kids home. What should I tell her?"

"I guess that's her privilege. Send for her children and let her take them home."

I turned back to Loretta. "Go on."

"Nancy started crying, so I said, 'What did you have to hit her for?' so she slapped me again. Then Timmy said, 'Don't hit my sister,' didn't you, Timmy?"

Timmy nodded as Loretta continued, "And then one of them slapped Timmy."

"Did they hurt you, Timmy?" I asked.

"Not much," he said.

"I guess they would have hit us some more," said Loretta, "if my friends hadn't come and chased them away."

"The girls from your room were able to chase those big girls away?"

"Oh, no. Not from my room. These were some big black girls from eighth grade. They're my friends."

"I see. How do you feel now?"

"Not too bad. I'm still shaking a little."

"I don't blame you. I'm sorry you were hurt. If you ever see those girls again or find out their names, let me know and I'll call the police. How is Nancy?"

"I don't know. She didn't come to school this afternoon. Outside of her nose bleeding, I don't think she was hurt much."

"Did they hit anyone else? Was anyone else attacked that you know of?"

"I don't know. I ran back to school to tell Mrs. Berta what happened. Then I went home and told my mother. She didn't want me to go back to school, but I told her I was all right."

"Did you see any other high school boys or girls around before or after this happened?"

"No, just those three."

"Well, tell your mother I'm sorry about all this, and if we ever catch those girls, I'll see that they're punished. At least, it's nice to know that your friends from eighth grade helped you. By the way, what happened to your comb?"

"Oh, I've got it. The girl who took it just threw it on the street and I picked it up."

"All right. You may both go back to your rooms now."

As I waited for a further response to my note, two more parents came to pick up their children. They had heard about the race riot. I didn't argue with them. That was their prerogative, I figured. I still didn't know what else had occurred. With three teachers informing me about the attacks and all those parents calling, there must have been other incidents. After about ten minutes, when no more students showed up, I sent the note around again. Then I remembered that Nancy, Loretta's girl friend who had suffered a bloody nose, had stayed home. There could very well be others who had been injured and had not come back to school that afternoon. I would have to wait till the next morning to find out.

I sent the note around again the following morning, and Nancy, who had returned to school, came to the office. She was all right, she told me. She was susceptible to nosebleeds, and she had been frightened, but she felt better now. Her account of what had transpired was essentially the same as Loretta's.

No other incidents were reported.

That was our race riot.

19. Discipline: The Perennial Problem

Time does not treat everyone alike. When I saw my colleagues once a month at district meetings, it seemed to me that some of them were aging prematurely—a reaction to the stresses and strains of their occupation, no doubt. I hoped I was not being similarly affected. A conversation I had with one of our students was not reassuring.

I was walking in the hall when a boy, about twelve years of age, addressed me. He had been contemplating a brass plaque affixed to the wall. "Sir, how old is the school?" he asked.

Pleased by his interest in historical data, I paused to reply. "Many years ago the school became overcrowded even as it is today, so they knocked out the wall and built an addition. That plaque commemorates the construction of the addition in 1939, but the original building was erected in 1903."

The boy was silent momentarily as he absorbed this information. Then he turned to me again and inquired respectfully, "Sir, were you the first principal?"

There is a well-known story about the great rabbi Hillel who lived several thousand years ago. When challenged by an unbeliever to explain the Bible while standing on one foot (that is, very briefly), he replied, "That's easy. 'Love thy neighbor.' All the rest is commentary." If I had to come up with a simple maxim for controlling a class, I might say, "Not by fear, but by respect." It's not as good as Hillel's, and it does require commentary, but then, with all due respect, Hillel never had to teach one of our seventh- or eighth-grade classes. I don't mean to belittle the travails of our primary teachers. I can recall a second-grade class that could have made a strong man weep.

As this is not a textbook, I suppose I could have avoided writing this chapter. Having presented my views on a number of educational topics, however, I feel obligated to say a few words—well, more than a few—about a problem that vexes so many teachers so much of the time. I've alluded to the subject before, even as far back as the first chapter when I cited a number of the "don'ts" which I consider important, so some repetition is likely to creep in. The charitable reader will, I hope, accept this as one of the inevitable symptoms of advancing age. Better still, he might look upon it as recapitulation for greater effect. As for the uncharitable reader, may he spend eternity teaching a class composed of a select group of students whose exploits are still vividly remembered by their former teachers as well as by me.

I can't offer any brilliant solutions to the problem of discipline. I learned by experience, mostly through trial and error. It was a little like learning to ride a bicycle. One day I suddenly seemed to get the hang of it, and then I wondered why it had taken me so long. However, while there is no substitute for experience, I believe that college education courses do not prepare their students adequately for what they will face in the classroom—at least they didn't when I went to school.

I attended a good college. I studied child psychology, theories of learning, and teaching methods, and absorbed a great deal of other valid and useful information—and some that was neither. We spent a lot of time learning to make lesson plans. In later years, I found that a good lesson plan does prevent discipline problems (though I never employed the complicated, time-consuming formula we were required to use in college). If the teacher can stimulate the students and maintain their interest, they are less likely to get into mischief. When students get bored or restless, some of them are inclined to engage in activities that are not educational in nature. However, a good plan is of little value if the teacher can't command the attention of the students to begin with, or, worse still, if there is so much noise that they can't hear the lesson. This problem was seldom discussed in my college classes. It should have been. I would say that a whole semester should be devoted to the subject of discipline. Obviously I can't cover it in one chapter.

Aspiring teachers ought to be informed that unless they can control the class they will be unsuccessful and perspiring teachers. Also (and principals will bless me for saying this) they should be taught how to keep an attendance book, prepare the monthly summary, write an accident report, and perform the other clerical functions which are part of the job.

Though I believe that some schools arrange to have their students observe good teachers in action, I never had that opportunity. I did have a semester of practice teaching prior to graduation. I assume that is a requirement at all schools. However, although the teacher whose class I took over monitored my performance, I never observed hers. I had a humbling experience at that time which should have forewarned me of the difficult year that was to follow.

I was teaching an eighth-grade history class. I had prepared my lesson well, and everything was going beautifully. The students were attentive, they raised their hands eagerly to recite or to ask questions, and I couldn't help wondering if the gray-haired old lady in whose room I was doing my practice teaching was jealous. I hoped not. I felt a little sorry for her. There she sat in the last seat of the last row grading her papers and hardly paying attention. Yet she couldn't help noticing how the students responded to my scintillating lesson. Here I was, just a practice teacher, probably doing a better job than this teacher with many year's experience who was almost ready for retirement. Then, one day, this unobtrusive little old lady slipped unobtrusively out of the room. For a few minutes the lesson went on as before. Then one student turned around and noticed that the teacher was gone. He whispered something to a classmate who also turned to look. Suddenly the students started talking to each other, a few spit balls flew across the room, and my beautiful lesson began to fall apart. Some students still tried to listen and to participate, but they were outnumbered. As I desperately shouted for the class to be quiet and wondered what was happening to me, the door opened and the little old lady returned—and almost miraculously order was restored.

How did this aging, gray-haired woman establish such control? Obviously not by superior strength. Of course this occurred many years ago, in the days when teachers knew how to discipline a class. Well, maybe so. However, about ten years later I volunteered to accept a practice teacher. One day this young teacher asked me if I would mind leaving the room while he conducted the lesson. My presence, he said, made him self-conscious. I had papers to grade and could work on them more comfortably in the teachers' room, so I was glad to oblige. It was a good class, and I didn't think my presence was really necessary. On my return, as I approached the room, I heard loud noises emanating from that direction. I opened the door and observed several students scurrying to their seats. The incident brought back memories. It was déjà vu in reverse. The wheel had turned full circle. I hoped I wasn't beginning to resemble a little old lady.

Well, there are two conclusions to draw from that chronicle: first—I know I keep repeating this, but it is very important—the value of experience; and second, that a substitute teacher operates at a great disadvantage. Both undeniably true, yet not necessarily so—by which I mean there are exceptions. Teaching is an art, not a science, and individual differences are as pronounced among teachers as among students. Some learn quickly; others never learn. The latter should find another profession. I don't intend this as a snide or derogatory remark. Some very fine people are unable to control a class. This does not indicate that they couldn't be quite successful at another occupation. As for the quick learners, I have tried not to be jealous of them. It took me a little longer, but I believe I finally made it. However, when teachers, especially inexperienced teachers, tell me that this class or that child is "impossible," I have to wonder. Improbable maybe, but not necessarily impossible.

At the beginning of this chapter, I referred to a second-grade class. I had a particular one in mind, the lowest of four homogeneous second-grade classes which we had at that time. There is a difference of opinion about homogeneous grouping. Let's just say that I favor it providing the bottom group can be kept to about twenty students. Unfortunately, due to our severe overcrowding, this class had a membership of about thirty-five, many of whom seemed to have a rather vague idea of where their seats were and what they were expected to do when they were in them. Their teacher, while not outstandingly successful, managed to battle them to a draw each day. Both she and the class survived, and she seldom sent students to the office. I was grateful for that. However, when she was absent and I had to assign a substitute, my aid was invariably required. In response to an urgent call for assistance, I usually removed two or three of the worst offenders and distributed them to other classrooms for the day. They were second graders; not really bad, just immature. That didn't make it any easier for the teacher, especially if she was a substitute. It got so that when the regular teacher was absent, I would try to visit the room during the first hour and remove a few students that I found running around the room (not always the same ones) to save the teacher the trouble of calling me later.

One day, when the regular teacher was absent, a pert, vivacious young redhead who had not been at our school before reported for duty, and I reluctantly assigned her to that room. Her cheerful smile, I reflected sadly, would soon fade, but I had no choice. Someone had to take that class, and she was the only one available. I planned to come to her rescue in a little while, for it was inevitable that she would need my help. However, I became involved with other matters and forgot all about her till shortly before lunch. Then it suddenly occurred to me that I had had no call for assistance, nor had the teacher sent any students to the office. My first thought was to leave well enough alone. This was followed by a mental image of a room in shambles and a teacher in a state of shock. Apprehensively, I walked over to the classroom—it was just two doors from my office—and looked in. The teacher was standing in front of the class, and the only student out of his seat was the one who evidently had been called upon to read. Feeling quite relieved, I was about to withdraw, but curiosity got the best of me, and I entered the room. The young teacher turned toward me, gave me a brief smile, and continued with the lesson. She did not look perturbed or disturbed. She was not even perspiring. It didn't seem possible. Perhaps the worst kids were absent. I looked around and identified the faces of those whom I had gotten to know all too well. As far as I could determine, they were all there. She couldn't have chloroformed them, for they were reasonably alert and were paying attention to the lesson, a novel activity for them.

"How's everything going?" I asked.

Again she smiled. "All right," she replied.

Her response was not too informative. However, I saw no reason to interrupt the lesson. I returned to the office. Well, just because the class was well-behaved when I entered didn't prove it had been that way all morning. Sometimes one comes in at a bad time. Maybe I came in at a good time. I would have to visit the class again in the afternoon to confirm what I had seen.

After lunch I got busy again—not an unusual state of affairs. It was ten minutes before dismissal time when I remembered that I had not revisited the second-grade class. I told my clerk where to find me if I was needed, hurried to the room, and walked in. The teacher was leading the class in a song. I don't intend to embellish the facts. Not everyone was singing, and among those who were, there apparently was a difference of opinion about the melody. Still, they (and the teacher) were evidently enjoying themselves, and no one was out of his seat—an accomplishment in itself for this class. I nodded to the teacher, she smiled and nodded back while continuing with the song, and I walked out. The class was obviously in good hands.

I instructed my clerk to ask this substitute to see me before she left. A few minutes later she walked into my office.

"How was your day?" I inquired.

"Fine," she said brightly. "They were a little 'antsy' but not too bad."

I was impressed. "I have an opening for a day-to-day sub if you're interested," I offered.

"I'm already working every day at another school. They had no vacancies today so they sent me here, but they expect to have an opening for me as an F.T.B. in a week or two. Sorry. Thanks anyway."

"Too bad," I said. "We could have used you. You did a nice job. If you ever need a position, let me know." She never called me or returned to our school, so I assume she received her appointment.

The moral of the story is that some teachers succeed even in a difficult situation, while others, when they have a class they are unable to manage, decide it can't be done. I admit there have been students I couldn't reach. That doesn't mean that someone else couldn't have done so. By the same token, I have succeeded with students that other teachers have given up on. When I failed, I consoled myself with the thought that I had done the best I could, and as I have often told my students, no one can do better than his best.

I must concede that we once had a seventh-grade class which no substitute, or at least none I had available, was able to handle. However, the circumstances were unusual. The regular teacher had managed the class quite effectively until he became ill. After that he was absent repeatedly, each time for a longer period. Due to his illness, he was unable to maintain order. The substitutes I assigned were equally unsuccessful. I kept rotating them (they refused to stay in that room for more than a few days) which did not help matters. Soon most of the students were completely out of control. I would walk in and quiet them almost every day, only to hear the noise begin again when I left. I even stayed after school with them a number of times. I sent for at least ten parents. I transferred some of the students to other classes. All these measures had only a temporary effect. There is just so much a principal or even a parent can do. The first line of defense is the teacher. Needless to say, some teachers blamed me for the situation.

The memory is depressing. I will balance it with a lighter moment involving a substitute, one whom I had assigned to a fifth-grade class. As she was signing out at the end of the day, she saw me in my office and approached the open door. "Thank you for disciplining those boys I sent you," she said.

"You're welcome," I replied automatically. I had taken care of a number of discipline cases that afternoon and sometimes they begin to blend together. She was halfway out of the door when I stopped her. "Just one minute," I called. "I don't seem to remember any boys from your room. What did they do?"

"They were fighting, and I sent them to the office."

"Oh, yes, I did take care of some boys who were fighting, but I thought they were from Mrs. Hammond's room. What were their names?"

The names she recited did not sound familiar. I was wondering if my memory was beginning to fail. "What did they tell you when they came back?" I asked.

"They said you gave them an assignment for homework."

"I did? What was the assignment?"

The teacher looked at me strangely. By this time she also must have been wondering about my mental capacity. "You told them to write 'I will obey the teacher and not fight in school' three hundred times."

"I see. Did you send them with a messenger?"

"Why, no. I gave them a note. They were gone about fifteen minutes. Then they returned and told me you had given them the assignment."

"Did they have a note from me?"

"I—I don't remember. I don't think so."

I saw she was becoming flustered. "Don't worry about it," I said. "This may be a learning experience for you. First, when you send kids to the office, it's a good idea to send a messenger with them. Second, you should not have admitted them back to class without an admission slip or a note from me. I imagine other schools have a similar policy. And third—of course you had no way of knowing this—I don't give stupid assignments like that. Your boys never came to the office—but don't worry. I'll take care of them tomorrow morning."

The next morning I sent for the two boys. It did not take long to arrive at the truth. They had torn up the teacher's note, had gone to the bathroom for about fifteen minutes, and then had returned to class with their story. They reasoned—and reasoned correctly—that a substitute would not be familiar with our procedures.

"And what was the assignment you said I gave you?" I asked them.

They glanced furtively at each other. Then one of them spoke up. "We said you told us to write 'I will obey the teacher and not fight in school.'"

"That's right. The teacher told me about it. How many times were you supposed to write it?"

"Three hundred times."

"Well, I never give an assignment like that. Certainly I wouldn't have made you write it three hundred times. If you had come to me like you were supposed to, I might even have let you off with a warning because, according to my records, you haven't been sent to the office before. But now that substitute is going to think our kids are liars. That will give our school a bad reputation. You wouldn't want that, would you?"

"No, sir," they both replied sheepishly.

"I'll tell you how we can fix that. You will each do that assignment three hundred times and give it to me tomorrow morning. If you don't have it, I'll call your parents. Then, if I ever see that teacher again, I can tell her that you actually told the truth, although you didn't know it at the time."

They did the assignment. Poetic justice, I thought.

Advocates of children's rights contend that children are often punished and even suspended for "crimes" which are not crimes at all in the adult world. School attendance is compulsory and children can be prosecuted if they are truant. Not so for adults. Children are punished for a variety of reasons—for making noise in class, not lining up properly, leaving their seats without permission, not doing their "work," violating the school dress code, being disrespectful, and infractions of other rules which have been promulgated by the teacher or principal—rules which are not applicable to adult behavior. These people paint a picture of poor, suffering children who are at the mercy of the teacher and the school system, are often treated unfairly, are judged and convicted without due process, and cannot appeal the decision. They make a strong case, and it is not without merit. There is no question that they can cite instances of gross injustices perpetrated upon children to substantiate their argument. I have witnessed injustices—too many of them—myself. But let's be fair. The people who make these accusations are usually lawyers or investigative reporters. I doubt if they ever taught school. If they did, they would find that the crimes of children are not always so innocuous. Teachers also have to deal with students who fight, bully other students, extort money from them, throw books in the classroom, set off fire alarms, steal, vandalize, and even intimidate the teachers. These students, especially if they are habitual offenders, are not easily frightened. Usually, the worst punishment that can be meted out to them is a suspension, and if their parents are unwilling or unable to exercise authority, a suspension soon ceases to be a deterrent.

As I have previously indicated, a principal cannot permanently remove a child from school. Parents and even some teachers do not seem to realize this. Here is a note, verbatum, as an example of the kind of requests (sometimes more like demands) that I've had from teachers:

"As of today I don't want Leonard in my class *EVER*."

How exactly did the teacher expect this to be consummated? He didn't say. He figured that was my job. As far as I can remember, Leonard's offenses were not sufficiently nefarious to warrant placement in Montefiore. Even if they had been, it would have required going through channels, making out a case report, etc., which could take months unless I could demonstrate that it was an emergency situation. Just because the teacher wanted him out didn't make it an emergency. Of course I could place Leonard in another room, transfer the headache from one teacher to another. Sometimes this works, sometimes it doesn't. I believe that's what I did in this case.

Some teachers have a simple, though hardly original, solution to the discipline problem. "Let's get rid of all the troublemakers," they say. "Expel them! Kick them out of school! They're not learning anything anyway, and they're not letting the other kids learn."

An intriguing idea, but how would it work out? What would happen to the crime rate with all these kids wandering around loose? I'll admit that many of them are not getting much of an education, but putting them out on the street where they would have no chance at all of getting one does not seem like the right answer. Juvenile delinquency and teenage unemployment are severe problems now. This would exacerbate both. And what an outcry there would be from the parents of these youngsters (in the interest of accuracy I won't call them students) and what a proliferation of lawsuits it would spawn. Well, as the Supreme Court has ruled that every child is entitled to an education, this is not a viable alternative. I'll mention my own solution again—more and better vocational schools with students admitted at age twelve. That too won't solve all the problems, but I believe it would be a step in the right direction—providing we can get good teachers for these schools. That won't be easy. Why should a good mechanic take a cut in salary to become a teacher?

When I was a teacher, I remember saying that if we only had a special class for the most disruptive students it would help tremendously. Some schools have such classes, and toward the end of my tenure as a principal I was finally able to establish one at our school. It helped a little but was not the panacea I had imagined it would be. For one thing, no teacher can be expected to handle more than a small number of such students. The maximum permitted in this class was eight. Removing eight students from their regular classes in a school with a membership of over sixteen hundred will not eliminate the discipline problems. While a few teachers benefited, it didn't make things much easier for me. It takes a special teacher to cope with this kind of student. The one we had was not equal to the task. Her students often slipped out to the playground or somewhere else in the building where they didn't belong. They still managed to get into trouble, and I doubt if they were getting an education. Needless to say, no school system can afford many such classes. Having one teacher for eight students is a pretty expensive proposition.

Let's get back to the situation in the regular classroom. It is true that some teachers are cruel and terrorize children in the name of discipline. It is also true that many teachers feel helpless, outnumbered, and surrounded by thirty or more "enemies." They want to teach, and they can't do it in a noisy classroom. They want children to be quiet, well-behaved, attentive, and eager to learn. The student who deviates from these standards is usually considered "bad." And if the teacher decides the child is bad, the feeling is likely to become mutual. When such a situation develops, the child can only be controlled by fear. Some teachers may want it that way; some think it's the only way. I have already made it clear that I disagree.

Throughout my teaching career, I tried to remember that we expect children to behave unnaturally—not to talk, not to move around, to do all the "work" we assign (some of which has doubtful educational value), and to restrain their normal desire to play and have fun, all for the sake of a nebulous future benefit which they can't see or feel—an education. I believe in that goal—I would not have taught if I didn't, and I don't think it can be achieved without some reasonable rules of conduct. However, I also made an effort to appreciate the children's point of view. This enabled me to curb my anger when they "misbehaved," and to refrain from shouting, bullying, name-calling, and unreasonable punishments. If I lost my temper, which I am afraid I did occasionally, I felt that I was as guilty as the child. As an adult and a professional I believed it was my obligation to exercise self-control. Sometimes, however, my anger was more pretended than real.

I learned that talking to a student after class, calmly if possible, was more effective than censoring him in front of his classmates. As he didn't have to put on a show for his friends, he was less likely to be rebellious and more likely to listen. There is one bit of advice that I have always given to young teachers. Avoid confrontations.

There may be a flaw in my logic, but I conjectured that the fewer rules I made, the fewer opportunities there would be for the students to be disobedient. Consequently, I wouldn't have to punish them as often, and this would make things easier for them and for me. During a written lesson I expected the class to be reasonably quiet, but I did not demand absolute silence. I could never bring myself to order children (especially upper-grade children) to sit with their hands folded on the desk. It is true that they can't get into much mischief while maintaining that position. However, I remember how I detested sitting that way when I went to school. I considered it asinine and degrading. I can't imagine adults being required to assume that posture.

At teachers' meetings which I have convened, I have observed, with secret amusement, the behavior of those teachers who were the most demanding in their standards of conduct for their students. They would sit in a variety of positions (forgetting that they expected their students to sit up straight), often pay little attention to the speaker, grade papers while a discussion was in progress, and sometimes make so much noise that I had to stop the meeting and wait for them to be quiet. Of course parents' meetings can be pretty noisy too. And although I have never attended one of their sessions, I understand that the United States Senate is seldom a model of decorum. I will confess that my own behavior in similar situations has not always been above reproach either. Strange that we expect so much more from children than we do from ourselves. What was it Robert Burns said about seeing ourselves as others see us?

And how do children see their teachers? Do they see them, as I saw mine, as cold, cheerless individuals with no sense of humor? I know most teachers would take issue with such a portrayal and insist that they have a very good sense of humor. And they have! Take my word for it. At parties they are just like everyone else. They usually have faculty parties twice a year, at which time they gossip and tell jokes, and no one appears to mind if the jokes are a bit off-color. The bar is quite popular too. A few individuals get very relaxed—some more relaxed than others. It doesn't get wild. Nothing happens that anyone has to be embarrassed about, but as the teachers themselves often say, "If our students could see us now!" Then, the very next morning they are back in the classroom (although a few may be nursing headaches), composed and serious. Well, that's as it should be. There is a time and place for everything. Still, I have often wished that a little of the relaxed, cheerful attitude that I have seen at the parties would carry over to the classroom (without the aid of alcoholic stimulants, of course). It rarely does.

The same teachers who enjoy a risqué story at a party are horrified when they intercept a profane note or salacious drawing from a student. The offending child is immediately carted down to the office and an urgent request is made that his (or her—for nice little girls are sometimes the culprits) parents be notified so they can be confronted with the damaging evidence. A parent, usually the mother, is summoned and, providing you can convince her that her little darling was indeed the guilty party, very properly expresses her anger and dismay, and punctuates it with a menacing aside in the direction of the offender—"Just wait till I get you home!"

I happen to dislike profanity and personally never use it. However, I was exposed to both the words and drawings when I went to school. In fact, I had a pretty colorful vocabulary myself at that time. My chief reaction, therefore, and this may be just a case of nostalgia, is that my contemporaries were better artists and spellers.

I do not condone the use of profanity by children, but I wish parents and teachers would not act as if it were the crime of the century, especially since most of them do not appear to be shocked when their friends use similar language or when they hear it in the theater or in a nightclub. I have known some parents who, when aroused, blurt out some lurid four-letter words themselves. Presumably it's all right as long as it's done by adults.

Although it is not necessary to call a parent every time a child offends the teacher's sensibilities, parents, if used discriminately, are still the best allies a teacher has. If the teacher's efforts with a child are ineffectual, it is advisable to elicit the aid of the parents. Some of them, unfortunately, have little influence upon the behavior of their children. There is not much the teacher can do about that except to deplore the state of society and the breakdown of our civilization, which may make the teacher feel better but won't solve anything. Forgetting about those parents (which isn't easy because their children are often the most disruptive), let's concentrate on getting the cooperation of the others. There is a little more to it than just arranging a meeting with the parent and enumerating the child's faults. The parent may be defensive and antagonistic for any of a number of reasons:

1. She has heard only one side of the story—her child's (whose version is sometimes a little biased).
2. She believes it is her duty to defend her child. If his mother won't, who will?
3. The teacher is picking on her child. She knows because he told her so. (It may even be true, though the teacher often feels it's the other way around.)
4. She believes the teacher is accusing her child unjustly. (Well, it's possible.)
5. She thinks the teacher is mean. (That's possible too.)
6. She is convinced that the teacher is exaggerating the problem. Her child isn't that bad.
7. She is antagonized by the teacher's attitude and decides that the teacher is more at fault than the child.
8. The teacher's criticism of the child implies that the mother is doing a poor job as a parent. No parent wants to admit that.
9. The mother's own school experience was unpleasant and she has developed a hostile attitude toward teachers.
10. She thinks teachers are not as competent as they were when she went to school.
11. She believes that when the child is at school his behavior is the responsibility of the teacher and the administrator, not hers.
12. She believes she has already fulfilled her obligation. She has told the child to behave.
13. She is tired of being bothered.
14. She is an argumentative, opinionated, stubborn, difficult, and thoroughly obnoxious person.

Well, with such sentiments and attitudes to overcome, what chance does the teacher have of gaining the parent's cooperation? A very good one. If approached properly, most parents are pussycats. They want their children to behave and to succeed in school, and they are usually prepared to accept the teacher as a competent professional. How the discussion proceeds is up to the teacher. I've seen many teachers in action who don't need my advice. They conduct a parent conference beautifully. For those who need help, here are a few suggestions:

1. Don't begin with a tirade about how bad the child is. Such an approach practically forces the parent to become defensive.

2. Be calm and professional. If you speak softly and without rancor, the parent will find it hard to believe the child's assertion that the teacher is always yelling at the children (even if it's true).

3. Try to think of something good to say about the child. (Maybe he comes to school on time, or he spells his name correctly. Think of something!)

4. Don't suggest that the child is a juvenile delinquent even if he is. You might say, "He is a very active child," or "He has a lot of energy." These are euphemisms for "This kid is driving me out of my mind," but they sound much better.

5. Make some positive suggestions, if you can think of any, as to what the parent can do to help. (Advising the parent to move to another neighborhood or to let the kid join the circus is not a positive suggestion.)

6. This above all: if you can convince the parent that you share her interest in the welfare of the child and that the purpose of the conference is to find ways to help him, not to punish him, you've got it made.

There can be a danger in sending for a parent. I have known a few who would punish the child so severely that I avoided calling them if I possibly could. The punitive parent may think it's for the good of the child, but it seldom works out that way.

I remember the time that my new assistant brought a seventh grader, a fourteen-year-old boy, to the office. "His father sent him to school like this," she said.

I knew the boy well. His teacher had referred him to me for discipline a number of times. He was walking very slowly and his eyes were downcast. His head was completely shaven.

"What happened to him?" I inquired.

"His father cut off all his hair," she replied, "but that's not all. Look at his legs."

At first I didn't notice anything unusual. Than, as he gingerly lifted his trousers, I saw that his legs were fastened together at the ankles with a heavy steel chain. He could just manage to take very small steps. It was reminiscent of movies I had seen about the Georgia chain gangs.

"Why did he do that?" I asked.

"For punishment," he mumbled. "He said I had to go to school like that."

"Punishment for what?"

He hesitated. "Go ahead, tell him," said my assistant.

"He caught me smoking a marijuana cigarette."

Smoking marijuana was something I strongly disapproved of, but his admission did not surprise or shock me. I knew that some of our students indulged in the practice. I had been summoned on a number of occasions by a teacher or student to check the boys' bathroom. When I arrived there, it would usually be empty, but the pungent, distinctive aroma of marijuana would permeate the air. However, I was seldom able to apprehend any of the culprits.

"What you do at home is not my business," I said, "though I don't think you should be smoking 'pot.' Right now we've got to get that chain off. You can't go around like that."

"My father said to keep it on."

"Your father isn't running this school," I said shortly. "I am." I turned to my assistant. "Take him to the shop," I instructed her. "Tell the teacher to put some soap or some grease on his legs and see if he can slide the chain off. If that doesn't work, he'll have to saw it off."

"What will I tell my father?" asked the boy. "He's gonna whip me if I come home without the chain."

"You tell him I gave the order to have the chain removed. If he doesn't believe you or if he has any objections he can come and see me."

I never saw his father. I was tempted to send for him but decided against it. Considering my feelings at the moment, I knew the discussion was not likely to be amicable. My assistant did contact him but with little success.

The father's stringent discipline at home apparently had a contrary effect upon his son's behavior in school. He bullied the other students and was insolent to the teacher. After several more visits to the office for discipline, I threatened, "If you can't behave, I'll have to call your father, and you know what he'll do to you."

"Go ahead," he said sullenly. "It doesn't matter."

I divined his meaning. "He beats you anyway, whether I call him or not. Is that it?"

He nodded. I assigned a punishment and placed him in another room for the day. I decided against calling his father. I didn't want to be responsible for another beating. His behavior did not improve.

Eventually, as he was over fourteen, I was able to transfer him to a vocational school.

A few years later, the city established an agency to investigate cases of child abuse. It is now mandatory for teachers or principals to report such incidents. Unfortunately, this agency did not exist at that time.

If a poll were taken, it would probably indicate that most people believe there has been a deterioration in parental supervision and control of children in recent years and an increase in the number of discipline problems in our schools. Many teachers will concur with that assessment and will maintain that the latter is a direct consequence of the former. Some people may view these as separate phenomena, each indicative of a greater permissiveness in our society. Whichever opinion one holds, are these beliefs based on fact, or are they the result of "the good old days" syndrome?

It is true that there has been a steady increase in the number of single-parent families and also the number of families in which both parents are working. Though they may still be increasing, neither is a recent development. In our school at least, many of our students who were sent to me for discipline had only one parent in the home—the mother—and her influence upon the student's behavior was often inadequate. If she was working during the day, she was even less able to deal with the situation. Nevertheless, I believe that most parents still can exert authority and could probably be more supportive of the teacher and the school if they made the effort—and if their cooperation was solicited in the right way.

For as long as I can remember, teachers have been telling me that conditions in the schools are getting worse. I heard that complaint when I first started teaching. It was not without foundation as the neighborhood was undergoing a change. It was becoming more transient and poorer, and the academic ability of the new students was generally lower. However, even when such a situation does not exist, there is a tendency to maximize present problems and cloak the past in a nostalgic glow.

I have read an article written by a young high school teacher, young by my standards anyway, directed to or, more precisely, at today's students. In it she launches into a scathing denunciation of their conduct and contrasts it with her innocent and virtuous behavior and that of her classmates when they were that age. She asserts that, unlike today's students, when she went to high school she arrived early, used the designated entrance, brought her own school supplies, did not deface her textbooks and library books with obscenities, and did not pilfer school equipment nor steal things out of gym lockers. The indictment continues. When she went to school the scent of marijuana and mace were not commonplace in the halls, there were no false fire alarms, the drinking fountains weren't filled with garbage, the toilets were not stopped up, most of the girls did not have babies of their own at home, and students were respectful to the teachers and principal. In conclusion, the teacher wonders, somewhat rhetorically, what her students will say when they are her age.

The conditions this teacher describes are deplorable, and her exasperation is understandable. While I can't offer any easy solutions, I can tell her what some of her students will say at her age. A few of them will probably become teachers and make similar statements to their students.

I am sure that many students do not smoke marijuana or stuff toilets, and I can't believe that most of the girls have babies of their own at home. Teenage pregnancy, though all too common, is still not that high. As to her assertion that she personally was not guilty of such transgressions, I can vouch for the truth of that statement. Where we part company is when she implies that these problems were nonexistent when she went to school.

It just so happens that I knew this teacher when she was in elementary school. I lived in the same neighborhood and taught at the school she attended. Although she was not in my class, I know that she was a very good student and that her teachers had no reason to complain about her conduct. We had homogeneous classes, and she was in the top group. Therefore, her classmates were also good students, and most of them—though not all—may have behaved well too. I can assure her, however, that the virtues she ascribes to her generation were not so prevalent in the student body as a whole.

In this middle-class community of home owners, the incidence of vandalism, both in the neighborhood and at the school, was actually greater than that which I encountered later in a much poorer neighborhood. There were some boys in the seventh and eighth grade who burglarized garages and stole cars. There were good students and poor ones and lazy ones as one finds at every school, though percentages may differ depending on the neighborhood. While the reading test results for the school as a whole were above average, there were plenty of poor readers. Nevertheless, the school did have a good reputation, probably better than it deserved. I remember the time that an experienced teacher, who had transferred to our school with high expectations, came to see me after her first week and confided, "I've got some real dandies in my room. They won't stop talking. Are all the classes like that?" I didn't have the heart to tell her that she had one of the better classes.

To summarize, the problems this high school teacher describes are not new. They existed years ago, though perhaps to a lesser degree, at the school in which I was principal—an elementary school, mind you. We had marijuana and mace, false fire alarms, damage and destruction of books, obscenities defacing the walls, vandalism, burglaries, and one or two pregnancies a year. It may sound worse than it was. Even as is true in the society as a whole, this antisocial behavior was not characteristic of the majority.

This teacher's benign recollection of conditions when she went to school is not uncommon, especially among female teachers. Most of them were good little girls who did their homework, got good grades, behaved properly, obeyed the teacher, and made friends with other little girls of a similar disposition. I don't say this disparagingly. Any teacher would be happy to have such students. Also, and this is an important consideration, they may have attended a school in a better neighborhood than the one in which they subsequently taught. Besides, their viewpoint was that of the student, not the teacher. They were dimly aware that there were some "bad" boys or girls in the class but considered them the exception. And maybe they were. In a class of thirty-five students, if twenty-five behave reasonably well, that leaves ten who don't, a minority to be sure, but more than enough to have the teacher reaching for the Valium. For that matter, it only takes one or two consistent, persistent, omnipresent troublemakers to raise a teacher's blood pressure several points.

The period this high school teacher recollects is really too recent to be called the good old days. That designation could more appropriately be applied to the time of my own school days which began about sixty years ago. As I try to recall them, I must include a caveat that I am describing childhood impressions which may not be entirely accurate. In fact, my memories of the first two schools I attended are so vague that I won't pursue them. The third school, which I entered in fifth grade, left a more lasting impression, although I only attended it for a short time. It was in a poor neighborhood and the rents were low, which was why my parents moved there. It was all they could afford. They soon decided, however, that they had made a mistake. I knew it before they did. The students were generally unruly, and the level of academic performance was low. Our teacher was pleasant, younger than most of those I remember, and she made an effort to teach and to maintain order. She had, at best, moderate success in both endeavors. Fights in the playground were common. I was often forced to defend myself and discovered it was possible to lose even when I won. When I lost, that was the end of it. The injuries were minor. When I won (which wasn't too often), I found that I had to face two or three of my opponent's friends the next day. It wasn't a happy situation, but it taught me to avoid fights. At any rate, my mother got tired of seeing me come home with torn trousers, scuffed knees, and an assortment of bruises which I tried to convince her were the result of tripping on the stairs or running into a door. For this and other reasons we soon moved to a better neighborhood even though my father considered it beyond his means.

The school to which I transferred had a reputation for enforcing good discipline and maintaining high academic standards. While the teachers received credit for this, I believe that the caliber of the students and the generally supportive home environments were more important ingredients. Certainly this was true in my family, where my immigrant parents were determined that their children would enjoy an easier life than they had endured, a very common attitude then and now. They were convinced that the only way to achieve this was through a college education, and that goal was impressed upon us at an early age. I imagine this view was shared by many of the parents in the neighborhood, which eased the task of the teachers considerably. While I can recall some students who were referred to as "dummies" and some who were "troublemakers," they probably constituted a smaller percentage than at other schools.

With one exception, my upper-grade teachers were feared and disliked. For several of them my feeling was closer to hatred. My friends and I often remarked that if they would smile their faces would crack. This was not true. I know because I saw them smile, though never at us. The smiles were in evidence when they stood in the hallway and engaged in a conversation among themselves. While this was going on, we would stand stiffly in single file, sometimes for five or ten minutes. I wondered if they had a contest to see which class could stand the longest without uttering a sound. If anyone whispered, they always seemed to hear it. Then one of them (maybe it depended on whose turn it was) would bellow in loud, threatening tones, "Now I don't want to hear one sound!" Sometimes the teacher in whose class the guilty student belonged would walk over to scream at him or at the entire class, intimating that she had been disgraced in front of her colleagues. Then, when the class was sufficiently cowed, she would calmly return to her conversation.

In the classroom, these teachers maintained order by staring at us with baleful disapproval, pounding on the desk, frequent shouting, bloodcurdling screams, intimidation, and the ultimate threat of sending for a parent. Though they would occasionally pull a student's ear or administer a sharp slap when they thought the occasion warranted it, their brutality was more mental than physical. For the teachers, those may have been the good old days, but not for the students. I did not like school.

As I said earlier, there was one exception, a tiny, middle-aged woman, well under five feet in height, who actually smiled at us, overlooked an occasional whisper, and tried to make the lesson interesting. We changed rooms for some subjects, and her geography class was always a welcome relief. Though there was a little more noise in her room than in the others, it never got out of hand. I guess there were good teachers and bad in those days even as there are today. However, if my experience is any indication, there are more teachers today who exhibit a sympathetic understanding of children than there were then. I had no thought at that time of becoming a teacher, but I distinctly remember promising myself that if I did become one, I would never treat children the way most of my upper-grade teachers had treated me. I believe I have kept that promise.

It might be argued that in spite of the strict discipline, or perhaps because of it, I did get an education. As I have already suggested, there were other factors involved. I am certain that one of them was my early discovery of a very important educational tool—the public library.

Throughout history, the younger generation has never lived up to the expectations of the previous one. One would hardly be surprised to hear these words from a parent today. "We live in a decaying age. Young people no longer respect their parents. They are rude and impatient. They inhabit taverns and have no self-control." The parent who wrote this, however, is supposed to have lived about six thousand years ago. The librarian I consulted tells me that this is a translation of an inscription found on an ancient Egyptian tomb. Another well-publicized quotation is attributed to a Greek writer or philosopher who lived about the time of Socrates. I can't vouch for its authenticity, but I've seen it in print several times. I'm sure many parents and teachers can empathize with these sentiments: "Our youths love luxury. They have contempt for authority; they show disrespect for their elders, and love to chatter in place of exercise. Children are now tyrants, not the servants of their household. They no longer rise when their elders enter the room. They contradict their parents, chatter before company, gobble up their food, and tyrannize their teachers."

Socrates himself was condemned to death for corrupting the youth of his day. He may have been a convenient scapegoat (after all, he was a teacher), but in that age of great enlightenment (when slavery was a common and accepted institution) one would think he would have been put on probation if his crime was only *attempted* corruption. Since his judges believed he deserved the death penalty, they must have been convinced that the young people were really corrupted.

Almost two hundred years ago, Wordsworth lamented that England "is a fen of stagnant waters," and wished that Milton were alive to bring back the days when people had "manners, virtue, freedom, power." And so in every generation we hear the despairing cry, "O tempora, O mores." Either we must assume that each successive generation throughout recorded history has become progressively worse—a most disconcerting thought—or people just think it has. Samuel Johnson said, "Every old man complains of the growing depravity of the world, of the petulance and insolence of the rising generation." I suspect there never were any good old days. So instead of glorifying the past, we might as well face the situation as it exists today and try to improve it. I'm all for learning from the past, but we have to live in the present.

I am not suggesting that those who want to "return" to strict discipline are bad people. Few of them would advocate a return to the brutal methods which were common in the English schools of the nineteenth century and were exposed by Charles Dickens. Fortunately, nothing like that could happen in this day and age. Or could it?

A news article describing the situation at a school in another city, which I prefer to leave nameless, might make one wonder a little. It revealed that no disciplinary action was being taken against teachers who were accused of tying unruly children to their desks, taping their mouths shut, and forcing them to crouch in awkward positions. The board called the classroom punishment ill-advised and imprudent but said it was "not cruel, inhuman, or abusive." There was also a statement from the attorney for the district. He said that the board found "no maliciousness whatsoever nor any abusive intent and that is the reason we do not recommend any change in personnel at this time. The board was very impressed with the presentation and intent of some of these disciplinary measures." He further affirmed that the majority of parents had supported the teachers' actions. Nevertheless, some of the parents were not too happy. They complained that "problem students were confined in a supply room, forced to stand for long periods in the hot desert sun, and tied to their desks." The board confirmed the charges and stated that such disciplinary measures were not acceptable under their guidelines. Yet they were impressed with the "presentation and intent" of these measures, whatever that means. Well, maybe my teachers weren't as bad as I thought.

I know that such practices are not typical. I just want to indicate that not only has this kind of discipline been employed but there are parents who approve of it. I suppose no one has asked the children how they feel about it.

It has been suggested by some educators that classroom discipline can be improved by the implementation of a technique called "behavior modification." As far as I can determine, its basic tenet is that the prospect of a reward is a more effective incentive than the fear of punishment. I certainly agree, though I fail to see anything new about this approach except the name. Animal trainers have been using it for years, and there is no question that it works with adults as well as children. People can be spurred to greater endeavors by flattery, testimonial dinners, the presentation of a plaque or a certificate of achievement, a more prestigious title, or a raise in salary. Children will respond to similar blandishments.

My mother used to give me a penny (when pennies still had some value) for going on an errand and sometimes for good behavior. Occasionally I received a small remuneration for bringing home an excellent report card, though usually this was taken for granted. My older brothers, unfortunately, had set such high standards that they had spoiled the market. My own children received a quarter for making the honor roll and often complained that they were being underpaid. Of course I contended that they were being compensated more liberally than I had been. In any case, neither my mother nor I were aware that we were practicing behavior modification.

While it is true that children appreciate material things, they also respond to rewards that are less tangible. A smile, a word of encouragement or approval, private or public recognition of a student's accomplishments—these are the stock in trade of any good teacher. I maintained charts embellished with silver and gold stars to denote the students' achievements in reading, spelling, and arithmetic. This was a lot of work, but the results justified the effort. Also, in recognition for good (or reasonably acceptable) behavior all week, I would permit the class to play a game during the last period on Friday. The game they usually played was called "Spelling Basketball," a concoction of my own based upon our spelling lessons. It was quite popular with the students, especially since it pitted the boys against the girls. I have always maintained that education can be fun and fun can be educational. And relying upon rewards instead of punishment is fine with me even if they call it behavior modification.

Some critics of our schools question the advisability of employing either reward or punishment as an incentive. They claim that the consequence of such tactics is to teach children, at a very early age, that the way to get along in school is to please the teacher by making the responses she considers correct or proper. This stifles or destroys their natural curiosity and kills the joy of learning. Ultimately, they say, many of the children become so bored or frustrated that they misbehave for lack of something better to do.

While there may be some truth to this assessment, I believe these critics overstate the case. I have had my share of boring teachers. Who hasn't? And I have observed teachers whose lessons could hardly be described as stimulating. However, many teachers work very hard on the preparation of their lesson plans and endeavor to make the class activities interesting. Nevertheless, contrary to what the critics imply, no teacher can stimulate all of the children all of the time. And although a good lesson plan can serve to deter disruptive behavior, it will not eliminate all discipline problems.

Discipline in the classroom is necessary so that the teacher can teach and the students can learn—I don't think anyone will disagree with that statement. But each teacher has to decide what kind of behavior she expects and what means she will use to obtain it. For my part, I will not endorse methods that are cruel, induce fear and hatred, and make the classroom seem more like a prison than a place of learning. We should remember that children who are brutalized often become brutal.

I have been told I sometimes get too preachy. So be it. I'll sermonize again. I've seen what I've seen and I know what I know. And I know that well-meaning people can often do as much harm as evil ones. So please, you teachers out there, and you would-be-teachers, and you parents as well, if you can't help the children, at least don't hurt them too much. School does not have to be a painful experience. I have seen teachers who can accept and like the homely child, the withdrawn child, the retarded child, and even the unruly child; who are kind, yet firm, and who treat all children fairly. To them I can only say, "Your job is not an easy one. It never has been. But I hope you persevere. The children need you."

Epilogue

Two boys had been sent to the office for creating a disturbance. As I considered what punishment would be appropriate, one of them burst out, "When we do something wrong we always get in trouble. How come it's all right if the teacher does something wrong?"

"You disrupted the class," I said. "I'm sure your teacher didn't do that."

"No, but he swears at us. That's not right, is it?"

"He swears at you? What does he say?"

"Well, yesterday he took the girls to gym. When he came back, I was out of my seat, so he said, 'Get your butt back in your seat,' only he didn't say 'butt.' He said something else."

"Are you sure?"

"I heard him," affirmed the other boy.

"Well," I temporized, "maybe it wasn't exactly the right thing to say, but I'll bet you boys have said much worse than that, haven't you?"

"Yes," replied the first boy, "but I'm not a teacher."

I don't remember my response. I've never forgotten his.